PRISONER
of
FAITH

A Journey from Hopelessness to Salvation

JAN SUMNER

Trilogy Christian Publishers
A Wholly Owned Subsidary of Trinity Broadcasting Network
2442 Michelle Drive
Tustin, CA 92780

For information, address Trilogy Christian Publishing
Rights Department, 2442 Michelle Drive, Tustin, Ca 92780.
Trilogy Christian Publishing/ TBN and colophon are trademarks of Trinity Broadcasting Network.

For information about special discounts for bulk purchases, please contact Trilogy Christian Publishing.

Manufactured in the United States of America

10 9 8 7 6 5 4 3 2 1

Library of Congress Cataloging-in-Publication Data is available.

ISBN 979-8-88738-351-4 (Print Book)
ISBN 979-8-88738-352-1 (ebook)

Contents

Introduction

Forty-five years ago my life was derailed from its path, or maybe it was the path God had chosen for me in order that I might write this book. It will take you on a journey that I actually lived and continue to live to this day.

My name is Jody Mobley, and my story begins from my earliest memories as a child. My father was killed in a truck accident when I was six years old while living in Gowrie, Iowa. That left my mother to raise three boys by herself. I was the middle son. My older brother later committed suicide, and my younger brother, unfortunately, followed in my life of crime.

I used to go to church by myself when I was around nine years old. My life at the time was filled with neglect, loneliness, and a lot of violence, so because of that, I lost all faith in the Lord and blamed Him for all the bad things in my life. As I got older, things got worse, so I ran away from home when I was twelve and have not been back since. I got caught up in fighting, drugs, and crime. I wound up in juvenile detention and did two years. When I first got caught, the authorities contacted my mom, and she told them to keep me. When I was twenty, my best friend put a shotgun in his mouth and committed suicide right in front of me. After that my life spiraled out of control, and I ended up in prison on a life sentence, which I'm still serving today.

In 2017 I was reading the obituaries in the newspaper and saw there was going to be a funeral service at Grace United Methodist Church in Denver, and I suddenly had this urge to contact them. This is how I met who would become my brother in Christ. My life was changing at the time, and my friend Jan was a beacon to turn my life back over to God. I'd already been in prison for twenty-nine years, and I was filled with anger and hopelessness, but God put me in touch with Jan, and over time we've become great friends, and the miracle of me opening my heart to God happened.

Prisoner of Faith is about my life and how I lost faith in God but in the end found my faith in Him. Some may say it's a miracle, and I think so, but it's also about God's power and shows that even in the darkest confines of prison, He can perform a miracle.

It should be noted that all the scripture quotes before each chapter were picked by Jody.

Chapter 1

Job 1:20–22—Job did not hide his overwhelming grief. He had not lost his faith in God; instead, his emotions showed that he was human and that he loved his family. God created our emotions, and it is not sinful or inappropriate to express them as Job did. If you have experienced a deep loss, a disappointment, or a heartbreak, admit your feelings to yourself and others and grieve.

* * * *

I lost my dad when I was six years old. I cried only one time after his funeral, and since then I've never properly grieved. At such a young age, I wasn't able to grieve, nor was I able to turn to God. The day my dad was killed changed my life. I pray that anybody who has had such a loss, or other tragedy in their life, can find someone they can turn to. I can tell you the one who will always be there to help and guide you is God. Don't be afraid to open up to Him. I wish I'd had the opportunity back then to turn to God, but I was too young, and I had nobody to guide me to Him. But God is with me now, and it is awesome!

Where does one start when talking about a miracle? You hear the term *miracle* used a lot, especially when something or someone is saved or prevented from disaster or further damage or even brought back from what appears to be sure death. I don't deny any of these, and without equivocation I believe wholeheartedly in miracles but never truly felt I was directly involved in what we would call a miracle sent straight from heaven. That was until now.

I guess the best place to start discussing a miracle is at the beginning. My name is Jan Sumner, and I am a Sunday school teacher at Grace United Methodist Church in southeast Denver for the middle and high school kids and have been for the past six years. That by itself does not merit or in any way give a good reason for what happened in early September of 2017. A letter was sent to our church from a prisoner in the Sterling Correction Facility in Sterling, Colorado. The pastor's wife opened it, read it, and for some inexplicable reason, gave it to me. To this day I don't know why except this had to be God's will, and believe me when I say I have wondered about His choice many times, but He is always right, so I have accepted it and now feel exceptionally blessed He would pick me to serve Him in such an extraordinary way.

Below is a copy of that letter and my response. As you can see, Jody's letter is well-written and straightforward but with a certain sense of desperation. I answered him the day I got the letter, having no idea what lay in store for Jody and me.

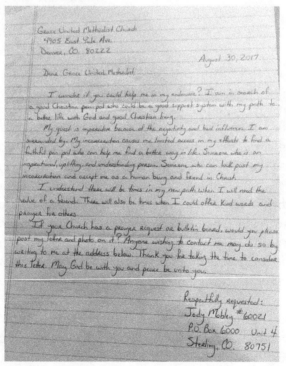

Jody Mobley #60021
PO Box 60021 Unit 4
Sterling, CO 80751

Dear Jody,

I am reaching out to you to let you know I would be more than happy to do what I can to assist you in your walk with the Lord.

I'll be very honest with you; I have no idea what it's like to be in prison or go through what you go through there on a daily basis. That being said, I do know what it is like to give your life to Jesus Christ, and I can say, without reservation, you will never do anything more important or life-altering. I obviously have no idea what you did to be incarcerated, but I'm sure there were many factors and variables involved. Whatever they were is none of my business. My only business is to help you in your walk with Christ.

I work with the youth (teenagers) at Grace and have worked with youth in Haiti and will soon, I hope, be working with incarcerated youth with Youth for Christ. But as we are told in the Bible, we are all children of God, so age is no factor when you believe in the Lord.

I'm sure you have access to a Bible, and I would suggest reading Matthew 14:22–33. This is one of my favorite passages. I've used it a lot with people I've worked with and would recommend it for you. After you've read it, keep in mind if you reach out your hand to Jesus, He will get in your boat (life) and will be there for you through eternity. Jody, I hope this helps, at least initially, and please consider me a friend of yours in Christ. I look forward to hearing from you.

Blessings to you,
Jan Sumner

* * * *

Matthew 14:22–33:

> *Immediately Jesus made the disciples get into the boat and go on ahead of him to the other side, while he dismissed the crowd. After he had dismissed them, he went up on a mountainside by himself to pray. Later that night, he was there alone, and the boat was already a considerable distance from land, buffeted by the waves because the wind was against it.*

Shortly before dawn Jesus went out to them, walking on the lake. When the disciples saw him walking on the lake, they were terrified. "It's a ghost," they said, and cried out in fear.

But Jesus immediately said to them: "Take courage! It is I. Don't be afraid."

"Lord, if it's you," Peter replied, "tell me to come to you on the water."

"Come," he said.

Then Peter got down out of the boat, walked on the water and came toward Jesus. But when he saw the wind, he was afraid and, beginning to sink, cried out, "Lord, save me!"

Immediately Jesus reached out his hand and caught him. "You of little faith," he said, "why did you doubt?"

And when they climbed into the boat, the wind died down. Then those who were in the boat worshiped him, saying, "Truly you are the Son of God."

* * * *

This then was the beginning of the most unique journey of not only mine but Jody's life as well. *As it says in 1 Kings 17:13–16, miracles seem so out of reach for our feeble faith. But every miracle, large or small, begins with an act of obedience.*

Chapter 2

Numbers 14:9—the path to open rebellion against God begins with dissatisfaction, then moves to grumbling about both God and present circumstances. Next comes bitterness and resentment, followed finally by rebellion and open hostility.

* * * *

I began to rebel for the wrong reasons and do things my way because I was hurting. My desire was attention from my mom; I wanted her love and attention, but it was not given, so I did bad things to get her attention. My actions were things God would not have approved of, but I was not familiar with God at that time. Seek God out before you thrust yourself into a cycle of negative behavior. The Lord can break that cycle, and if you ask for His guidance, He will help you make better decisions.

Jody's next letter was full of trepidation, and yet there was a sense of hope in it. Hope that something good would happen and maybe there was a possibility his life could change for the better, and maybe, just maybe, God could orchestrate that change.

* * * *

10/23/17

Dear Jan,

Thank you for reaching out and contacting me. It really means a lot that you are kind enough to want to assist me on this journey. I will be perfectly honest with you. This path is a choice that is difficult for me. I've been

5

in trouble most of my life and religion has not been a part of my life since I was a child. So this is not going to be an easy road for me. So thank you again so much for reaching out to me.

Let me tell you a little about myself. I was born in Iowa. Will be fifty-one years old on November 16. Originally came to prison for felony theft, criminal trespassing and second degree burglary. Did a few years in prison from '88 to '93 over all of that. Paroled in '93 and didn't care much about anything. Was drinking one night and woke up in jail on an armed robbery charge. Was only out for twenty-three days. So it has been a long, hard, lonely road I've been on. Have made a conscious choice to give myself to the Lord and see if I can salvage some inner peace and maybe find a good friend along the way.

Prison life is a lonely one. A lot of cruelty and hatred behind these walls. I want to change and try to become a better person. When I was fourteen I was in the juvenile institution called Mountview School for Boys and I had a really good individual in my life from Youth for Christ named Rich Van Pelt. After losing contact with him was when everything went downhill for me. I miss him.

I have requested a Bible from the chaplain's office. As soon as it is issued to me I will be reading what you have suggested—Matthew 14:22–33. Won't lie to you Jan. I'm a bit scared because this is a very new path for me. Am willing to take the steps for Christ to be my guiding light. Am looking forward to hearing from you.

Your friend,
Jody Mobley
Jody Mobley #60021
PO Box 6000 Unit 4
Sterling, CO 80751

11/1/17

Dear Jody,

It was great to hear back from you! I know this journey you're starting is not only difficult but, I'm sure, might seem unattainable given your current situation. Remember nothing is impossible for our Lord. I don't know if you're familiar with the apostle Paul, who didn't come onto the scene until after Jesus' death, but his goal in life as a young man, then called Saul, was to kill Christians, and he was good at it. His life changed on his way to the city of Damascus, where he was hoping to slaughter Christians. On the road there, Jesus literally knocked him off his horse and asked him, "Saul, Saul, why do you persecute Me?" This story in the Bible, Acts 9, converted Paul into possibly the most prolific author in the Bible. He eventually wrote over half of the New Testament, and some of his greatest writings were written while he was in prison.

Jody, I guess what I'm saying is prison, although lonely and dangerous, in no way will hinder your relationship with the Lord and His Son, our Savior, Jesus Christ. If you invite Him in, as you are doing, He will change your life, not your environment but your soul. As Paul discovered, God can touch and speak to you anywhere, anytime; you just need to open your heart to Him. I think the fact that you're reaching out to Him is an obvious sign you want Him in your life, and believe me, He will come and make you a new man in Christ.

Thank you for telling me about your past life. I can't imagine what it was truly like for you, and I'm sure at soon-to-be fifty-one (happy birthday, by the way) you feel like so much of your life has been spent on wrong choices. Even though you are where you are paying for those choices, you have now made the greatest and most life-altering choice of your life, and He will not disappoint. I personally think God has already begun a work in your life. You mentioned in your letter Youth for Christ and Rich Van Pelt. It so happens I'm beginning work with Youth for Christ and was telling my supervisor about you after receiving your letter. I mentioned Rich, and he told me he knows Rich and will talk to him about contacting you. Now, if that's not God at work, I don't know what is.

Jody, please let me know if you're allowed to have your own Bible because I'd like to send you one. Also, are visitors allowed? And what are the requirements for that? Because I'd like to come up and see you. Look forward to hearing from you, and God bless you, my friend!

Jan

Acts 9:

Meanwhile, Saul was still breathing out murderous threats against the Lord's disciples. He went to the

high priest and asked him for letters to the syna-
gogues in Damascus, so that if he found any there
who belonged to the Way, whether men or women,
he might take them as prisoners to Jerusalem. As he
neared Damascus on his journey, suddenly a light
from heaven flashed around him. He fell to the
ground and heard a voice say to him, "Saul, Saul,
why do you persecute me?"

"Who are you, Lord?" Saul asked.

"I am Jesus, whom you are persecuting," he
replied. "Now get up and go into the city, and you
will be told what you must do."

The men traveling with Saul stood there
speechless; they heard the sound but did not see
anyone. Saul got up from the ground, but when he
opened his eyes he could see nothing. So they led him
by the hand into Damascus. For three days he was
blind, and did not eat or drink anything.

In Damascus there was a disciple named
Ananias. The Lord called to him in a vision,
"Ananias!"

"Yes, Lord," he answered.

The Lord told him, "Go to the house of Judas
on Straight Street and ask for a man from Tarsus
named Saul, for he is praying. In a vision he has
seen a man named Ananias come and place his
hands on him to restore his sight."

"Lord," Ananias answered, "I have heard
many reports about this man and all the harm he
has done to your holy people in Jerusalem. And he
has come here with authority from the chief priests
to arrest all who call on your name."

But the Lord said to Ananias, "Go! This man
is my chosen instrument to proclaim my name to the
Gentiles and their kings and to the people of Israel. I
will show him how much he must suffer for my name."

Then Ananias went to the house and entered it. Placing his hands on Saul, he said, "Brother Saul, the Lord—Jesus, who appeared to you on the road as you were coming here—has sent me so that you may see again and be filled with the Holy Spirit." Immediately, something like scales fell from Saul's eyes, and he could see again. He got up and was baptized, and after taking some food, he regained his strength.

Chapter 3

Deuteronomy 33:20–21—the people of the tribe of God received the best of the new land because they obeyed God by punishing Israel's wicked enemies. Punishment is unpleasant for both the giver and the receiver, but it is a necessary part of growth. Understand that realistic discipline is important to character development. Always strive to be both just and merciful, keeping in mind the best interests of the person who must receive the punishment.

* * * *

My actions that caused some of my punishment may have been justified, while others not so much. Obviously, I was the recipient of the punishment, and to a certain extent, you need to discipline children, but God does not approve of abuse. My mom and Terry never kept in mind the best interests of my brothers and me. I didn't know it at the time, but God was there helping me survive in order that I could do work spreading the word of His power and love. God puts punishment in play to facilitate discipline, but abuse will destroy!

In the following letter, Jody is beginning to open up a little about not only his life but what might have caused his life to take the shape it did. This was also the start of his desire to know what God's Word was all about and whether it could actually be applicable to his past and present circumstances.

* * * *

11/24/17

Dear Jan,

Was really nice to receive your letter. Receiving mail from time to time is nice. Thank you. They called me to the chaplain's office the other day to issue me a Bible. It is my first one since I was just a child. First thing I did was read Matthew 14:22–33. Jesus walks on water. Don't understand why Peter lost faith. If he believed in the beginning and got out of the boat to walk on the water to Jesus and was walking on the water, you would have to assume his belief would have gotten stronger. Even with the wind right? Or is that scripture supposed to teach us that even if our faith may falter at times, He is still there for us? Can you explain your understanding of that passage?

Yes, this journey I've decided to take is not going to be an easy one. When a person lives a certain life for so long it's hard to make life altering changes without support and friendship. I ran away from home at age twelve and my mom told them when they picked me up and put me in Zeb Pike Juvenile Detention in Colorado Springs to keep me. Made me think I wasn't worthy of love or a good life. As I got older life got more difficult and I ended up in Mount View School for Boys at age fifteen. Actually fourteen and that's when I met Rich. When I got out on November 19, 1982, I had an okay life. Occasionally I found myself in trouble, but not major trouble. Then on December 20, 1986, my best friend put a shotgun in his mouth and committed suicide in front of me. It caused me to have severe PTSD and major depression disorder. My older brother hung himself in January of 2003. I've lost pretty much everybody that was close to me over the years. From 2013 to now I have had five attempts. But for some reason, I've not gone to the next life. Now don't get me wrong Jan, these are not things I normally tell anybody, nor are they ment to get anybody to feel sorry for me. I'm only telling you because you need to know me and the things I've been through. Plus I believe I should be open and honest with you on all levels in order for you to know who I am without judgment. I also feel safe talking to you.

Yes, I've heard of the apostle Paul, but am not at all familiar with his trials and tribulations. Had no idea he was in prison either. I know a lot of devote followers back then were persecuted and made to live hard lives.

And as you mention in your latest letter the Lord and His Son, our Savior, cannot change the environment I'm in but can change my life. That is what I'm looking forward for. A better quality life. I've had opportunities in life to go down a better path but never made the turn. I have an opportunity now with your support to make that turn. Thank you for responding. It truly makes me believe that somebody is looking out for me. It strengthens my faith for this journey and makes me not so scared. Thank you again. I really hope this is the beginning of a new wonderful love filled life and a great new friendship with you!

Wow—I can't believe Rich is still around! That's cool. Think it is awesome you will be working for Youth for Christ. I know you will make a great amount of success there. It only takes one person to make a difference in a person's life.

You asked if you could send a Bible? You can. It has to come directly from the store with a receipt, and a copy of the receipt should be sent to me for a record. But I'd love to have my own personal Bible. As for visits I will have to get the forms for that and send them to you. Will do that in my next letter.

How did your Thanksgiving go? Ours was okay. We ended up in lockdown around 7 p.m. An incident in another pod happened and put the unit on lockdown. Other than that it was okay. My birthday was okay also. A few of the guys in here ordered some items off canteen and made me nachos. It was very thoughtful and it was nice of them. Hope you had a great Thanksgiving. I've got a lot to be thankful for this year. A new path with Jesus Christ, a new friendship with you, and a better feeling in my heart. The Lord has definitely blessed me this year. Am also thankful Rich is still living his life. He made a huge impact on my life in 1981–82. I look forward to hearing from you and please feel free to give me some scripture to read that we can discuss. Take care.

God bless you my friend—always and forever.

Jody
Jody Mobley #60021
PO Box 6000
Sterling, CO 80751

12/7/17

Dear Jody,

It was great to hear from you. Your letter was certainly honest and help-ful in understanding you as a person. I can't remotely imagine what it's been like for you, given what you explained in your letter. Unquestionably, there are things in life you can't unsee and certainly can't forget, as you described. At age twenty my dad, a Kansas farm boy, was fighting in WWII in Europe. He had to kill and saw his closest friend killed right in front of him. He was cap-tured and was a prisoner of war. He escaped when the Russians were attack-ing the prison camp he was in. He talked about it just one time in my life, and I was stunned to hear it. As with your life, Jody, there were many things he could not unsee and never forget, but he became a great man of faith and let God handle his past. He and I were baptized at the same time when I was a baby and he was home from the war. He turned to my mom and said, "Do you think God forgives you for what you've done in war?" The answer, of course, is yes! God and Jesus are in the forgiveness business.

You asked me about Matthew 14:22–33. I love all of Jesus' parables, and this is one of my favorites. All His disciples, including Peter, had seen Him perform any number of miracles, as well as what had just happened, feeding thousands with two fishes and five loaves of bread, and yet when He walked across the water, only Peter stepped out. So, of all the disciples, only Peter had the faith to step out onto the water. I don't know about you, but if I saw a man walking on the water and He told me He was the Son of God, I'd probably believe it, and yet they all, even Peter, had doubts. You're absolutely right, Jody; even when we doubt, and everyone does, He is still there for us; we just need to hold out our hand and take Him in our boat (life) with us. A side note: Peter was crucified years later, and he made them crucify him upside down because he said he wasn't worthy of being crucified the same way His Lord and Savior had been. His faith did grow stronger and stronger until the end of his life.

You indicated this journey you've decided to take is not going to be easy, and I would not disagree with that, but of all the journeys you've taken in your life, this one is the most important and will absolutely be the most rewarding. You said in the past four years you've attempted suicide five times but for some reason have not gone on to the next life. I certainly don't know God's plan for you, Jody, but I can tell you He does have a plan, and that plan can only be completed if you're here to finish it. I can also tell you His plan for you will be fulfilling, exciting, and gratifying beyond anything you can imagine. All you need do is be open and patient. As you stated, you had opportunities in the past to go down a better path but never made that turn; well, my friend, you're making that turn now, and you'll never have to look back.

Jody, I mentioned to you in my first letter that I work with the teenage youth at our church. As a group we work on the Christian beliefs of giving, compassion, and forgiveness. I hope you're okay with this; I've talked to them about you and what you're facing in prison and how you're now reaching out to the Lord. They think what you're doing is wonderful and inspiring. My reason for talking to them is I want their input on what they might do to help you. Again, I hope you're okay with this; if not, just let me know, and I'll stop. They were hoping you'd be okay with it because, as one of them put it, "He'll have six more people praying for him and trying to help him." Again, you let me know how you feel about it, and that's what I'll do.

Thank you for the encouragement about Youth for Christ. I'll certainly give it my best, and God willing, it will work out. Thanksgiving was great. I have two daughters and seven grandkids, so it's always a little crazy. It sounds like your Thanksgiving was cut short, but your birthday was good. You can't beat nachos, and that was thoughtful of them to do that for you.

Jody, I've been wondering what prompted you to start this journey. Back in August our church received a letter from you, which the pastor's wife gave to me. I remember at the time wondering how you found our little church, but I'm sure glad you did. You mentioned you have a lot to be thankful for this year, a new path with Jesus Christ, our new friendship, a better feeling in your heart, and that the Lord has definitely blessed you this year. I can't tell you how awesome that sounds. There must have been a point when He spoke to you and put you on this path. In Psalm 119:105 it says, *"Your word is a lamp to my feet and a light to my path."* Let's keep at it, Jody, and it wouldn't surprise me that someday you'll be doing Bible studies for others who are seeking a better and more hopeful life.

As for Scripture there are two things I would suggest. First, I'd learn the Lord's Prayer, Matthew 6:9, if you don't know it already. This is how Jesus taught us to pray. Second, I'd recommend starting Psalms. It's in the Old Testament and teaches us how to rise from the depths of despair to new heights of joy. David of David and Goliath wrote around seventy-five of them, and they are comforting and inspirational. I think you'd get a great deal out of them. One of the girls in Sunday school class works at Barnes & Noble, so we're going to get to work on sending you a study Bible, and I'll wait to hear from you about a visit.

Take care, Jody, and trust in the Lord. God's blessing to you!

Your friend,

Jan

Chapter 4

Exodus 2:23–25—God's rescue doesn't always come the moment we want it. God had promised to bring the Hebrew slaves out of Egypt. The people had waited a long time for that promise to be kept, but God rescued them when He knew the right time had come. God knows the best time to act. When you feel God has forgotten you in your troubles, remember God has a time table we can't see.

* * * *

I believe going to church that first time with Ralph and his family was God attempting to rescue me from the tragic events going on in my life. God may not have pulled me completely from the abyss I was in, but His timing was perfect to keep me going, so I could survive and eventually end up coming back to Him when He saw the time was right. Now, here I am in God's hands, hoping that by doing His work, it helps you.

This was our fourth letter in the span of a little over three and a half months, and as you can see, our letters crossed in the mail. Jody had learned the hard way not to trust anyone, and rightfully so, and to be honest, I wasn't sure I could trust him. We've all heard stories about prisoners who have found God and are now transformed by their faith in the Lord. I wasn't sure that was not what was happening here, but if that was the case, what was his angle, and was I just being used?

* * * *

12/28/17

Dear Jan,

It was really nice to receive your letter and card. Thank you! Your words are very uplifting. You are certainly correct when you say there are things in life we can't un-see. It would be nice if we could, but I guess the things we go through in life get us to where we are going. Thank you for the story about your father. It's hard to imagine that God is so forgiving. Knowing that God and Jesus do forgive us for our sins is very comforting for sure.

I did not know Peter was crucified upside down. Peter 1:13 is a verse that I really like. My mind has been in a place that was not good, but by believing in Christ prepares me for tomorrow. My mind is open, and I can take in the knowledge that Jesus is there whether we see him or not. That revelation alone makes tomorrow a brighter day. Not sure if my words make much sense to you, but they do to me. As Peter's faith grew stronger with time, so will mine.

You ask what prompted me to take this journey. Well, as I mentioned in my last letter I've tried to move on to the next life and for some reason there is a force keeping me here. Began wondering if God and Jesus Christ are involved. A lot of soul searching and trying to figure out why I'm still here has brought me to this point. Then I took a shot in the dark and sent a letter to your church. Received a reply from you. What are the odds that three out of those five attempts I should have not come back from. Then, what are the odds that out of all the churches in Colorado, I send a letter to yours and you respond?

I don't believe this is a coincidence, nor do I believe it's blind luck. Something is happening. Why else would I feel this pull toward God's Word and His Son our Savior? What would put me in your path? Only God and Jesus Christ have the power to make all this happen. That is my belief anyway. So here I am on a journey with God, Jesus Christ, and my new friend and guide Jan.

Am not real sure about having the teenage youth knowing my trials and tribulations, but I do know that I trust you and believe you are only trying to help. So I am okay with what you are doing.

Wow—seven grandchildren! I bet that can be quite a handful. Am glad I don't have any children. Life in here is hard enough. Wouldn't want to have children growing up without a father. I went through that. My father passed away when I was only six. Think I would've been a good father if the chance was there, but not from in here.

Have read the Lord's Prayer and have a question. It says, "Do not heap up empty phrases as the Gentiles do." Don't understand that. What is an empty phrase? Or what is the meaning of an empty phrase?

Am enclosing a visiting form that, once filled out, must be sent to the facility and not to me. I was so excited to finally be getting a visitor after so many years and now have bad news. In July I was at my worst with the whole prison and the way we are treated, and decided that it was time to move on. I did a shot of heroin and went to sleep. My cellmate and two others found me not breathing and gave me CPR until they got help. Was taken to the hospital, where I came back. Was going to be charged in court for possession of and use of a narcotic. They dropped all charges, but the CDOC charged me with the use of a drug through a hot UA that went into effect November 27, 2017. Am not allowed visits or phone calls until November 27, 2018. You asked what brought me to God and this new path? It was all started over this last incident in July. Didn't want to mention his earlier because I thought they may let me slide, but I had to wait nonetheless until final word came from the warden at Sterling. Didn't want to get anybody's hope up until I knew for sure what was going on. You can still submit the form, but I think it has to be updated every six months to a year. I'm not sure, it's been a long time since I've had any visits.

Will be reading Psalms and studying that. Think it will be good to have you or the youth recommend scripture to read and study. Not only will it help guide me, it will also showcase what the youth have been learning.

For now take care, and I apologize for the visiting situation. Hope you will be willing to visit in the future. With the Lord's Prayer and God's blessing to you.

Your friend,
Jody—Have a very happy New Year!

First Peter 1:13:

"Therefore, preparing your minds for action, and being sober-minded, set your hope fully on the grace that will be brought to you at the revelation of Jesus Christ."

Jody Mobley #60021
PO Box 777
Canon City, CO 81215

12/28/17

Dear Jody,

I got your Christmas card, thank you! I hope you got mine; I sent it on 12/7. If you didn't get my card and letter, please let me know, and I'll resend them. I hope your Christmas was good with the knowledge that our Lord and Savior came into the world on Christmas day.

My Christmas was very blessed, and thank you for all your well wishes. I truly count my new relationship with you as an additional and profound blessing. This week I'll start working on getting you your own Bible, and hopefully I can get it to you sooner than later, and I'd still like to come visit you at some point.

I, too, am proud to be on this journey with you, Jody. As Jesus said in Matthew 14:20, *"For where two or three are gathered together in my name, there too am I."* And there is no doubt you and I are gathered in spirit in His name.

I just wanted to drop you a quick note to let you know I got your card and am aware of your address change. Here's hoping that in the new year, Jody, your journey with God continues to grow and brings you peace, understanding, and contentment. As I said, I'm proud and honored to be along for the ride. Take care, my friend, and may God bless all things in your life.

Jan

* * * *

As you can see by this letter, he says he is starting to trust the Lord and me, which I found somewhat curious this early on; however, I was in no position to judge him, and I kept thinking God didn't bring us together for wrong purposes, so I needed to persevere and trust in the Lord.

Chapter 5

Malachi 2:14—the people were complaining about their adverse circumstances when they had only themselves to blame. People often try to avoid guilt feelings by shifting the blame, but this doesn't solve the problem. When you face problems, look first at yourself. If you changed your attitude or behavior, would your problem be solved?

* * * *

When things are bad and we're young, we tend to blame others for our problems. I began to blame God since He'd created me. My belief in Him faded, and we became enemies. He was to blame for all my problems when in reality God was preparing me to help others and bring me back into His family. I had no idea my life would never see any peace, but that all changed when I decided to stop blaming God and let Him into my heart. I may be in prison and dealing with the daily grind in here, but now I'm able to do it with an inner feeling of peace because God has eased those feelings of blame, and I can now see things much clearer with Him by my side.

In this letter from Jody, there is a certain sense of expectation about the new year. That maybe 2018 could be different in a positive way and that God could be the answer.

* * * *

1/9/18

Dear Jan,

Am so glad the new year is here. This last one was rough, but my new path has put a joy in my heart and a new friend in my life! Haven't been on this new path long, but the difference is how I feel with our Lord and Savior by my side; it is so profoundly different from what I've felt previously.

I've been learning the Lord's Prayer and hope it helps me. Have no doubt it will. I do have a question. What is the difference between Bibles if any? The reason I ask is I have one given to me by the chaplain at Sterling. It's an English Standard Version from the World Bible School. But there are some that say King James Version and others. What is the difference between them.

My new year so far has been good. We get put on lockdown a lot here, but that's okay. Give me time to study the Bible and familiarize myself with it more. I set aside time each day to study. One passage that really made me think the other day was John 11:25–26, when Jesus was talking to Martha. Was a really deep revelation in my mind, as you can imagine.

Last night I relaxed and watched the college football championship game. I do like sports. My favorites are NBA, NFL, tennis and college football. Never had the opportunity to go to college, except when I was in minimum security facility in Rifle, Colorado. They allowed us to take classes at the Colorado Rocky Mountain Community College there. Did two semesters there. The first semester we had to do just general studies and only with the facility. The second semester we were allowed to take classes with people in the community. Was able to do that because I studied and took my GED in Denver County Jail. So I have accomplished some things while locked up. Of course, my biggest accomplishment was making the decision to give my life to the Lord.

Hope all is well with you and your family. Take care and my God bless you in every way.

Your friend,
Jody

John 11:25–26:

*"Jesus said to her, 'I am the resurrection and the life.
The one who believes in me will live, even though
they die; and whoever lives by believing in me will
never die. Do you believe this?'"*

Jody Mobley #60021
PO Box 777
Canon City, CO 81215

1/12/18

Dear Jody,

I got your letter—well done and honest as always. I went into the ConnectNetwork.com and then to the Colorado Department of Corrections, and naturally there was a lot there, so I'll sort through that in the next few days and see what I can figure out. Being able to send you messages would be great, and I'm sure we'll be able to work that out once I set it up on my end.

All the disciples were put to death and tortured for following Jesus. I'm sure when they started their discipleship, they had no idea how it would end, and had they been told, you have to wonder what they would have done. Jesus, of course, knew and groomed them for what their future would ultimately be. He also knew their reward in heaven was far more than they could have ever imagined. Christ will prepare you for your tomorrows and even better for your eternal life with Him in heaven. You've told me how you tried to move on five times and never succeeded. Had you been successful before, now you wouldn't have had the chance to give your life to God and reap the rewards that come with His love. Maybe you've stayed here so you can fellowship with Him and His Son, Jesus Christ, and who knows what He has planned for you? But it is His plan, and I know it will be something great.

Jody, I've thought many times how amazing it is that He brought us together. As you said, out of all the churches in Colorado, you picked the one I'm at, and the pastor's wife, out of all the people in the congregation, gave your letter to me. When God wants something to go a certain way...it does!

You were right; it was not blind luck or coincidence; it was God making sure our paths crossed. Yes, something is happening, not only for you but for my Sunday school class and me. They have a genuine concern and interest in how you're doing and how your walk with the Lord is progressing. I'm going to have each one of them write you a letter. I'll be anxious to see what you think and how their perspective makes you look at the journey you're on.

I can't imagine what you go through on a daily, weekly, or monthly basis and have for years. But up until now, you were trying to handle it alone, and now you have a cheering squad and, even better, the greatest coach in the universe, God. I work with baseball pitchers over the winter, getting them ready for their spring seasons, and I tell them, "Hey, when you're out there on the mound in a game...guess what? I can't be there with you." But, as you well know, God and our Savior Jesus Christ are with us every second of every day for eternity if we'll let Them. I think as you're finding out, there is nothing more comforting than that knowledge.

I'm so sorry about your last attempt and the fallout from that, but that doesn't change one thing for me. I'll fill out the visitor form, and when I can, I'll come see you. I can tell you it would have been an immense tragedy had we not connected, so thank the Lord. He had other plans for both of us.

Yes, I, too, love Peter 1:13, which you're in the process of doing, living a holy life. You asked about "what an empty phrase/prayer is." Certainly, since the time of Jesus and right on through to today, many people like to make a show of praying. They're saying, "Oh, look at me; I'm praying. I must be holy...right?" Wrong! As Jesus says, "Pray privately to your Father in heaven, and He will hear you." Now, that's not to say praying in public is wrong; it's not, but God knows your heart, and He knows when it's for show and for real. I hope that helps.

I think another piece of scripture you will find helpful and enlightening is John 1. The basic premise is God and Jesus saying to all who follow, "I've got your back no matter what!" It clearly states who Jesus is and why He came. He's come for you, Jody, and I can't tell you how tremendous it is that you're opening the door to let Him in. That's not to say we won't have problems in our lives; we will, but we won't be facing them alone. You've had to deal with many life-altering and overwhelming things in your life, which persist even today, but now you have God to guide you through the rough spots and bad times—He's always there for you; just ask for His help and understanding.

Well, I guess that's it for now, but let me know if you still want your own Bible, and I'll let you know about the internet hookup. Take care of yourself, my friend, and know God's right there with you always!

Jan

First Peter 1:13:

"Therefore, with minds that are alert and fully sober, set your hope on the grace to be brought to you when Jesus Christ is revealed at his coming."

* * * *

Between his last letter and this letter, Jody was moved from the Sterling Correction Facility in Sterling, Colorado, to the Colorado State Penitentiary in Canon City, Colorado. Here's a little background on those two facilities—Sterling Correctional Facility (SCF) is the largest prison in the Colorado Department of Corrections system with a capacity of 2,585 prisoners. Colorado State Penitentiary (commonly abbreviated CSP) is a level V maximum security prison. The facility is located in the state's East Cañon Complex with six other state correctional facilities of various security levels, including Florence Super Max.

Jody was moved because of his suicide attempts, and the warden apparently saw him as a persistent problem who needed more stringent security.

Chapter 6

Job 2:10—many people think that believing in God protects them from trouble, so when calamity comes, they question God's goodness and justice. But the message of Job is that you should not give up on God because He allows you to have bad experiences. Faith in God does not guarantee personal prosperity, and lack of faith does not guarantee troubles in this life. God is capable of rescuing us from suffering, but He may also allow suffering for reasons we cannot understand.

* * * *

Turning against God and letting my faith diminish into obscurity, I got lost in darkness. I felt abandoned, scared, mad, and my belief faded. I begged God for help, but it wasn't coming fast enough, so Satan weaseled his way into my life. I fell for his play, and any connection I had with God was gone. It's so much easier to be bad than good, so stay strong in your belief in the Lord. Think about what's really important, your faith or the dead-end path we take when God and Christ are not with us. Keep your faith, and believe me, it will pay off.

You can see in the following letter Jody is starting to see and feel God's presence in his life, and although, as he puts it, seeming childish about it, it's taking hold, and you can sense he wants that and wants it to grow stronger.

* * * *

1/28/18

Dear Jan,

Received two letters from you. As always it's good to hear from you. It's definitely a good feeling to receive mail at mail call. Thank you!

Was reading Genesis 1–3 this morning and actually reading those verses it's amazing the clarity it brought. Everybody, or mostly everybody, is familiar with God creating the world and heaven and earth. All these years I've never put each day to a day of the week. Funny how something so obvious and something of common sense can bypass your thought process. Also I never knew God created Adam from dust and breathed life into him by blowing it in through his nostrils. Nor did I know Eve was made from a rib bone taken from Adam. Was familiar with the serpent being a snake, because all the pictures you see of that story you see the snake hanging in the tree talking to Eve. And how fitting is it that good old serpent was made a snake by God. A conniving, manipulative creature. If you look up the definition of a snake in the dictionary God was perfect in His creations. My thoughts on all of this may seem a bit childish in interpreting it all, but in reality I am just a child in all of this. The feeling you get from reading the verses are kind of euphoric I guess you could say. The feelings I'm going through are ones I've never really experienced before much. They are great feelings for sure!

You are so correct in not being able to imagine what we have to go through in here on a daily or weekly basis. Seems to be designed and run to sap all hope and good feeling from you. But—and they say that is a word you should never use, but since taking this new path with God and His Son Jesus Christ, I've felt better and have made progress in being able to leave the darkness behind. Has also helped just by knowing you and knowing my past and current situation is not under judgment by you. You have accepted me as I am and that feels so good you do not even understand!

On the empty phrase/prayer—thank you for your interpretation. I've always seen or heard people pray they get this or that, and it made me think—how could prayer be beneficial if all you do it for is personal gain. Shouldn't it be good enough we have been forgiven our sins and to strive to be better than we were yesterday? Just a thought.

On the 11ᵗʰ I was taken to DRDC in Denver and spent till the 16ᵗʰ there. Had to go to the eye doctor on the 12ᵗʰ at the Denver Health Center. Normally those trips are day trips and you go to them and back in one day. Am supposed to have safety glasses due to my eye condition and the injury I sustained in Sterling. I have glaucoma and am totally blind in the right eye. The injury was getting hit in the left eye with a handball accidentally while I was working out. Yeah, it caused some damage but things are going okay. I've had a pretty hard life Jan, but I'm going to make it. I have God, Jesus and you. I'm fine.

Thank you for offering me a good Bible. Can't wait for the day it arrives. It will definitely be put to good use. Well I plan on reading the Genesis scripture about Cain and Abel a little later today. Will write more later. For now take care and bask in the Lord's love as I will.

Your friend,
Jody

Genesis 1:3:

In the beginning God created the heavens and the earth. Now the earth was formless and empty, darkness was over the surface of the deep, and the Spirit of God was hovering over the waters.

And God said, "Let there be light," and there was light. God saw that the light was good, and he separated the light from the darkness. God called the light "day," and the darkness he called "night." And there was evening, and there was morning—the first day.

Jody Mobley #60021
PO Box 777
Canon City, CO 81215

1/24/18

Dear Jody,

I got your letter—we seem to be passing in the mail. You can't imagine how great it is to hear you say how glad you are the new year is here and that you've started on this new path that's put joy in your heart and that you have a new friend for life…you do! As you say, you haven't been on your new journey long, but look how fast the Lord has changed your heart and soul. Believe me, it's only going to get better.

I'm glad you're learning the Lord's Prayer. I say it every morning when I get up. It covers all your bases for the day, and as you move forward, it's a great piece of scripture to study. As for the difference in Bibles, I'm not familiar with the World Bible School and the English Standard Version. I looked at their website, and it appears it's a place you can study to become a minister online. I don't know if what you have is a study Bible, but I'm going to send you a good study Bible, where below all the scripture writings is an explanation of what they mean and in the back is a section called Concordance, where you can look up anything like jealousy, prayer, or sections of scripture. It's fantastic and will really help you in your studies. I use it constantly.

I'm glad your new year has been good so far. I'll tell you the difference between your first letter to the church in August of last year and now is dramatic and awe-inspiring. I'm sure you're not aware of how inspirational your story is to people like the kids in class and me. God is using you, Jody, not just to help yourself but to aid some of us. One of our major goals as Christians is to spread the good news, and that's exactly what you're doing through your continuing walk with the Lord.

That's interesting you mention John 11:25–26. I've actually discussed that passage with the kids and asked them what they thought it meant. It also became a relevant passage to me back in the summer of 2016. Jesus certainly could have saved Lazarus from dying but, as you know, waited four days to go to his grave. It's a great lesson in being patient with the Lord's ways and timing in our lives. I won't go into the whole story, but back in early 2016, I connected with a Christian mission in Haiti called Respire Haiti. It's a remarkable story of one young girl's battle against evil in the desperate and poverty-stricken country of Haiti. I'll send you a copy of her book, *Miracle on Voodoo Mountain*. So I contacted them about bringing baseball to Haiti. They went nuts—"Yes, please bring baseball to our little island." I planned a trip there in March of 2016 but caught the flu and had to postpone. Tried again in April, and we got hit with a major snowstorm here in Denver, and the flight was canceled. I then had a hard time communicating with them and, thinking I was in charge of this, got mad about it. I remember saying to God, "Well, am I supposed to go or not?" Can you believe the audacity of that? He responded and set me straight. One night while lying in bed I was about to go to sleep when this strong voice said to me, "This isn't about you; it's about Me!" John 11:25–26 at work. "Be patient, and I will take care of it," and He did. I wound up going at the end of May, and what an experience it was.

That was great you got your GED, but you're right; that will pale compared to what you're doing now, giving your life to the Lord. None of us can do anything more life-changing or rewarding than opening the door and inviting the Lord and His Son, Jesus Christ, into our lives.

I checked into the messaging thing, and it appears I can't do that with the prison in Canon City. I'll check it out further and let you know. Well, my friend, keep those letters coming and walking the walk, and may God bless you and continue to guide your every step. Take care, Jody!

Jan

* * * *

Jody appears to be taking a genuine interest in God's Word. He appears to be searching for how the Bible might help him understand his past and maybe give him some hope for the future. He's also opening up a little about his life, even to the point of kidding about it. I'm certainly hoping that this will continue and he'll not stall out due to the environment he's in. For the majority of his life, Jody's only known prison, and, as he says, you have no idea unless you've been there, so this is an immense challenge and completely contrary to anything he's ever done. However, the undeniable truth is he's got God in his corner, and he's starting to see and feel what that means.

Chapter 7

Matthew 5:38–42—when we are wronged, often our first reaction is to get even. Instead Jesus said we should do good to those who wrong us! Our desire should not be to keep score but to love and forgive. This is not natural—it's supernatural. Only God can give us the strength to love as He does. Instead of planning vengeance, pray for those who hurt you.

* * * *

At the time this was all going on in my life, I wanted everyone to feel as bad as I did. God and Jesus were not there for me, so my anger was focused on them because they were supposed to save me. I couldn't trust anybody and felt like I had to get away from it all. I was just too young and not knowledgeable about faith and trusting God. But it is never too late to come back to Him. Fortunately for me, God whispered in my ear, "It's time!" Now, here I am, doing His work, which He prepared me for.

Jody Mobley #60021
PO Box 777
Canon City, CO 81215

2/6/18

Dear Jody,

First, I wanted to let you know I ordered you a study Bible, the same one I use. You should get it around the 13th/14th of next week. I think you'll find it very helpful and insightful. I also sent in my visit request, so whenever that can happen, I'm there. Things have been pretty busy, but I'm still working on the messaging thing.

It looks like you're reading the Old Testament, which can be pretty heavy, especially Job. For the most part, the Old Testament was all the rules and regulations, so to speak, God ordained. The New Testament is about Jesus explaining all those rules and regulations. One of the things I love about the Bible is there is no situation, circumstance, or problem in life that is not addressed in the Bible, and you feeling euphoric reading the Scriptures is absolutely fantastic!

Yeah, I'm sure the prison is run by very strict rules and regulations, but, as you say, since you've been on your new path to glory, God and Jesus can sidestep those and deal directly with your heart and soul. As for not judging you, I have no right or interest in judging you, Jody, now, then, or ever. The only one who can and will judge any of us is God. I do think, however, it is one of the hardest things to do not to judge people, especially those who seem to be all about themselves and apparently have no interest in helping others. I had a great pastor once who said, "As God requires, you have to love everyone...but that doesn't mean you have to like them."

I hope my empty prayer explanation helped. It's amazing when you think about it that we can pray anytime; He's always there listening. No matter where we are, where we're going, or what's happening to us, He's there. When you said, "Shouldn't it be good enough we have been forgiven for our sins and to strive to be better than we were yesterday?" you were right on the mark! God sent His only Son, who died a horrific death, to take on the sins of the world. That's almost too much to comprehend, but it is a fact! I feel a great responsibility to thank Him for that each and every day.

Sorry about your eye. Yeah, playing handball or racquetball without goggles is dangerous. I played a lot of years of racquetball and saw a few guys not wearing eye protection do some serious damage. Yes, you are right, Jody, you have had a hard life, but now that you have the Lord and Jesus as your personal trainers, I'm guessing your physical and spiritual life is going to take off.

It's amazing how God puts things in our lives, and of course, we have no idea the ramifications of those things as we move through life. Baseball has been that for me. It's been a part of my life since I can remember and has opened many doors, many of which have led me to the Lord. Atlanta Braves, eh? Well, I'll let that pass...just kidding. They certainly have had some great pitching over the years, so I'll give you that. LOL. Hey, don't feel like the lone ranger; none of us are what we used to be, at least physically; we are, however, new creations in Jesus Christ.

Let me know when you get the Bible and if I can help out with books for the library. Always good to hear from you, Jody—may God bless you every minute of every day!

Your friend in Christ,

Jan

Dear Jody,

I wanted to send you these first two letters from two of the girls in class. I hope you find them encouraging and sincere. The other kids in class are working on letters to you, but I don't push them; I want them to genuinely think about how they feel and what they want to say to you. I asked them to tell me the last time they thought they actually witnessed a miracle. None of them could really come up with anything, although I think we see miracles every day, but hey, I'm an old dude, so maybe I'm paying more attention. Anyway, I told them they're involved in one right now... you, Jody. When you reached out to our church, I'm sure you had no idea you would be touching so many lives and bringing those lives closer to God through your experiences and your journey with God. It has been profound and wonderful...thank you!

Anyway, I wanted you to have these and to know we're all with you. I hope by the time you get this, you'll have your new Bible. Take care, Jody, and know besides God, our Savior Jesus Christ, and me, you have the youth of Grace United Methodist Church walking with you and cheering you on!

Yours in Christ,

Jan

* * * *

Dear Jody,

I do hope the Scripture gives you strength in yourself and through God. Just remember that God is here for you when you need Him. He may not answer you right away, but He will answer you when the time is perfect, and He will give you His love if you give all of yourself to Him. I will pray for you and hope this letter gives you the strength and faith you are looking for. Take care of yourself, Jody, and please keep that strength with you!

Sincerely,

Cindy

Hi, Jody,

With Jan, we have talked some about miracles and what they mean. You and your journey have really stood out to me as a miracle, and I fully support you in this new path. You reached out to our church, out of any others, and I think that is a miracle. You are trying to get closer to God, and God sees how much you are trying; therefore, He is trying to get to know you better, which is a miracle as well. If you keep trying and don't lose hope and faith, God will learn more about you and you, God.

Sarah

* * * *

2/18/18

Dear Jan,

Thank you so much for the study Bible. I really like it. Really like the explanations at the bottom of the pages. It really helps to understand what everything means. Thank you again.

Yes, I was reading some from the Old Testament. I go back and forth into the Old and New Testaments. Take for instance the anger and resentment we tend to feel in prison toward the guards and staff. Went from reading Genesis on Adam and Eve to Matthew 5:43–48, "Love your enemies." Even on this new path it's not easy to put that anger and resentment aside. Prisoners can tell you story after story of being mistreated, abused, put down, disrespected and many other things that breeds those harsh feelings. "Love your enemies and pray for your persecutors" is not an easy task in here. However, it's becoming somewhat easier with each day that passes. I'm so glad our Savior and Lord Jesus Christ is so forgiving because I do falter at times. One thing I am learning having God and Jesus in my life is it doesn't matter if you falter from time to time. What matters is picking yourself up and trying to do better in their eyes. Something else I've learned is the harder you try the amazing the feelings are.

So all the kids you work with—do not get into trouble. We take so much for granted in life. Waking up and being able to just walk outside and smell the fresh air is one thing I never really thought about. Walking barefoot in the soft grass or listening to the birds singing on a warm summer day. A good meal with your family. Oh and a soft bed. Being bad is easy. Being good is the chore. It's one chore I am working on having back in my life. With the help of our Lord and Jesus I'm finding it easier. Faith will conquer all.

Received the letters you sent to me from Cindy and Sarah. Tell them thank you—some smart kids. If I ever did get out I really would consider working for and with kids. If I could prevent any kids from ending up in places like this my life would be complete. Who knows—maybe that's God's plan for me. I don't know, but whatever His plans are I welcome them with open arms!

Hope this finds you all in good health and spirits. Take care and enjoy each day we have with our Lord and our Savior Jesus Christ.

God bless,

Jody

Matthew 5:43–45:

> *Ye have heard that it hath been said, Thou shalt love thy neighbour, and hate thine enemy. But I say unto you, Love your enemies, bless them that curse you, do good to them that hate you, and pray for them which despitefully use you, and persecute you; That ye may be the children of your Father which is in heaven: for he maketh his sun to rise on the evil and on the good, and sendeth rain on the just and on the unjust.*

* * * *

I love the way Jody is starting to talk about his anger and resentment and how his attitude with both is starting to shift from retaliation to measured acceptance through the Lord. Jody's beginning to understand God's forgiveness is real, and although we all falter, as he puts it, God knows our hearts, recognizes our shortcomings, and still forgives us.

My Sunday school class consisted of three girls and three boys, all in their teens and up to twenty years of age. Once Jody and I began corresponding, I started discussing him, his history, and his new attempt at connecting with God. Teenage life, as we know, tends to be very egocentric for the most part. It's always been that way and always will be to greater or lesser degrees. But this was something new and certainly different, and they became engaged fairly quickly. Here we had a prisoner with a gruesome childhood who'd been on the streets since he was twelve and had now spent all his life either homeless or in prison. This was not something any of them, including me, had ever encountered before, so it didn't take much to hold their interest. Before I had them write Jody letters, we discussed what those letters should pertain to. I remember asking them what they'd say to Jody if he were sitting in class with us. This, of course, drew blank stares and silence. Apparently, I'd asked this in French because they had nothing. So I asked them, "If Jesus was sitting here, what do you think He'd say to Jody?" Well, this seemed to loosen things up, and they began to respond. One said, "Do you believe in Me?" Another said, "I forgive you!" and so it went. I think this helped lay the groundwork for their letters. I told them I'd have to read all their letters before I sent them to make sure we didn't get out of bounds with Jody or the prison system.

The girls in the class seemed a little more comfortable with the letter writing, and they wrote the first few I sent. The boy's letters were a little less comforting and more questioning, but they were all supportive and encouraging in different ways. One of the boys, however, wrote a letter that was, well, unsettling. He talked about his own insecurities, lack of emotions, and basically how dissatisfied he was with his life, and believe me when I say he presented the exact opposite personality in every way. He was an exceptional student, popular, and had a great sense of humor, so the fact he penned this letter was beyond shocking to me. It bothered me so much that I took him to lunch to discuss it and find out where this was coming from. He reiterated it was all true, and he thought Jody might be able to commiserate with him. I told him to a great extent we were talking apples and oranges, but I'd send it, and we'd see what Jody thought. Off it went, and within about ten days, Jody wrote a separate letter to this boy, and it was awesome! He not only commiserated, but he also offered encouragement and told the boy if God could help him, Jody, He could and would help anyone. The letter was truly inspirational and, beyond that, amazingly insightful. A week or so after I gave the letter to the young man, I asked him what he thought of it; he looked at me almost tearfully and said, "That was incredible and powerful." The young man has since gone off to college and joined a Bible study group, and to my knowledge his parents never knew any of this happened. God works in mysterious ways, and this is the personification of that.

Chapter 8

James 1:5—by wisdom, James is not only talking about knowledge but the ability to make wise decisions in difficult circumstances. Whenever we need wisdom, we can pray to God, and He will generously provide what we need. Christians don't need to grope around in the dark, hoping to stumble upon answers. We can ask for God's wisdom to guide our choices.

* * * *

When I was running away and causing problems, it was because my circumstances were not what I wanted them to be, and I made decisions that created more problems. My refusal to turn to God for guidance was a bad decision, but I didn't trust Him anymore. I understand now that I should have asked for His guidance. If you truly believe in God, you will be led down the right path. My path to joy and happiness is happening now, so don't waste your life like I did and wait until it's too late. With God it's never too late, even in the worst of circumstances. He has brought light into my life, and now I feel the grace and joy of our Lord every day…so can you!

Jody Mobley #60021
PO Box 777
Canon City, CO 81215

3/5/18

Dear Jody,

Sorry, it's been a while; I came down with the flu, which has laid me low. Glad you got the Bible. I know you'll enjoy it. I use mine constantly.

You spoke of forgiveness, which is certainly one of the most difficult things to do. It seems to be a natural instinct to want revenge. However, I did hear a minister once say, "The sweetest revenge of all is forgiveness." That, of course, is easier said than done. And for you, given your severe conditions, it has to be all that more difficult—I can't imagine. I am, however, constantly reminded of how, while hanging on the cross, Jesus said, "Forgive them, Father, for they know not what they do." I use that as a constant reminder of how my forgiveness is absolutely necessary, so I can be forgiven. Yes, you're right; we all falter and always will. It's just who we are because only one person never faltered, and He died for our sins. But as you said, the harder you try, the bigger the reward. A great scripture here is Psalm 103:12, *"As far as the east is from the west, so far has he removed our transgressions from us."*

Glad you're continuing to work out. I know that has to be a challenge with the conditions and meals you face, but that's a tribute to you that you keep at it. You said you'd like to work with kids and prevent them from making the same mistakes you did and that maybe that's God's plan for you. Well, Jody, I wouldn't doubt that for a second. As we've discussed, He reached out and touched you for a reason, and only He knows what that is, but the fact you would like to do that and are preparing yourself to do that might indicate that's exactly what He has in mind for you. I can tell you if that's His plan for you, it will happen! He does have a plan for you, and it's got to be pretty inspiring to think about and ponder the possibilities. There are kids out there right now who need your help, understanding, and guidance, and I have no doubt it will happen in God's time. You have given yourself to Him, and He will continue to light your path.

I read your letter to the kids on Sunday, and it really hit them when you talked about taking so much for granted, such as breathing the fresh air and walking barefoot in the soft grass. You're exactly right; we out here take all that for granted and tend to not appreciate it like we should. Now that they know you through your letters and our discussions of your circumstances, they take it to heart when you talk about what you don't have and what they do. Believe me, they are not lost on them—your words of reality. As I've told you before, God's impact on you is now reaching out to the kids and me. It's interesting that you want to work with kids when you get out, and yet here you are, working with kids while you're still in prison. Isn't God amazing!

It's always great to hear from you, and again, sorry for the delay, but this feisty bug doesn't seem to want to move on. Hope to hear from you soon, and hang tough with God as He will with you!

All God's blessings to you, Jody.

Jan

3/22/18

Dear Jan,

Hello! Hope this finds you doing well. That flu can really be a doozy. Have been really lucky this year and haven't gotten any of the viruses going around. While at Sterling that was horrible. Got sick more times in the eight months I was there than in the entire past fifteen or more years. Seemed like at least half of the facility was sick all the time. Some places are like that.

On the 15th I was taken to DRDC in Denver to stay for a few days so I could go to an eye doctor appointment at the Denver Health Center. Was given fairly good news. My eyesight has not diminished any further, and the pressure is back to a good number. Not sure if I've told you, but I have glaucoma and have already lost the sight in my right eye entirely. Eventually I go blind, but know this, ever since taking the steps to change my path and go with the Lord things have stabilized. I feel all my hard work and struggles to stay the course has showed God and His Son that my new path is very serious to me. Believe they both are blessing me by keeping my medical issues stable. My heart and soul even feels so much lighter and my attitude is so much more positive. Yes—I still have the occasional meltdown and get very angry at some things, but our Lord and Savior lets me stumble then pick me up and guides me to greener pastures. A perfect scripture that really hit me hard was Psalm 103:3. It just shows how exact His words are in my life. When I read scriptures like that, my strength in the decision to take that step in changing my life with God and Jesus is boosted a hundredfold. Something wonderful is happening Jan and I'm so happy you are a part of it. I read Psalm 103:12, the scripture you mentioned. The true meaning of that one is eluding me a little. What's your interpretation?

Yes—if I ever get the chance at freedom I would really like to work with kids who are struggling to make it. Children are our future and this is definitely not the place for them to end up. Trust me I know! Am hoping that's

God's plan for me, but whatever it is I will be more than happy to do it. No matter what it is.

Am glad my words have an impact on you and the kids you work with. Especially the taking things for granted. There is so much about the life inside prison that people don't understand or realize. Take for instance cold. It's always cold in here. It's done on purpose. They feel that if you are in your bed and covered up all day then there's less trouble. If you want to get warm you go outside. Which we only get three hours outside a week. That's only if we aren't on lockdown for that particular hour. Then you have the financial side of things. They give me around $8 a month to survive on. They take 20% of that to pay for my court costs. Most kids spend that much on lunch every day. I used to take people's canteen and other stuff just so I had things to eat, toothpaste, soap, toilet paper to use. You are given one roll of toilet paper per week. If you need more you have to pay for it. Stamps, paper, envelopes, pens, everything you don't worry about we struggle to have. If you don't have family or friends you go without. No, I don't take people's things anymore. I go without. The Lord takes care of me now. Throughout one day think of the things you bypass with no thought. Look at the colors you see every day. Hearing the birds singing or a dog licking your face cause they are happy to see you. Walking on carpet, opening a door. People don't think about that. They reach for that door knob and just expect that door to open. When you wake up, what are the sounds you hear every morning? What do you smell? There is so much we just assume will always be there. Take the time to look, smell, feel the things you never think about.

It's amazing how God's plans affect your life. If you take the time to actually appreciate all He created for us, you'll find just how much. I'm slowly learning myself.

It was really good to hear from you Jan. Am really enjoying the friendship we are building, as well as enjoying walking this new path with your support. It is a tremendous help to have a friend to share all this with. God has blessed me in ways I would never have imagined. Take care and be well.

With God's love and blessings!

Jody

Psalm 103:3:

"Who forgives all your sins and heals all your diseases."

* * * *

It appears Jody is beginning to trust God with all phases of his life, but with that there is a longing that his past could have been different. When he talks about what we take for granted out here in the non-prison world, you can sense his yearning to go back and relive his life with an upbringing of love and compassion.

Chapter 9

Luke 15:3–6—it may seem foolish for the shepherd to leave the nine-ty-nine sheep to go search for just one, but the shepherd knew that the ninety-nine would be safe in the sheepfold, whereas the lost sheep was in danger. Because each sheep was of high value, the shepherd knew it was worthwhile to search diligently for the lost one. God's love for each individual is so great that He seeks each one out and rejoices when he or she is found. Before you were a believer, He sought you, and His love is still seeking those who are yet lost.

* * * *

This is where I lost my battle. The choice to trust and believe in God was over, so what little good presented itself I tended to destroy. My destructive path was harming me more than I ever realized until the last few years. It's only been the last few years since I've found my way back to God. He has shown me that He can bring good out of bad, and I'm living that right now. Prison is a bad and evil place, but God has brought a lot of good into my life, and it doesn't seem like the end of the world anymore.

4/3/18

Dear Jan,

Hello! I hope this finds you in good health and spirits. I'm doing okay. Got a note from my case manager yesterday. She said you called to see if I was okay because you haven't heard from me for a while. Well that's a bummer because that means the letter I sent you around the 22ⁿᵈ of March never reached you. The good thing is the good Lord was looking in on me.

A lot has gone on in the past couple of weeks. On the 15th of March I went to Denver to DRDC and spent the weekend there due to an eye doctor appointment on March 16th. The pressure in my eye was about back to where it should be and they said the vision had stayed the same since my last visit in January. So that was all good news. The only bad news was the doctor's orders for me to wear safety glasses 100% of the time has not been followed by DOC. That's a bit scary since that puts me at high risk of getting injured again. Which the doctor has told DOC any more injury could cause me to go blind. I pray everyday nothing bad happens. He has looked after us this far and I have no doubt He will continue to look after all of us!

In the facility we have been on lockdown for close to two long weeks. There has been some stabbings, one of which happened in my pod. It was not on my tier, but the entire facility is being shook down. They are looking for homemade knives. They just come in Sunday to our pod and took all of our property to the e-scanner and searched out cells. Now we are just waiting for them to finish the rest of the facility. Could be another week or more. All depends on how long it takes them for the rest of the units. Think there is only two units left.

I was reading John 11:51-52 about God bringing us into a new family. Even the children of God scattered abroad. Sometimes I feel I'm one of the scattered who has finally been gathered up. Of course it is great feeling to know none of us have been left behind. It may have taken some longer to be gathered up than others, but in the end we are all under His umbrella. Safe and in the best of company. My studies are never on a set path. I will read a little here and then a little there. What I find intriguing is the fact everything our Lord did He did for all of us. Amazing what one individual gave for so many others. Taking this path has been the best part of my life by far.

Am glad the kids took what I said about taking things for granted to heart. Not only do people take for granted the most simple things like going out in a nice green grass yard, but think about this. For one person per month, all up just your basic hygiene items. Shampoo, soap, lotion, razors, shaving cream, toothpaste. What's that, around $7-$8? Now add stamps, envelopes, writing paper, pens, another $4-$5 per month, for a total of say $13 per month. A normal kid spends that per week on goodies. Going to *a movie is probably more than thirteen for one person these days. Normal everyday things are just expected by people to be there cause it's always been there. They give me right at $8 per month to live on. And if you need to go to medical in here it's an automatic $5. So if you get into trouble what do you decide to go without? Do you not write your loved ones or do you not brush your teeth for a month? Think that's one reason it took me so long to come around and take this path in life. You go into survival mode and resort to past ways of life in order to survive.*

When you take the path of Jesus Christ you're letting Him take care of you. I think I'm doing pretty good. The anger can still get me, but to be honest it's not really an issue anymore. My heart is lighter and I can let more go as time goes by, and I learn more about what Jesus sacrificed for us, things become easier.

Hope to hear from you soon and I hope I didn't worry you too much, but I did send a letter out after I returned from my medical trip. Take care and God bless.

Your friend,
Jody

John 11:51–52:

"Now this he did not say on his own authority; but being high priest that year he prophesied that Jesus would die for the nation, and not for that nation only, but also that He would gather together in one the children of God who were scattered abroad."

* * * *

Jody Mobley #60021
PO Box 777
Canon City, CO 81215

4/6/18

Dear Jody,

Great to hear from you as always. Yes, finally got over the flu; always a ton of fun. I'm glad you have been able to avoid it and hope it stays that way. So sorry about your vision, which you did mention before, but your attitude and belief in the Lord and how He has helped you and, as we know, will continue to do so is what true faith is all about, and you have that, Jody. I can't tell you what an inspiration your faith in God has been to the kids and me. As a matter of fact, I've been asked to speak at a Methodist men's breakfast in a few weeks, and they want me to talk about you and your journey to God's grace. I hope that's okay with you; I won't use your name if you don't want me to, but your story is so inspirational God's people should hear it. If you'd rather I didn't do it at all, I won't, but I don't think God has taken you, me, and the kids on this journey so we can keep quiet about it.

Many years ago, when I returned to my walk with the Lord, I had this fantastic pastor who I got to know fairly well. His story was pretty amazing, not as much as yours, but very interesting. I'm sure I haven't told you this, but I'm an author, having written nine books, and I wanted to write one about finding faith and use him as the common thread running through the story. He was a very dynamic guy and had been offered a radio ministry to go along with his church ministry. Apparently, some of his congregation wasn't too thrilled about the radio gig and told him so. I guess they were afraid he'd become popular and leave the church. He asked me what I thought about it. I told him, as I remembered, Jesus only preached for three years, never wrote anything down, and never went further than sixty miles, and I certainly don't remember Him saying to His disciples, "Now, I don't want my preaching to spread." He threw his head back and laughed. He went on to a great radio ministry and is now a very popular preacher in Georgia. I guess my point is your story is far more moving than his, and I truly feel, Jody, God wants people to know about it. That being said, it is still your call.

You mentioned Psalm 103:3 and how much that scripture is in your life now. You also said something wonderful is happening and you're so happy that I'm a part of it. Well, you have no idea how happy I am about it. I truly feel this is a blessing from God. As for Psalm 103:12, which I had recommended for you, it says east and west can never meet, which is symbolic for God's forgiveness. When He forgives our sin, He separates it from us and doesn't even remember it. It's wise for us to forget it as well, as we know He does, and model His forgiveness when we have to forgive others and the sin they committed against us. I just thought that might be valuable with regard to your circumstance and the people you have to deal with.

I couldn't agree with you more when you say children are our future. Sadly, today I think we undervalue children. In this lightning-speed society, they need all the help they can get, and I find that the kids I work with many times have a difficult time relating their lives today to faith and following Jesus. People like you, Jody, who have been through so much, can touch a chord with them I can't. For them to see where you have come from and where you are now is something they will never forget. I, obviously, have no idea what God's plan is for you, but I also don't think it's a coincidence you are reaching out and touching kids right now. I've felt I'm serving as God's pipeline with these kids, and now I'm serving as yours as well. What an honor and wonderful responsibility.

I have enclosed three more letters from the kids, and I will be interested in seeing your response to one of them, the one from Mike. He's a great kid, a senior in high school who has always appeared very self-confident and was sure he knew what God had planned for him. When you read his letter, you'll see that he has changed and now he's feeling unsure of himself. I told him his troubles might seem trivial to you, given your past, but to him they are very real and concerning. You've mentioned several times how we take so much for granted, and he and I talked about that, and he clearly understands that. I think he is so hung up on what his future holds it's become overwhelming. As you and I both know, our future belongs to God, not only what will happen but when it will happen. I was troubled enough that I took him to lunch, and we talked about it, and he told me our conversation helped, but he is anxious to hear what you have to say.

I always look forward to hearing from you, Jody, and as a matter of fact, since I hadn't heard from you for a couple of weeks, I called the prison to check on you. They connected me to your case manager, and I left her a message. I haven't heard back, but that's a moot point now since I got your letter. I also signed up for JPay.com and sent you $40 to help with your needs. By the time you get this, you should be aware of that and hopefully have been able to put it to good use. One of Jesus' proclamations was we need to be servants and help when we can. I sent this to you as one of His servants.

Jody, I, too, am enjoying this friendship we are experiencing, and I'm thrilled to be part of your passage with the Lord. There is no greater journey, and when you get to travel it with someone else, it makes it all the more glorious. God's blessing to you, Jody; take care of yourself and be safe!

Your friend,

Jan

* * * *

The Three Letters

Dear Jody,

I'm sorry I have taken so long to write to you. I find it near impossible for me to even feel emotion, much less write it down on paper. I think about you, your circumstances, and everything Jan has told us about you almost every day. You are a reminder to me of God's overwhelming power and goodness. Not being able to feel emotion has been a blessing and a curse at the same time. I've had my entire life planned out since third grade. So far, everything has gone exactly as I planned; the whole time I believed it was God's plan. Now I'm not so sure. Everything is falling apart because of circumstances outside my control. My life is falling apart, and I just feel nothing. I want to trust in the Lord, but I just…I'm sorry for this. I just thought maybe you would be able to relate to this feeling of no control. Jan said that this might be the one opportunity in our lives to help someone, to truly help someone. I know that I should help you, and I want to help you, but I'm not sure how I can help anyone when I can't even help myself. Maybe I just need to pray more. When I do pray, I always make sure to ask the Lord to look out for you. Jody, I'm sorry for whining about my life to you. I just don't know anyone who might be able to relate to this. I read this Bible verse recently, and it might be able to help both of us, "*I lift up my eyes to the hills. From where does my help come? My help comes from the Lord, who made heaven and earth*" (Psalm 121:1–2). It's strange how I find confidence in a man I have never met. Maybe that is why I find confidence in you. I don't read the Bible, so I'm afraid that I can't exactly point you in the direction of scriptures. I feel like this letter hasn't helped you at all, but in a weird way, it's helped me a little—thank you. Thank you for listening to my pity party. Maybe, just maybe, I might have helped you in your quest for the Lord. I want to thank you for that opportunity also.

Sincerely,

Mike

Dear Jody,

Hello, my name is Beth. I think it's wonderful that you want to find God. God can be a light in the darkness for you to follow. Sometimes when bad things happen to me, I blame God and get angry at Him. Do not lose faith! I know you are in a bad situation, and I might not be able to feel what you feel like, but I am here for you. Enough of the religion talk. You can pick yourself up again, and I think you can! You sound like a reasonable man from what Jan has told us. I think it is really cool you are writing us. But why us? Why do you want to find God? If you believe God is with you, He is. Since you have accepted Christ Jesus as Lord, live in union with Him, keep your roots deep in Him, build your life on Him, and become stronger in your faith as you were taught. And *"be filled with thanksgiving"* (Colossians 2:6–7).

Beth

Dear Jody,

It is amazing what God can do when He wants something, and I believe it wasn't luck that made you write to this church. It is so cool that you have come all this way from being a person who barely thought about God to a strong Christian. God does not care what you did in your past, just what you are going to do in the future, and He will always forgive you. Just remember if you forgive yourself, God will forgive you.

From Alex

* * * *

Jody's letters are starting to be a little more conversational and open about his feelings and past. With me and the kids now being involved in his life, albeit remotely, I think he's, probably for the first time in his life, feeling like he belongs to folks who truly care about him.

Chapter 10

First Kings 17:10—in a nation that was required by law to care for its prophets, isn't it ironic that God turned to ravens and a widow to care for Elijah? God has help where we least expect it, and He provides for us in ways that go beyond our narrow definitions and expectations. No matter how bitter our trials or how seemingly hopeless our situations are, we should look for God's caring touch; we may find His providence in some strange places.

* * * *

As you can see, God tried to reach me through Rich Van Pelt, but I never really gave it much thought at the time, but looking at it now, God was there. We just need to open our eyes and hearts to see Him. Mine were closed, and because of it, I missed a huge opportunity to have Him back in my life. Don't blind yourself to God as I did. My life could have changed at that time if I hadn't been so caught up in being self-centered and self-defeating. It's never too late to open up to God…don't wait!

Here are two letters from Jody and one from me that sort of crisscrossed, but given it was the only way we could communicate at the time, things didn't always go smoothly.

4/4/18

Dear Jan,

Just sent out a letter to you the other day, but yesterday I received a JPay from you. Not sure what prompted you to show me such kindness, but I'm hoping it was done because you wanted to do that, and not because

I could use the help. If it was brought on by anything I've wrote, that was not my intention for saying anything. When I write it's more for the kids to understand you don't just lose your freedom. You lose more than you can imagine. Even yourself at times. So when I talk about the struggles of prison it's written in hopes maybe one thing will make something click in the minds that this is not a place for anybody to end up. When you're young, or even our age, we take life's joys for granted. So I want to instill the losses so they can understand.

What a wild turn of events. I was a runaway at age twelve. I've not been home since. Rich Van Pelt was doing Youth for Christ and took me under his wing. Still ended up in prison at twenty-one. Still just a kid. Now years later here I am on a new path with Jesus and my goals are to work and help the younger generation learn about, and stay away, from places like this. Now I met Rich in 1981. Here it is thirty-seven years later and I've taken Christ into my heart and life and I feel better and good things are happening. The power of God and His Son is really something to be cherished! It's been a long time since I've shed a tear for anything. I'm losing some now, but not from sadness. These are tears of joy and it's an experience I've never had. All I can say is wow!

Thank you for being a part of this, Jan, and thank you for your kindness. You will always be in my prayers.

Take care,
Jody

4/23/18

Dear Jan,

Hello my friend. May God's love shine on you, and I hope this finds you in good health and spirits. Received your letter along with the others. As always it's good to hear from you.

Am glad to hear you made it through that flu bug. As for my eyes it's pretty scary. Just the thought of the possibility of going blind scares the bejeebers out of me. I have all the faith in the world the good Lord will look out for me. Unfortunately, if my sight goes in here, I have no idea what I will do. One thing is for sure, you cannot live in this environment without sight. So it's pretty darn scary to even think about. My prayers will guide me.

So great you've been asked to speak. I'm okay with using my story for inspiration and the power God's words can do for people, but I'd rather you not use my name. I agree my story is something that can give a lot of people hope and inspiration, but I just don't feel putting my name with it is a good idea. I've been told by a lot of different people in here that I should write a book on my life. The only problem is I wouldn't be able to use my own name. There are reasons behind that, which I will at some point get into. That is so crazy you're an author and somebody that I consider my friend on this journey I've taken. Everybody in life needs guidance and supportive influence no matter how young or old you may be. Boy—the more I learn about God and our Lord Jesus Christ, the more amazing this whole ordeal is. And yes Jan, I am very happy you are a part of all this. Not just for friendship but it shows me just how true God's Word is. It proves that He has put good, kind, caring people on this world to help guide the newcomers to the Lord.

In your letter you discuss Psalm 103:12 about God's forgiveness and how we should model ourselves after Him in our forgiveness to the people who have committed sins against us. That's a passage we can all learn from there. More so in here because of all the different types of people and emotions that go through people in here. That's a great passage to keep in mind always in here. We tend to forget that forgiveness is one of the most important things we can do for another as well as for ourselves.

There is no doubt people today undervalue the children. We have to teach and educate and show them their potential. They all text all day now. I remember when I was a kid, we would be outside playing or going to see a friend. We didn't sit in our bedrooms glued to a smartphone or whatever they have these days. People used to visit each other and go out together, and go on picnics and all that good stuff. The only thing I really like about all the new technology is the music. I will admit, that is what keeps me grounded. I like rock and roll and I found a band the other day: "LEAH." I believe it's a Christian rock group. Not real sure. The songs are right and the words, but am not totally sure, because it doesn't tell you the kind of music except for like rock, country, jazz etc. Could you find out for me? The singer is awesome. Her voice is beautiful. Hate to admit it, but I did order a month's worth of music with some of the $ you sent. Music is a big outlet for me. I put some Christian rock on and my mood gets so much better when I am not doing good. Its still a challenge at times for me not to resort to old ways, but it's been so much more fulfilling with music. The Lord's words just flow into my head and all frustration dissipates and I feel good. Of course music has been an outlet for me since I was a grade schooler. I had been diagnosed back in 1979 with anger control problems and depression. Music was my escape and soother. With this tablet I now can listen to gospel rock. Unfortunately it's short lived, but it is better than nothing. Don't worry, I did stock up on my hygiene, paper, stamps and envelopes. So thank you!

Read Mike's letter and I must say—that's the type of things that interest me in helping kids. His troubles are not at all trivial. They are pretty darn serious if you ask me. I probably read more into it than you because I've been through all those feelings, and they can quickly bring a person into ruin. So I really hope what I write him will help and get him to take a step back and look at his life. He is destined for a great life with the Lord and will be inspirational to all around him given the chance. Ya know I ran away from an abusive childhood at age twelve and now I am fifty-one. I do have a serious question. You didn't tell the kids I have tried to end my life have you? Not sure the young need to hear that. My story may be great, but some things I feel are for a more mature mind. I don't even know why I told you. It just felt right to be completely honest with you. There are things I haven't told you yet, but in time I will. I feel I can trust you completely already. Pretty sure God played His cards right by putting us in touch. God bless God! The other letters from the kids were refreshing. A very bright bunch of kids for sure.

Really hope this finds you, your family and all the kids you work with in the best of health and spirits. Look forward to hearing Mike is doing well. God has really blessed me more than I could have imagined and it feels really good to be with Him and Lord Jesus Christ!

God bless you my friend!

Jody

PS. I'd like you to do me a favor? With Mike I'd prefer he not take my letter home. Unless you think different. My reasoning is, even if I'm trying to help him and change my life, a lot of people, regardless of who they are, do not think we are worth much because of our incarceration. I will leave that deci-

60

sion up to you. What's best for Mike is what matters. I can be judged and I'm okay with that, but I don't feel he should be judged because of me.

Jody Mobley #60021
PO Box 777
Canon City, CO 81215

5/5/18

Dear Jody,

I got your letter and the letter to Mike. First, let me say your letter to Mike was outstanding. He wasn't at church last Sunday, so I'm giving it to him this coming Sunday. I did call him and tell him you had written him and that it was a letter he not only wants to read but keep. Jody, you've mentioned how you want to work with kids, and as I told you, you are, and if that's an example of your insight into kids, it's something I know God will help you continue to pursue.

Yes, I, too, have thought and prayed about your eyesight and what will happen should you go completely blind. I've wondered how we'll correspond, but every time I start thinking about it, it's as if I get a message from the Lord saying, "I'll take care of it," and you and I know He will.

Well, due to our minor mix-up in letter exchanges, I've already given my speech, and I can't tell you how touched everyone was when hearing about your story. I called the speech "Have You Ever Seen a Miracle?" As you and I have discussed, this is truly a miracle and was right from the very beginning. As for your name, I only used your first name; I hope that's okay, so they don't know who you really are other than a man who has found the Lord and is on one of the most amazing journeys they've ever heard of. I also had three of the kids from class come and say a little about the impact your story has had on their lives. You would have been proud of them, Jody...I certainly was.

As for a book about your life, I do think that should be done someday, some way. What's happening here is a story that absolutely needs to be told, and I can tell you from the reaction I saw at my talk it only confirms that. That being said, it's your story and should only be done when you're ready to tell it. Yes, I am an author, having written nine books, and I can flat-out tell you I would be honored to write your story if that's of interest to you. Again, isn't it amazing, well, maybe not, that God put us on the same path?

Yeah, you're right; kids today spend waaaaay too much time on their iPhones and tablets. Sadly, they're losing the ability to talk to each other or anyone else. During our Sunday school class, they have to put their phones away, and we talk face to face for an hour or more. I'm hoping they learn to enjoy that and use it elsewhere.

Yes, I, too, love music, always have and always will. I grew up with rock and roll but love smooth jazz and classical. As for Leah, here's what I found. Her name is Leah Shafer, and here's a little about her.

Her philosophy of faith:

"I am always growing, learning and changing through the help of the Lord. His grace and strength and prayer has saved me many times," says Leah.

She is a strong believer that you should never get too comfortable in this life because that is when you will be spiritually attacked. "We must always be on guard with your heart and spirit." That is why she is such a huge proponent of family unity and praying together daily as a couple and family. Leah is emphatic, "Through my faith, nothing is impossible."

Leah says, "Music is a non-threatening way to communicate your heart and hope to others." Leah's music has opened doors to relate to the brokenness in others who are overcoming abuse and tragedies. She is a huge advocate for the program Celebrate Recovery, a Christ-based recovery program. I took this off her website. I hope it helps when you listen to her.

So you spent the money on music, huh? Just kidding, you spend it on whatever you need or want. We are all to be servants as Jesus showed when He washed the feet of His disciples at the Last Supper, so just consider me a servant of the Lord sent to help you, and please, Jody, when that money gets low, let me know so I can serve you and the Lord some more. I am honored to do it, and I know you'd do it for me if our roles were reversed.

Yes, Jody, I did tell the kids about your suicide attempts, but keep in mind kids today see things on TV and the internet you and I would never have dreamt of when we were kids, so I knew it wouldn't be shocking to them. But more importantly, I thought it showed just how far you've come in your journey with God and was probably what prompted you to start down this road in the first place. I apologize if I overstepped my bounds, but believe me, it made your story all the more compelling. I'm sure you wouldn't have told me had not God wanted you to, and as for the other things you've not told me, I'm sure God will put it on your heart when the time is right. I know many of those things are just between you and our Lord.

As I said, I'm giving your letter to Mike this Sunday, and I think I'll let him decide if he wants to share it with his mom and dad. He really is a pretty mature kid, and I know he'll make the right decision. You are right about people judging those in prison, but people do that about skin color, religion, weight, etc. You and I both know there are wonderful people in prison (you) and out of prison, Black, Hispanic, Asian, skinny, and overweight. I feel truly sorry for those who have to tag people with labels because of where they are or how they look or what religion they follow. The kids and I have talked at length about judging others when we know judgment day will come for every one of us. Jody, you should feel wonderful about your walk with the Lord, and I know you do. Trust me, you have a lot more faith than a lot of people who go to church every Sunday, pray, sing hymns, and then spend the rest of the week doing what they want. I know because I was one of those people years ago, but God gathered me up, and here you and I are, sharing our faith in our Lord Jesus Christ.

Well, as a sidebar, I'm having my left hip replaced on May 21st, so wish me well and pray for me. I'm sure it will go just fine, and I'm looking forward to eliminating the constant pain. God bless you, Jody, and everything you're doing in the name of the Lord. I couldn't be more honored to call you my friend and walk this glorious path with you!

Yours in Christ,
Jan

Chapter 11

Genesis 49:3–28—Jacob blessed each of his sons and then made a prediction about each one's future. The way the men had lived played an important part in Jacob's blessing and prophecy. Our past also affects our present and future. By sunrise tomorrow, our actions of today will have become part of the past. Yet they will already have begun to shape the future. What actions can you choose or avoid that will positively shape your future?

* * * *

Everything I'd done in my past had already shaped my future. Even though I was free and Stan allowed me to stay with his family and things were looking good for me, my neglecting God was about to play a big part in my future. Without Him I was doomed; I just didn't realize it. My decisions and actions of the past had already shaped my future. You have the chance to make better choices than I did. If you are a person of God or are thinking of becoming a person of God, I encourage you to take that step and let Him in. Your life and future will be better for it!

5/10/18

Dear Jan,

Hi! Received your letter the other day. As always it was a great day. It always is when I hear from you. Am glad you thought the letter I wrote to Mike was good. The Lord guided my writing. Plus my insight into kids is pretty good. God has given me those tools and it's a great feeling to be able to impact someone's life. Hopefully it will give Mike something to look to for inspiration. As we get older we tend to forget what it's like to be a kid and the problems they go through. Starting to believe God has put me on this path with you to give me a chance to make a difference in someone's life. If He wants me to help kids, which I believe He does, then I'm in 110%. I'm not a real big believer in coincidences. God wants me to share my story and help the kids of our future, and He wanted you to be a force in my life. I will do my best to show Him I can do this. There is no other explanation for all of this coming together like it is if this isn't what He wanted.

Yes, that's okay you used my first name. That's pretty awesome how my story could be such a powerful one. It instills the fact that our Lord and Savior works some pretty spectacular miracles. Pretty cool you took some of the kids with you. Never would have ever thought I'd be a person who could inspire or touch so many with my story. As far as a book of my life goes, if there is a possibility of it helping others it may be a good idea. Not to mention it could help me support myself in here and possibly help me get a good lawyer.

Really would love to get out and help and work with kids. Have no idea how to start it or any of that though. It's not a happy story until you get to where I am now. I've actually been wanting to share my story for a long time, but I had no idea that this would be where I am at this point. Not the fact I'm in prison, but my place with God. This is all like a fairytale you read in a book. You never think this would be me in this spot. I never thought it anyway. Not sure where everything changed. All I do know is God changed my path and my life is so much better with Him in it!

Thank you for looking up the information on Leah. Her music is really good. I like it a lot. Her philosophy on faith is great. I always wonder what my life would have turned out like if I wouldn't have lost faith at such a young age. My views of God changed from good to bad when I was just nine or ten years old. I used to go to a Lutheran church when I was a child. I would go by myself every Sunday. My younger brother was too young to come with me and my older brother was in a boy's ranch. Bad things kept happening, and I asked God one day why He would put a child through all I was going through. That's when my faith faded, and a dislike began brewing. It lasted all this time. So much transpired throughout my life. I just couldn't believe He would put me on earth to suffer so much. And now here we are. He is my guiding light. I'm okay with everything now. He made it all okay.

Here are my thoughts on asking for things. Yes, it would be nice to have the things I'd like to have in here. It would be great to get a little canteen each week, but I've learned that people tire of being asked to send this or that or do this or that. It is one of the reasons I've lost everybody in my life. I've watched others go through the same ordeal. Asking for things is the quickest way to lose people while in prison. I don't want to ruin our friendship over that. Thank you for the offer, but the best I can do is tell you we are only allowed to order $25 in canteen per week. That includes hygiene, stamps, food, writing material, and any other items offered. What you do with that information is entirely up to you, Jan. God is with me, and you are with me. I couldn't ask for anything more!

Will be honest, the thought of the kids knowing about my suicide attempts is a scary one. Just don't what them to think that is an idea people can turn to when things are hard. It's certainly not anything I'm proud of and nobody knows in here except mental health. There is no doubt in my mind you wouldn't say anything to the kids that would be traumatizing. So no, you didn't overstep any boundaries. It's scary that people know. I told you because it played a part in my coming back to the Lord. I trust your judgment. For others, it's just one more reason to judge us. And it sucks to be judged when the people judging you know nothing about you. We all do it at some point or another, but that is because our minds detect friend or foe signals subconsciously from people. We don't even know it's happening unless we can train ourselves to recognize the signs.

Take care of yourself Jan, and I pray you have no pain in your hip once healed. I'm very honored to have you as a friend. God bless you always.

Brothers in Christ,
Jody
Jody Mobley #60021
PO Box 777
Canon City, CO 81215

5/30/18

Dear Jody,

Well, came through the surgery fine, and I'm feeling better every day. It's amazing what they can do now for destroyed hips, knees, and shoulders. The surgery was on the 21st, and I'm walking around now without using a walker or cane, and best of all, the constant pain is gone. Thank you for your prayers.

I read every page of the clinical mental health report you sent, and over and over in my mind, I kept saying to myself, "Wow, this isn't the man I know now." As you've mentioned in previous letters, your life has been filled with trials and tribulations, and you've questioned why you're still here. I think, given your current circumstances, we know the answer to that now. I believe in my heart God wants you to work with kids in one capacity or another. As we've discussed, it's already started with the teenagers at Grace, and only He knows how big and far-reaching it will get. I don't know about you, but I can hardly wait to find out.

As for a book about your life, I think it could be profoundly helpful to kids around the world. It's one thing to touch the kids at Grace Church and quite another to impact kids in England, Argentina, Chicago, and Los Angeles. As we know there are kids around the world who are Christian or trying to become Christians or just don't know about Jesus Christ. What you went through as a boy, teenager, and young man will resonate with who knows how many young people looking for answers. Kids can relate to the fact you've been there and done that, and look how God has turned your life around as a follower of Jesus Christ. As Jesus said, "We are to be servants of the Lord," and that's what you're doing, and I'm sure will continue to do with His guidance. On a personal level, I know God will help you with supporting yourself and acquiring a good criminal lawyer. In that regard, I used to do investigative work for one of the big defense firms here in Denver, and if and when you want me to look into obtaining a lawyer for you, I will be more than happy to do so.

Putting money into your canteen is something I want to do, Jody, not something I feel obligated to do. As I mentioned before, it's part of the servant mentality God wants us to have, and I'm honored to do it, and trust me, it will never come between our friendship!

I know your suicide attempts are a part of your past you're ashamed of, but, Jody, it's helped bring you to where you are now, as strange as that seems, and as we well know, God forgives all. I have no idea the dark places you were in when you made those attempts, and neither does anyone else. So I wouldn't worry about being judged by people who have no idea what they're talking about and, I'm sure, have plenty of problems of their own. You turned it from the worst negative into the most glorious positive we can know. You said the most interesting thing about our minds detecting friend or foe signals subconsciously. I'd never thought of that, but you're absolutely right, which immediately turns into judgment. I guess it's always been a part of life and always will be; look how those who had no clue judged Jesus. This is all part of your improbable journey, and I'm thrilled to be part of it.

Well, time for some hip therapy. Always great to hear from you, and hope to hear from you soon. Take care, Jody, and may God bless you always!

Brothers in Christ!

Jan

* * * *

As Jody stated above, he sent me the mental health report from the Department of Corrections filed in March of 2014. It verified everything he's been telling me was true and detailed what they had determined was going on with him and what treatments they had used. I certainly learned some things about Jody he's not told me yet, but the most interesting part of all of it for me was that he trusted me with this information. As you can see by his letters above, his trust in the Lord and me is growing daily, and even now I can't imagine what a liberating feeling that must be for him.

Chapter 12

Romans 1:24–32—these people chose to reject God, and God allowed them to do it. God does not usually stop us from making choices that are against His will. He lets us declare our supposed independence from Him, even though He knows that in time we will become slaves to our own rebellious choices—we will lose our freedom not to sin. Does life without God look like freedom to you? Look more closely. There is no worse slavery than slavery to sin.

* * * *

My choices during these times made me a slave to sin, which eventually led to my being in prison and a life of hatred and blame. The question of, "Does life without God look like freedom to you?" is a good one. I've come to find that true freedom only comes with faith and belief in God. If you feel your choices are causing more problems, then take a good look at those choices in faith and God's Word.

6/7/18

Dear Jan,
Received your most recent letter. As always, it has brightened my day and life. Really enjoy seeing what you have to say, or what your mind's thoughts are. This change of pace and new journey is amazing. The things that are transpiring, the feeling I'm going through and just the joy I feel makes me sit back and wonder, "Why did it take so long to realize that God has maneuvered my life to where I am going?" Finally, I feel good with my future, no matter how it turns out. I know I'm on the right path as a servant of the Lord!

71

Yeah, the mental health report really gives a person an idea of a lot of the trials and tribulations I've gone through. It's been an extremely rough life for sure. There's so much I've been through. Everything I've suffered through or have had to deal with has made it possible for me to really relate to and understand what kids go through. God has given me the tools to help the younger generation. For years now I've questioned or asked myself, "What purpose in life do I have? I'm not living, I'm just existing!" The scripture John 17:25-26 I believe says it—God has had a plan for me and now I can have purpose and meaning, which I was lacking in the past. Ephesians 1:3-6 also says some about God's eternal purpose for us. So as much as I dislike a lot of the things I had to endure in my life, I'd like to use what I've gone through, and all I've learned to inspire kids. And if I can save one or two from having to end up in here, that will be an accomplishment I can be proud of. So yeah—I would like to do a book and if I can get out I want to travel and talk to kids. That is my calling. I want to do it. I'd like my story to start from as far back as I can remember. There is a lot I don't remember. Psychologists say I have a pretty serious blockade up. Like most people remember birthdays, Christmas and other holidays I can't remember any birthdays or holidays as a child. Most of my memories from childhood are not good. So if you are willing I'd like to tell my story and I'd like to have you as the one I open up to. I trust the Lord put you in my path for a lot of reasons. This is one of them. I would be honored to have you on this project. To be honest I don't think I'd want anyone else to do it.

Boy, it sure would be nice to have a good lawyer, but at this point I need to find out if I have any options on getting in front of a judge. I did write a bunch of lawyers with issues I thought might be grounds to get back in court. Got one response and was told everything I bought up was time based. So have to look at things at a different angle. I need to do more research. If there is a chance I don't want to mess it up by being in a rush. Have to be patient with this as God was with me.

This is actually a lot for me to digest at one time. If you look at it from my point of view it's like a fairy tale. Made the choice to take this journey to renew my faith, and all of a sudden everything I've had on my mind for years is all dropping in my lap.

Really is pretty shocking to say the least. I wanted to do a book years ago, but never had the right people in my life. I've always dreamed of being a big brother type and working with kids. I wanted to reach out and find somebody who could help me on my journey. I've dreamed of being able to get a lawyer. It's a bit surreal. This is my skeptical side talking. I want my faith to be complete and here I am wondering if this is all real or will it all be gone tomorrow. Do you see where I'm having problems? How many churches are in and around Denver? How many millions of people? Now how many of them do you think are authors, previous investigators for a big defense firm, and work with kids? The odds are astronomical. That tells you a miracle is taking place.

Yeah—I know all I've been through and I will go through is all preparation for where I end up. But there are still things I'm a bit ashamed of. Being judged by those who have to clue what another has gone through still hurts. It's like my ties to the gang, no matter how far I distance myself from, or how far or long ago I left them, DOC will always have me as a high ranking member and when anything happens I will also be punished. I was sent out of state to Wisconsin in January of 2005. They still threw me in seg and investigated me, even though I hadn't been in contact with anybody. So I'm constantly judged by society if they find out I was a former gang member. Yes Jan, I've done a lot of craziness, been in a lot of craziness, but no matter how strong my faith is, no matter what I do in life, people will judge me and label me for the rest of my life. They will never believe a guy like me can, or will change. I'm not the only one who has changed. There are several, but that part of my life will be kept a secret. I'm just hoping that my inspiration will touch those who also struggle and help guide them to a better life with God!

Hope this finds you in great health and spirits. My prayers are always with you. Take care!

Brothers in Christ!

Jody.

John 17:25–26:

"Righteous Father, though the world does not know you, I know you, and they know that you have sent me. I have made you known to them, and will continue to make you known in order that the love you

*have for me may be in them and that I myself may
be in them."*

Ephesians 1:3–6:

*Praise be to the God and Father of our Lord Jesus
Christ, who has blessed us in the heavenly realms
with every spiritual blessing in Christ. For he chose
us in him before the creation of the world to be holy
and blameless in his sight. In love he predestined
us for adoption to sonship through Jesus Christ, in
accordance with his pleasure and will—to the praise
of his glorious grace, which he has freely given us in
the One he loves.*

Jody Mobley #60021

PO Box 777

Canon City, CO 81215

6/18/18

Dear Jody,

Yeah, the surgery was a big success and just in the nick of time. I got
up and around pretty quickly, and just as I did, my wife became very ill and
is still recovering at this writing. It's been a fun few weeks, but we know God
is always with us. As you well know, as we get older, health issues continue to
grow, which is just part of the aging process. It certainly can be frustrating and
painful, but the final reward will make it all worth it. In heaven that all goes
away, and we can bask in the glory of God!

You mentioned in your letter why it took you so long to realize that God
has maneuvered your life to where you're going now. One of my favorite pastors once said, "It's like we're standing on the bank of a river flowing by. We
can see where it came from and where it is right in front of us, but we don't
know where it's going." That's how God sees our lives—only He knows exactly
where it's going and how it's going to get there. This whole time you've been
in prison God knew where your life was going, but He also knew you had to

be ready to make that journey, and now He knows you are and has started you down that path; however, you still don't know how far or how long, but He does and will guide you every step of the way. I don't know exactly what made you write Grace Church, and maybe you don't either, really, but He does, and He knew it was the exact right time to begin this. It is beyond exciting to me that He has allowed me to be part of this, and only He knows where it's going and the impact your life will have on others, who at this very minute are out there walking around, living their lives and have no idea Jody Mobley will enter their lives in a profound and life-changing way. But God knows who they are and how you will affect them, just as you did in my life and the kids at Grace. God's miracle of life at work through you, Jody!

You asked in your letter, "What purpose in life do I have?" I've heard, as I'm sure you have, all lives have a purpose, but that's hard to comprehend given all the tragedy and horror in the world. Certainly, that can't be God's purpose to create chaos and sadness. Jody, your path has been dark since you were a little boy, and that was not your fault. You made some bad choices as you grew up, again, many of which were based on your life experience to that point. I know this sounds strange, but it may have been God's way of preparing you for now. There is no way you could relate to and honestly discuss life choices with kids and young adults had you not been down the road you have. You sacrificed so much of your life, and I'm sure it never crossed your mind you were doing it for God. I know I wouldn't have felt that. But He was preparing you for His work now.

Jody, I don't know if you've ever heard of Father Damien. He was a priest who moved to the island of Molokai in Hawaii in 1864. Molokai was the leper island. For sixteen years he lived in the midst of the lepers, learning their language, bandaging their wounds, embracing these bodies no one else would touch. He preached to their hearts and organized schools, bands, and choirs. He built them homes so they could have shelter, and he constructed two thousand coffins by hand so when they died, they could be buried with dignity. He offered them hope. He was not careful about keeping his distance. He dipped his fingers in the poi bowl along with the patients. He shared his pipe and did not always wash his hands after tending to their sores. He got close, and they loved him. Then one day, he stood up and started his sermon with two words, "We lepers!" He was not just helping them; he'd become one of them. He, of course, got leprosy. With an arm in a sling, a foot in bandages, and his leg dragging, Damien knew death was near. He was bedridden on March 23, 1889, and on March 30th, he made a general confession. Father Damien died of leprosy at 8:00 a.m. on April 15th, 1889, at the age of forty-nine. In April of 2008, 119 years after his death, he was canonized at the Vatican and made a saint. I'm guessing his reward in heaven came on April 15th, 1889, and it just took the world 119 years to recognize his complete devotion to serving God.

I only tell you this because I would bet you as a young man Father Damien had no idea what God had planned for him and the impact his life as a servant to the Lord would have on so many.

Father Damien shortly before he died.

He who gives a lot shall receive a lot. I think there are a lot of great things ahead for you and the work you'll do for God.

As for a book on your life, as I've told you, I would be honored to do it. I've done several biographies, and they are always interesting, but I'm thinking none will have been more remarkable than yours. This will, however, present a unique challenge in that I usually get to sit down with the subject and conduct several interviews. Obviously, we can't do that right now, so we'll have to make do with what we have. We certainly have enough through your letters to me and the prison report to generate a starting point. Jody, my suggestion would be for you to start as far back as you can or choose to remember and start chronologically arranging your life from birth to now. I know you said there are things you're ashamed of and/or have chosen to forget or just can't remember. That's fine. Just do what you can and put down what you think is important or relevant to your life story. This is, after all, your life, so you put in or leave out whatever you want. I know you're unsure about how some people will judge you based on what you've done and question whether you're being sincere now. Well, as I've grown older, I've determined that people who are going to judge you are simply not worth your time. You know you have much bigger fish to fry, and many of those people wouldn't believe you no matter what you said or did, so to heck with them! How many people on earth today still don't believe Jesus was or is the Messiah, even though He died for their sins? If He can't convince them through what His life was and still is, what chance do you and I have? Ultimately, the only judgment that counts comes from our Father in heaven.

I can't even imagine how surreal this must seem to you. I'm sure you question from time to time if, in fact, this is actually happening and if it will continue or suddenly disappear. I don't blame you for a second. Hey, you dropped in my life last August, and I had no idea what I was in for. I'm sure if someone had come up to me and said, "Well, you know this is going to happen, and then this will happen," etc., etc., I would have probably told them they were crazy…but look where we are now. As you and I have discussed, God didn't bring us together and put you on your journey to desert us now. As you said, how many churches, how many people are authors and former investigators? Only God knew and made it happen! If this isn't a miracle, then I don't know the meaning of the word.

You said in your letter you'd been a member of a gang and are still feeling repercussions from that. You're right—there will always be people who can't see past that, and I'm sure the Justice Dept. is one of them. But, you know, and more importantly, God knows that's ancient history for you, and best of all, He's forgiven you. Those people and that institution will never forgive you and certainly never forget, but you and I know God is bigger than all of them put together, and so is His plan for you. His plan for you, Jody, will supersede and grow far bigger than anything they can or will do to stop you. The Lord is in charge of this and cannot be stopped. His will be done, not yours, not mine, and certainly not theirs. Stay the course as you're doing, and you cannot fail!

Well, my friend, this just gets more interesting and exciting all the time. I don't know where this is all heading, Jody, but with God in charge, I know it's going to be glorious. Take care of yourself, and let me know how your supplies are holding up; the servant needs to know. You're in my prayers every day!

Brothers in Christ,

Jan

* * * *

Jody's realizing that his past, albeit brutal, violent, and I'm sure to him seemingly wasted, now seems, through God, to, in fact, have purpose. I think Jody seeing his life does now have an objective and that God's goal for him could well be working with and helping young people who are either lost or on the path to destruction has given him hope, which until now was only a desire to survive.

Chapter 13

First Timothy 1:12–17—people can feel so guilt-ridden by their past that they think God could never forgive and accept them. But consider Paul's past. He had scoffed at the teachings of Jesus hunting down and murdering God's people before coming to faith in Christ. God forgave Paul and used him mightily for His kingdom. He can forgive and use you.

* * * *

My past was obviously riddled with shame. It's hard to move forward sometimes and follow the path of righteousness, which was the case for me. My past dictated my future, and that turned out to be a downhill road for decades. Then God came to me and gave me a push to do something I never would have done on my own. Now, I'm trying to assist Him by helping others. Don't let your past mistakes hold you back or push you further down a road that leads to nowhere. Rejoice in the fact that God will forgive you and show you a better path.

6/24/18

Dear Jan,

Hi! How have you been? Good I hope. Am doing okay myself. The other night I was just lying here and had the urge to go talk to an old boss of mine. It was really strange to be honest. I played the whole scenario in my mind. On how I would find him, knock on his door and sit and talk to him. Wanted to apologize for being a bad employee after all he went through to try and help me. Then I wanted to thank him for being the person he was and giving me so many chances. Wanted him to know I was not the same person anymore and I would never forget his kindness. Don't know why it was so important for me to do that, but if I ever do get that chance, it is at the top of my list of things to do.

Besides that, I am continuing my studies in the word of God and the Bible. My prayers include you and all the kids, who I hope are all well and enjoying this beautiful weather. Hope you are too. We got to go to the yard today and it really was nice out. When we came in and mail was passed out, I received your latest letter. I was extremely happy and excited to read it. Like I was saying earlier, the feeling of wanting, or needing, to let my boss know how I felt and feel today about his kindness, and all that has gone on since I mailed that letter to Grace, I have relinquished all doubt about if this is real or not. As you said—if this isn't a miracle, I don't know the meaning of the word. I feel the exact same way. This is all truly a miracle and I'm going to soak it all in. My hope and goal is that my journey, life, and story will inspire, help and guide other to a better quality life. Also want to thank you for all you've done for me, or will do for me, but most of all I want to thank you for accepting me and not judging me. Your words are inspiring me and help me stay on my course. God has done what I prayed for. I needed a person whose faith in God was real and true to help keep me focused and guide me along, and be a positive supportive individual. He sent you and it really means a lot to have you be a part of all this that's happening.

Its funny that in your letter you talk about writing what I think is important in my life for things in the book, and you say, "I know you are unsure about how some people will judge you based on what you've done and question whether you're being sincere now." This is so true! The reason I mention this is just the other day a situation came about. They moved me to a different unit, and when they do that you have to be locked down the first twenty-four hours. That first night they were turning in laundry bags. The female guard that was working I've been around and have know for a few years. I needed a zip tie which they pass out to tie the bag closed. She didn't have one and said, "I'll put one on for you." Of course I was concerned about that cause if you lose any laundry they charge you crazy prices to replace those lost items. So I said, "Make sure you put it on good so I don't lose anything," and she said, "You just said earlier we've known each other for a long time, don't you trust me?" My response was, "Do you trust me?" She instantly said no. Told her, "Well if you don't trust me, why should I trust you?" She said I made a good point and she understands my concerns. Its just a good example of how we are judged just because we are in prison. Other reasons it bothers me isn't really because of myself, people will judge you and look down on you just because you're in contact with me. However, I don't believe that is anything you are worried about, and I truly believe God would not put you in any position He thought you could not handle.

As I sit here writing I'm going through all these different types of feelings. They are good ones and are hard to put words to, but I will admit, it's been a very long time since I've felt good like this. Sure is a heck of a lot better than being angry all the time.

The story of Father Damien is very inspiring. I've never heard of him until now. Definitely like his style for sure. Don't know if I'll change anyones life on the level he did, but if I can inspire just one person I've accomplished something special.

You know Jan, I'm not really too concerned about whether DOC or anybody else for that matter, believes my past is just that—in the past. As you said—the Lord is in charge, and what He wants He will get. I'm willing to put my all in whatever plans He has for me. I'm not going to let what others believe, or don't believe, cloud my path. Sure, there will be some lumps and bumps that go along with this new path, but bring it on—I have God on my side, and a great friend to help me when things get rough. This is a glorious time in my life and I want to soak it all in and enjoy it all until we meet our Father in heaven. That will be a glorious time as well.

With that said—take care of yourself and my prayers are with you and your wife. Hope she is feeling well.

To my friend and brother in Christ.

Jody
Jody Mobley #600217/3/18
PO Box 777
Canon City, CO 81215

Dear Jody,

I, too, look forward to getting a letter from you. This is such an unusual and fantastic journey we're on, all under God's guidance, that the expectation of what's next is truly inspiring.

That's so interesting that you want to connect with your former boss and apologize and let him know you're a completely different man now. This is just my opinion, but I think you would only feel comfortable doing this because you have forgiven yourself for your past, and that can only happen because you know God has forgiven you. I have no idea what his response would be, but there is no way he wouldn't recognize you're a different person than he used to know, and that's the most important part of your apology. If you want me to try and find him, I will, and, if nothing else, you could write him a letter. You let me know if that's of interest.

Jody, you mentioned how you prayed for God to put someone in your life to help you on this journey, and He chose me. First of all, when God chooses you for anything, it's really overwhelming. I had no idea when I got that first letter where this would lead, but I can tell you I've prayed to God for some time to let me work with kids on His behalf. First were the little kids at Grace and then the teenagers, and now, through you, the possibility to reach who knows how many kids, all in the name of the Lord. When you step back and look at it, you realize how infinite His power is and how He picks those He knows will fulfill His desires and continue to spread the good news. It's an immeasurable blessing!

You remarked about your conversation with the guard and her lack of trust. I'm sure she has no idea how you've changed and probably wouldn't care and/or believe it. Well, all I can say is forgive her for her lack of understanding. Sadly, she's the one missing out on the born-again Jody. That being said, as we've discussed, she certainly won't be the last, and each and every one of those people is not aware there is, in fact, a miracle taking place. Maybe with time others will recognize you are a changed man and a man of God and be more accepting. We can only hope, but in the meantime we can continue to follow God's path, knowing He has a grand plan for you, and those of little or no faith will, unfortunately, fall by the wayside. As for me being judged due to my relationship with you, you're exactly right; I couldn't care less what someone might think. That hasn't happened yet, but I'm sure it will, and I'm sure my first instinct will be to tell them to get lost, but I know that's not what God would want, so I'll forgive them and hope that at some point they will see this for what it truly is…a miracle!

I'm so glad you're feeling good about your life. As we know, only God can do that. When you think about it, your environment and circumstances haven't changed that much, but He has come into your life and soul and changed you. He knows who He wants, and He wants you, Jody! You talk about inspiring just one individual and how special that would be; well, guess what? I think you've already done that with Mike. I know you've certainly changed my life, and several of the other kids always ask about you. You've already started helping kids, and there is no doubt in my mind it will just continue to grow and grow. There's a scripture I'd like you to read and then give me your take on it. It's Mark 5:25–34. It's about an ill woman who touches Jesus' cloak as He's walking in a crowd. I see a parallel in your life and hers and would love to know what you think.

This is a glorious time in your life and my life, and to think the best is yet to come! Our Father in heaven is magnificent and has put us on a glorious path; I couldn't feel more blessed. I don't think I've ever said this, but thank you for writing to Grace Church! By the way, my hip is awesome, and my wife is feeling great, so thanks for your prayers. Take care of yourself, Jody, and God bless you!

Your friend and brother in Christ!

Jan

Mark 5:25–34:

And a woman was there who had been subject to bleeding for twelve years. She had suffered a great deal under the care of many doctors and had spent all she had, yet instead of getting better she grew worse. When she heard about Jesus, she came up behind him in the crowd and touched his cloak, because she thought, "If I just touch his clothes, I will be healed." Immediately her bleeding stopped and she felt in her body that she was freed from her suffering.

At once Jesus realized that power had gone out from him. He turned around in the crowd and asked, "Who touched my clothes?"

"You see the people crowding against you," his disciples answered, "and yet you can ask, 'Who touched me?'"

But Jesus kept looking around to see who had done it. Then the woman, knowing what had happened to her, came and fell at his feet and, trembling with fear, told him the whole truth. He said to her, "Daughter, your faith has healed you. Go in peace and be freed from your suffering."

* * * *

I think it's interesting how Jody wants to reach out to a former employer he apparently treated badly and seek forgiveness and maybe reconciliation. I also love how he says he knows there will be lumps and bumps along the road, but *bring it on!* Because he now has God on his side, and for the first time, I'm sure, in his existence, said, "This is a glorious time in my life!" For a man who has spent almost all his life either homeless or in prison, I can't remotely fathom how this must feel for him.

Chapter 14

Matthew 9:22—God changed a situation that had been a problem for years. Like the leper and the devil-possessed men, this diseased woman was considered unclean. For twelve years she, too, had been one of the "untouchables" and had not been able to live a normal life. But Jesus changed that and restored her. Sometimes we are tempted to give up on people or situations that have not changed for many years. God can change what seems unchangeable, giving new life and hope.

* * * *

This was where I was at because, for years, I felt unneeded and unwanted. As a child it breaks you to believe nobody wants you. As you grow up, it's hard to change that thought process, but the power of God can change anybody. If He can do it for me, He can certainly do it for everyone. God's power is great, and He will show you His grace, glory, and love if you just give Him a chance. Jesus and our Lord never give up on us, and we should never give up on Them!

7/8/18

Dear Jan,

Received your most recent letter. As always it was good to hear from you! This journey has only begun and already it's more exciting than anything I've ever been through. God sure has His way of making a person feel good and at peace, even under the most intense circumstances! Am excited and really looking forward to my future under His guidance.

Am really glad to hear Mike is doing good. Makes me feel pretty good I could help him in any way. I send my blessing to him and hope all he wants in life comes to fruition for him. Seems to be a very bright young man.

I can just imagine the surprise you got when the pastor of Grace handed you my letter! Do you think we can really reach kids all over the world? Just to think about it is amazing. It's a little overwhelming for sure, but it's something I really want to do. I am so blessed! Not just to be with God but to have Him put a friend like you in my life. I've been alone for so long. Now I have our heavenly Father with me, you, and a purpose. Makes a person feel like a complete person!

I totally agree with you—most won't accept or believe the changes in me or my life, but I'm not too worried about it. What God has in store for us is bigger than my imagination would take me. I know where my faith and heart lie. That and what God's plans are, are all I need to worry about. People are people. Some of us can change, some refuse to, others can't. Some are unwilling to change there views on forgiveness. Others choose to forgive and move on in life. At the end of the day only one person's view matters—God's!

Thank you for the canteen funds. They have things on catalog order that we are allowed to order once a month. Like shoes, undergarments and a variety of other things. Thanks to you I am able to order a knee brace. Thank you.

I really hope the kids at Grace Church are all doing well and enjoying the summer. Tell the kids I am always hoping the best for them and their futures. And if you have ever wondered why kids are so important to me, this is why. Not only have I had a pretty bad childhood, but from my time in prison I've ran across so many who have raped, molested, beaten, sold and murdered children, it's always been heartbreaking to me. I was beaten and given away to be raised by the state. Children are the most innocent people in the world. We lived by a code as I grew up. My anger and violence was terrible, but the one thing I've always lived by was no women—no children. And since my childhood wasn't good, I want to help other kids in our society have good childhoods. Does that make sense? I'm still changing and some things are harder to let go of, but I'm learning to forgive even the people I once despised.

Since I am not in CSP at the moment I'm unable to read Mark 5:25–34 until I get back. So once I'm back I will read it and write you my thoughts on it. Oh, I've started writing my story down. Once I get enough done I will send it to you. You can go over it and ask me questions and whatever. Will send the parts as I go. Your questions may jog a memory or two that I can't get to at the moment. But I have started.

For now I will close and pray my eye appointment goes well tomorrow. This glorious journey and adventure is just beginning and I'm so bless you will be here to watch it all unfold with me. My prayers always include you and your family and the kids.

May God's blessing be with you always my friend!

Jody

Jody Mobley #60021

PO Box 777

Canon City, CO 81215

7/19/18

Dear Jody,

It was good to get your letter, as always. I'm so sorry about all the problems you're having with your eyes, and for some strange reason, you're not getting any help with your condition. It would seem to me if you're given a prescription for eyewear, the prison would have to honor that. Please let me know if you get that resolved. If not, maybe I can do some checking on what can be done. I don't blame you for being scared; I would be too. But I also know in my heart God will take care of it the way it's supposed to be handled.

You mentioned me getting the letter you sent to Grace. Actually the pastor's wife gave it to my wife, Karen, who brought it home to me that day after church. I don't know if I was surprised as much as I was puzzled. My first thought was you had probably sent out a number of letters to different churches hoping for a response from someone. Now, when I found out ours was the only church, yes, I was surprised, and that's probably the first time I began to think God had a hand in this. Now, of course, you and I both know this was all His doing. Praise the Lord!

As for your book, you bet we can reach kids everywhere. I wrote a western, which is only an ebook, thinking it would sell best in the US...wrong. It has sold the best in Australia and New Zealand. Your story, which would have a much broader interest, could touch kids and adults in lots of places. However,

I will tell you putting a book together is a time-consuming process, but it will be well worth it.

Glad I could help you get a knee brace and some other essentials. Keep me posted on how your funds are holding up. I have started volunteering at Children's Hospital here in Denver on Tuesdays and Fridays. It's a huge and fantastic hospital, one of the best in the nation. I volunteer in an area called the Tween Zone. It's for sick kids ages ten to eighteen. We have a pool table, foosball, big screen TV with any and all kinds of video games, arcade basketball shoot, small movie theater with virtual reality, and all sorts of arts and crafts. I'll tell you, Jody, it's tough to see kids come in there on death's door and fight for their lives, but this gives them a chance to get away from their room and doctors for a little while and have some fun and laugh a little. God blessed me with the ability to make kids laugh, so I have at them, and they love it. It's funny, but I'll call them by wrong names intentionally, and they love it. We have one girl whose name is Heather, and I call her Debbie, and it just slays her. She now tells anyone who will listen I call her Debbie, and of course, she now calls me Jim. It's both rewarding and difficult, but I truly felt God called me to do this. I'm also involved in trying to help put on a big fundraiser for Respire Haiti. I think I told you I went there to try and start baseball, but that poor country is in such dire straits I don't think that will ever happen. There is no educational system in Haiti, but at Respire, a wonderful Christian mission, they are educating kids, which, as we know, will be the only way Haiti survives. The fundraiser is in November, and our goal is $175,000 for the kids there. We'll see how it goes, and with God's help we'll hit our mark. Other than that, in the summer, my grandkids keep me moving. The hip is excellent, and I now don't even think about it being titanium.

All the kids at Grace are doing well and ask about you often. They, too, are excited about what's happening in your life and the possibility of a book about it. Yes, when you talked about the people you've seen and met in prison who have brutalized children, especially given what you went through, I'm sure it's beyond difficult for you. God made it very clear that people who do things to children have a special place in hell. I have never understood it, nor will I ever understand it. We all come into this world helpless and innocent and for anyone to take advantage of that is staggering to me. Sadly, it happens more often than we want to think about. Now, here you are, going in the opposite direction to help them. Isn't God glorious! And yes, it makes all the sense in the world you want to do this, and more importantly, He wants you to do this. I can tell you your ability to forgive any and all who hurt, harmed, or did you wrong in any way will free you up to do what you need to do here. You will see them in a new light, a light of forgiveness and understanding, which in turn will open your heart to see the world in a new and magnificent light (Matthew 6:34).

Jody, as for writing down your life, and I'm glad you've started, don't try to write a book; just put things down as they come to you. You'll probably find one memory leads to another and so on. Don't try to sequence them right now; just put them down on paper. We can arrange them in order later. When I wrote my book about my experiences with the Colorado Rockies, I'd be writing along, and out of nowhere another instance or memory would pop into my head. It took me over a year to write that book, and even after all that, I forgot one significant story. Don't be in a hurry; thoughts and memories will come and go, which is par for the course. Eventually, it will all be there, or at least what you want to be there. I think you'll find it very exciting, probably somewhat disturbing, but all in all, healing. Good luck—let the adventure begin!

You're in my prayers every day, Jody. I pray God will continue to smile on you and what He has planned for you, and I thank Him for letting me be a part of it. He will take care of you, and nothing will change the path He has you on. Take care, my friend and brother in Christ; looking forward to hearing from you!

God bless you, Jody!

Jan

Matthew 6:34:

> *"Therefore do not worry about tomorrow, for tomorrow will worry about itself. Each day has enough trouble of its own."*

* * * *

I think for the first time in his life Jody is starting to feel like he is part of a family. He has God and His Son, Jesus, guiding and leading the way and me and my wife, Karen, and the kids at Grace Church, all supporting him in every way we can. He has never had any of this in his life up until now, and it seems to be consuming him in the best possible way. He then responded to me about Mark 5:25–34.

7/17/18

Dear Jan,

Wanted to respond to your request to read Mark:5 25–34 and give you my thoughts on it.

After reading it a few times and thinking on it, there are an amazing amount of similarities with the ill woman's plight and my life. Not in the medical way. Where she has suffered with discharge of blood for years, I relate with being in prison for years. Where she had suffered from all the physicians, I relate with suffering under the hands of DOC, and no matter what I tried, it seemed like things always got worse. We both heard and knew about the Lord Jesus Christ. We both came to a point in our lives where our faith became very strong. Even with all our struggles in life, we began and fully believed, with Jesus, we would be, and will be saved. Her touching His garment. Me by learning His Word and trusting Him. Our faith in Jesus has renewed our spirits and saved us from the suffering we've been enduring in our lives. It shows that no matter who you are, where you are, what your circumstances are, as long as your belief and faith is true, you will be saved and suffer no more.

So this is how I perceived these writings. I'm curious to hear how you saw the parallels in both hers and my life, and how close our thoughts on this are. I look forward to hearing from you soon!

My prayers are with you, your family and all the kids. Take care and be safe.

Your friend and brother in Christ,
Jody
Jody Mobley #60021
PO Box 777
Canon City, CO 81215

7/27/18

Dear Jody,

Got your letter about Mark 5:25–34, but first, let me know how your eye appointment went. As for the scripture, you nailed it! I thought the parallels were amazingly similar. She was deemed to be unclean, and by touching Jesus she knew she would make Him unclean, but her faith was stronger than her fear, as is yours. He knew she had been healed the second she touched His robe but asked, "Who touched My clothes?" He wanted her to know it was her faith that healed her, not the touching. I don't know, but I'm wondering if the moment you wrote that letter to Grace Church wasn't your moment of touching Jesus' robe. Given what's happened since, it seems like a match to me.

Some news! I'm leaving Grace Church. I know I never told you this, but when I was a teenager, I walked away from the church and God. I'd been raised an Episcopalian, but once I hit high school and college, I just didn't have time for it. I always believed God was there, but I was just too busy for Him. I was brought back to the church some forty years later by an atheist who is now a devout Christian. It's a long story, and I'll tell it to you sometime. When I did return to the church, it was at Colorado Community Church with an incredible pastor, Mark Brewer. I got involved in the church and actually started a book called *Ascend*, which is about people who, all of a sudden and for no apparent reason, open their hearts to God; sound familiar? Anyway, when I met Karen, my second wife, we started going there and did for several years. Her elderly mother was attending Grace and needed help going to and from church, so that's why we moved to Grace years ago. As for now, I'm down to one teenager for Sunday school class at Grace. Believe me, Jody, I have prayed and prayed about this and truly felt God has guided me back to Colorado Community. I called the head of the youth there, and he told me they have over a hundred teenagers. I really believe God wants me to work with more kids, not fewer, and as a sidebar, imagine how many more kids you're going to be able to reach. I told the youth director about you and what we're doing, and he was very excited to learn more because they have a special program just for troubled youth. I'm going to start immediately, and I'm very eager to get involved. Your story and what we're doing should be such a natural fit into their troubled youth program, as well as the youth in general. As you and I have discussed, none of this is a coincidence or happened by accident. In 1

Chronicles 14:13–16, it talks about seeking out God's guidance in each new situation so we can avoid unseen dangers, and I have. It also says if you seek God's leading in new circumstances, change won't appear as a threat but as an opportunity to let God work in new ways in your life. I truly feel God has directed me this way, and since you and I are brothers in Christ and have a story to tell, well, here we go!

Our journey continues, Jody, and I'm sure it will get more interesting and more exciting with each passing day. Hope you're doing well. I pray for you every day and look forward to meeting you someday…maybe November. Take care, my friend, and may God's blessing be with you always!

Your brother in Christ!

Jan

First Chronicles 14:13–16:

Once more the Philistines raided the valley; so David inquired of God again, and God answered him, "Do not go directly after them, but circle around them and attack them in front of the poplar trees. As soon as you hear the sound of marching in the tops of the poplar trees, move out to battle, because that will mean God has gone out in front of you to strike the Philistine army." So David did as God commanded him, and they struck down the Philistine army, all the way from Gibeon to Gezer.

Chapter 15

Lamentations 3:21–2—Jeremiah saw one ray of hope in all the sin and sorrow surrounding him. God's compassions never fail. Compassion is love in action, and God willingly responds with help when we ask. God's compassion is greater than any sin, and He promises forgiveness.

* * * *

We all sin at various times in our lives, but the severity of those sins varies for different reasons. We find ourselves in situations where sinning is the easier choice, or so we think, but as you can see in my story, it's easier to be bad than good. In order to change, we really need to give ourselves to the Lord because we are far better off with God in our lives. His forgiveness is there for us all the time; all we have to do is ask for it. I will try and be a blessing to all who ask because I thought there was nobody who would give me forgiveness, but God did, and now I'm doing His work and enjoying every bit of it. Join me, and you'll find it is better than you can possibly imagine.

7/30/18

Dear Jan,

As always, it was good to hear from you. Want to thank you for the canteen funds you sent. You have definitely been kind in that area, and I am very appreciative for all your kindness.

Yes, the situation dealing with my eyesight is one I worry about. I know God is looking after me and will do what is needed when it is needed, but it is still a scary ordeal to be going through. As Psalm 103:3 says, "Who forgives all your iniquity—who heals all your diseases" I trust He will take care of me.

The story of how I picked Grace Church is very strange. It was right before I OD'd last year. I wasn't feeling good about life anymore and I was reading the newspaper. I came to the obituaries and read some of them and there was a service being held at Grace Church. Got a feeling that I should write and see if Grace would help me with putting me in touch with some-body that could help me move forward on my journey with God. I was going to give it a little time, and then if nobody responded, I'd try to write another church. That's how I chose Grace Church—through reading the obituaries. If that's not strange I don't know what is!

Really glad to hear the kids at Grace are doing well. Let them know I'm always hoping the best for them and I said hi. I did not know God had made it clear that people who do things to children have a special place in hell. Seems as if they have to live in two different hells. Their lives in here are, and always has been a living hell. God teaches us to forgive those who have hurt us or wronged us. I will be honest with you—it's not easy when it comes to those who have hurt a child. I can forgive them to a certain extent, but I would never associate with them or hang out with those who have done crimes against a child.

The understanding part is difficult as well, because I see children as they are, honest, innocent, helpless and trusting to a fault. So to prey on them is so wrong. I think of the kids I was around when I was free. If you ask a question you get a real answer. They don't know how to lie yet. They trust you to protect them and keep them safe. God sure doesn't make things easy, but that's where faith comes in. You have to have faith that He knows what He is doing. So I forgive—to a certain extent. Maybe as time goes by, and I get stronger in His Word, forgiveness will become easier. It's hard sometimes, but by His will I'm doing pretty good if I do say so myself.

As for my lifes story? No, I'm not going to rush it. It will take some time, but its going good. My younger years are going to be easier to write about due to the mental blocks from trauma. As I grew older things get clearer. I am just going through time frames right now cause I don't recall the years or ages I was at the beginning. Once I get far enough I will send you the pages for you to look at, ask questions and get whatever information you can from me. I am already enjoying the thought of this inspiring others. As I go I will just write what I remember. However long it take it takes.

Certainly agree with Matthew 6:34—not worrying about tomorrow, unless just planning for tomorrow, is good habit to be in, as it says, today has enough to worry about. Believe it or not you learn that passage in here. Prison actually teaches you to not worry about tomorrow. There's too much to worry about today, and tomorrow can't be stopped from coming so why worry about it. Take care of today, today and take care of tomorrow—tomorrow. It's kind of amazing to see all the correlations between life, our circumstances and our living conditions, and how the Bible and Word of God coincide. Everything fits in harmony no matter where you are. God's words put it all together and give you a look at just how powerful His words are. It's probably not as amazing to you as it is to me because you have been on your path with God much longer than I have. How did you come to be so devoted to God Jan? Was it early on in life, or did something happen that opened your eyes and mind to Him? Am curious as to how your journey began.

Well, they came through and took all the tablets today. We don't know if or when we will ever get them back. They may be gone forever. They were nice while they lasted. I'm going to miss the spiritual music.

My friend—know you and yours are in my prayers as well as the kids of the world. I am enjoying God's path and your friendship. Thank you for being my friend and brother in Christ. It really means more to me than you can imagine.

God bless.

Jody

8/12/18

Dear Jan,

Received your letter about leaving Grace Church. First, I just returned from Denver yesterday. They took me Tuesday to DRDC and went to my appointment on Wednesday then back to Canon City on Thursday. Am not real thrilled about going to DRDC and held there for a few days because I am put in segregation while there. The drive and scenery are good. Love to see the sky, clouds, trees, cars, grass, houses and all the stuff I only see on TV. The doctor said that all my visits since September of last year, they have been telling DOC

I need safety glasses. Am pretty concerned that DOC is refusing to do what the doctor says 'cause I really don't want to take any more chances of something happening and losing my sight. I feel God will watch over me and let me keep my vision since I will need it to write and touch the kids through my letters. However, it's still very scary because this is prison, and you can't control what others do. My faith will have to do the hard part for me on this. With that I know I will be okay in the end.

Am personally looking forward to your move. I'm excited for you and Karen. Been a long time since I've felt this good about anything. You probably already know this, but Galatians 6:1–3—wow! When I read the explanation at the bottom on these scriptures I came to understand your meanings from previous letters and I want to strive to be a person of such good heart as you and Karen. What a new thought process and outlook this has given me. I've got to be honest, all that has happened, all I'm learning from the Bible, the more understanding I get of it all, the stronger our friendship grows—I am so overwhelmed! Keep telling myself over and over to watch my step because I don't want to screw anything up. I'm talking about me with God, helping and inspiring kids as well as others, your kindness and friendship, your support in learning God's Word and following Christ. Just don't want to mess anything up. Oh yes, there have been several stumbles when things began going good, but am hoping and praying this continues to flourish. In the past I had no real belief in what I was doing, or where I was going. Now that belief is stronger than anything I've imagined.

Our journey is moving at a fast pace. This whole process is so interesting and exciting. It will only get more interesting and exciting. Even writing to you is amazing for me. The jubilation and joy it gives me. These feeling aren't new—they've just been lost and buried for so long, they seem new.

I've been ordering books from the library, but they never seem to have the ones I'm asking for. Was given a book by another guy that is pretty interesting called "Confucius From the Heart." There was something he and one of his pupils were discussing, and I found it pretty amazing. It went like this: Confucius said, "I am thinking of giving up speech." Zigong asked him, "If you did not speak, what would there be for us, your disciples to transmit?" Confucius answered very calmly and matter of factly, "What does heaven ever say? Yet there are four seasons going around, and there are hundreds of things coming into being. What does heaven ever say?" What is so amazing about this is, if you think about it, God has complete control of the heavens, and the 4 seasons, and the hundreds of things coming into being, but what has He really said? He talked through His Son, Jesus Christ, and that's how we know His words. Through Jesus and His disciples. So it's pretty profound when you really think about it.

Yes, I am well. Thank you for asking. Hope this finds you, Karen, your family and all the people we reach in great health and spirits! You are in my prayers always. Am looking forward to November. Really want my visits back so I can meet you. Be safe and take care, my friend. May God's love and blessings bring you joy and happiness every day!

I am and always will be—your brother in Christ!

Jody

PS. I would like a picture of you and your family. Thank you Jan.

Galatians 6:1–3:

> *Doing Good to All*
> *Brothers and sisters, if someone is caught in a sin, you who live by the Spirit should restore that person gently. But watch yourselves, or you also may be tempted. Carry each other's burdens, and in this way you will fulfill the law of Christ. If anyone thinks they are something when they are not, they deceive themselves.*

Jody Mobley #60021
PO Box 777
Canon City, CO 81215

8/19/18

Dear Jody,

Two letters to read from you…fantastic! I'm sorry your eye situation is so unstable and, for some reason, is apparently confusing to the DOJ. Hopefully, one of the attorneys you contacted will step up and help you, but as you said and we know, God will be there for you no matter what.

Now that you've told me the details of how you contacted Grace Church, it makes all this that much more inspiring and just strengthens my belief this is absolutely a miracle completely conducted by our Father in heaven! I don't know whose funeral that was, although I could find out but have chosen not to for various reasons. But the very fact God would use someone's passing to ignite your journey with Him is almost too much to imagine. As it says in the Bible, "His ways are not our ways," and thank goodness for that because there is no way any of us could have thought this up, let alone carry it out. Only the supreme power in the universe could have made this happen.

At the new church I'm at, we have a lot of kids—103 at our opening night registration and fun night, and some of them are from unprivileged families and have had to deal with drug and alcohol issues and child abuse. Jesus talks about child abuse in Matthew 18:6–14. We just had a case here in Colorado where a father killed his pregnant wife and two little daughters and put them in oil barrels at an oilfield site where he used to work. He strangled his three- and five-year-old daughters to death, and apparently it was all over financial problems he was having. As you mentioned, and as we've discussed, we need to forgive, but I don't even know where to start with this guy. Ultimately, it's not up to me to forgive him, thank goodness, but God will have the final say in what happens to him. I will just never understand the abuse and killing of children. As you said, they are innocent, pure, and certainly have not learned to sin against anyone. Maybe that's why Jesus said we must enter the kingdom of heaven as children. It's a big responsibility to work with, to teach, and mentor children, especially in the name of the Lord, and there have certainly been those in the past who took advantage of kids in God's name. I can't even imagine what they must face when going before God. I pray daily that He lets me finish my life serving Him by bringing the good news to children and kids of all ages, and obviously bringing you into my life was part of His plan. Thank You, Jesus!

I'm sorry they took your tablet, but you still have the tablet the Ten Commandments were written on, at least in your heart and your Bible. Who knows, maybe they'll give them back; I hope so.

You mentioned Galatians 6:1–3. Is that right on or what? I certainly know people who are more about themselves than others as I once was, and

I now have a hard time relating to them. I know everyone has to do what they think is right for themselves, but if you can help others, you really need to. God is helping you and me, and we, in turn, are trying to help children and kids in His name. I know I speak for both of us when I say nothing feels better than that. You also mentioned how it all seems to be coming together so cleanly and you don't want to mess it up. Jody, you know we're going to have some missteps and setbacks, but He didn't put us on this path to watch us fail. This miracle we've been privileged to be a part of is so much bigger than you and me that it's hard for me to envision what the final outcome will be, but I know it will be great because He wants it to be. You and I, like the disciples and so many wonderful priests and pastors before us and those to follow, are merely God's messengers. The fact that He would pick you and me and then put us together is beyond my comprehension and my ability to truly thank Him.

It's interesting that you said your newfound feelings are not, in fact, new but have simply been buried for so long they seem new. Throughout all your ups and downs and hard times, God knew your heart and was just waiting for the right moment to set it free. It's always interesting to me that most but probably not all of the time, the Lord steps into our lives during adversity. When He knows we're at the end of our rope, He is suddenly there or apparently suddenly there when, in fact, He was there all along just waiting for us to turn to Him and open our hearts.

That was interesting—what Confucius said—and it is so true. I don't know if you've had the chance to read Job yet, but for me it is the heaviest book in the Bible. It's also the oldest book in the Bible, and what He says to Job—well, it gave me chills. Without question, no one who has ever lived had it harder than Job, and yet, through it all he never lost his faith...unbelievable! Let me know what you think.

Yeah, November is going to be here before we know it, and I'll head south and schedule a time to meet you in person. That should be beyond amazing; can't wait!

Here are a few pics for you.

Here I am giving my sermon in Haiti to a bunch of Haitian kids—I'm on the right in the red ball cap with Josh Anderson, who runs Respire Haiti with his wife, Megan.

Karen and me at a fair in my hometown of Independence, Kansas, a couple of years ago. Don't have an up-to-date photo of the whole family—there are too many of us to fit into one picture.

Well, Jody, let the journey continue knowing God has us in the palm of His hand. I, too, pray for you and your well-being daily and thank Him for this opportunity to serve Him. Take care of yourself, my friend; enjoy God's love, and know He is with you always!

Your forever brother in Christ!

Jan

Matthew 18:6–14:

Causing to Stumble
If anyone causes one of these little ones—those
who believe in me—to stumble, it would be better
for them to have a large millstone hung around their
neck and to be drowned in the depths of the sea. Woe
to the world because of the things that cause people
to stumble! Such things must come, but woe to the
person through whom they come! If your hand or
your foot causes you to stumble, cut it off and throw
it away. It is better for you to enter life maimed or
crippled than to have two hands or two feet and be
thrown into eternal fire. And if your eye causes you
to stumble, gouge it out and throw it away. It is
better for you to enter life with one eye than to have
two eyes and be thrown into the fire of hell.

The Parable of the Wandering Sheep
See that you do not despise one of these lit-
tle ones. For I tell you that their angels in heaven
always see the face of my Father in heaven.
What do you think? If a man owns a hundred
sheep, and one of them wanders away, will he not
leave the ninety-nine on the hills and go to look for
the one that wandered off? And if he finds it, truly
I tell you, he is happier about that one sheep than
about the ninety-nine that did not wander off. In
the same way your Father in heaven is not willing
that any of these little ones should perish.

* * * *

You get a feeling Jody is getting more devoted to God's Word and what he perceives as God's presence in his life. There just seems to be a more relaxed way he's talking about his life and the hope he has for his future.

Chapter 16

Deuteronomy 1:22—the spies had been sent into the land to determine not whether they should enter but where they should enter. Upon returning, however, most of the spies had concluded that the land was not worth the obstacles. God would give the Israelites the power to conquer the land, but they were afraid of the risk and decided not to enter. God gives us the power to overcome our obstacles, but just as the Israelites were filled with fear and skepticism, we often let difficulties control our lives. Following God regardless of the obstacles and difficulties is the way to have courageous, overcoming faith.

* * * *

God would have given me the power to conquer my fear of letting Him back into my heart if I had just tried to keep my faith back then. Now, I didn't know it, and you probably don't either at times, but God was there for me and is there for you if you just look at the obstacles you've already overcome. We have shown strength, and now we need to show strength in our faith. It is far easier than any of us think; just give it a shot and see the changes it brings.

8/26/18

Dear Jan,

As always it was great to receive your letter. Things here are good, although it has been a long week. There was a staff assault last weekend and we have been on lockdown ever since. No, it didn't happen in this unit. It was in B unit. There are six units in CSP (A, B, C, D, E, F) with eight pods in each unit. Each pod has sixteen cells. Eight cells on the bottom tier and eight on *the top. Total of 768 people here. In all units except B and D and half of F, we get four hours out a day. We come out with only the seven other people on our tier. I'm on the bottom tier, so our times out are Sunday, Monday, Wednesday, and Friday from 11:45 a.m. to 1:45 p.m. and 6 p.m. to 8 p.m. On Tuesday, Thursday, and Saturday, we come out at 7:45 a.m. to 9:45 a.m. and 2:15 p.m. to 4:15 p.m. B pod is transition. It's where you go when you're getting ready to leave this facility and you are out all day and you go to classes. D pod is the incentive unit for all the workers and people are out all day. F unit is three pods segregation; one pod is death row and the rest are like A, C and E. Also there are certain pods in some units that are protective custody. A lot of different levels here. All cells are single cell. Every pod except for segregation pods have a TV hanging on the wall and a micro-wave. The only thing I don't like is not knowing what time it is. We used to have our watches, but for some reason they don't allow us to have them anymore, but they do store them so we will get them back when we leave this facility. They do sell a digital alarm clock, which you have to order off catalog on the first Friday of each month. Then you'll get it the following month. I'm saving $18 out of the funds you just sent and am going to get the alarm clock. Speaking of canteen funds, thank you for sending some. You have no idea how much it has helped. Thank you for your kindness Jan.*

Was trying to read some of Job today, but my eye won't focus enough. I don't focus all the time clearly. Every now and then reading is not possible because my sight is blurry. Other times I have no problem. Good thing is, if not today, then tomorrow. I have a lot of time to study the Word of God.

Oh, there is no doubt God has His own way of doing things. The fact that our meeting each other came through the obituaries is insane really. I'm not going to question His way of doing things, but it is one of the strangest ways I can think of. I wasn't even looking at who was the person passing. Was actually looking for a church to help me with my journey. I wanted to reach out and I had no other way of getting in contact with a church. Keep going over it all and just the fact I picked Grace Church and the pastor gave the letter to Karen and you wrote. It really is a miracle that is mind blowing. Here is a question to think about—how long do you think God has had this planned? The supreme power of the universe has really pulled off a doozie. I'm amazed!

Today is Sunday. Yesterday I had a hard time trying to read, today no problem. I just read the intro to Job. The last small paragraph really hit me hard. "It is easy to think we have all the answers. In reality, only God knows exactly why events unfold as they do and we must submit to him as our sovereign. As you read this book, emulate Job and decide to trust God no matter what happens." The reason it hits me like it does is because of how he put us together, and my question of, "Do you think this has been his plan all along?" That small paragraph answered it all. Will be back in a little bit. Want to read some of Job while everything is clear and I want to read Matthew 18:6–14. Whoa! Just reading up to Job 4 sure shows the manipulation of Satan. Job's faith is something to emulate for sure. It does make me wonder where my life would've taken me if I could've kept my faith throughout. The main thing for me right now is the fact I found what was lost and my life with God is back on track.

Okay—just read Matthew 18:6–14. Makes me feel good about what we are doing. We both have grown up in two different worlds, and both have the same goals regardless of our life situations. You are able to help kids in a different way than me, but our work together will be amazing for the kids. I had no idea God was so hardcore when it came to the little ones.

My heart tells me God has always been there, just not visible to me because of all that has happened to me I chose to look away. Now the more knowledge I learn about God, the more I realize He has always been there looking after me. It's a good feeling to have that understanding.

Thank you for the pictures you sent. You and Karen look good together. Independence, Kansas huh? Looks like we are both a couple of country boys. My hometown is Fort Dodge, Iowa. I love those town fairs. Would always go to them if I had the chance. Just lots of fun.

With that I hope your days are filled with joy. With God's guidance we will be doing a lot of good, and I'm excited! Take care, and know you are both always in my prayers.

Your friend and brother in Christ!
Jody
Jody Mobley #60021
PO Box 777
Canon City, CO 81215

9/2/18

Dear Jody,

I don't know if you're aware of this, but I just received your nineteenth letter…incredible! You sent your first letter to Grace Church on August 30 of last year, and I responded a few days later, and look at us now. We have both come so far in God's grace and understanding, and my sense of it is we are only at the beginning of this miracle journey.

You're right about how we connected through the passing of another. It is beyond strange, at least to us, and no matter how many times I think about it, it still baffles my mind. You asked how long I think God had this planned. I think He had this planned before you and I came into existence. I know that seems impossible to us, but to Him, Creator of the universe, it was nothing to put us together. I think about Paul, killer of Christians, changed into author of over half the New Testament; Mark Brewer, the pastor I found when I returned to my walk with the Lord, who at twelve walked away from the church only to return when he saw his girlfriend killed; my friend Steve, who was an atheist most of his life, then changed into a devout Christian after a devastating divorce; and me, brought back to God by that very same Steve. He knows our hearts, Jody, and He knows when we're ready to accept Him and His ways. In Revelation 3:20, it talks about Jesus knocking on the door of our hearts. He wants to have fellowship with us but will not barge in. We must open the door and let Him in. There is no doubt in my mind that fifteen years ago, neither you nor I would have believed, let alone accepted, what has happened to us now. God always knows the perfect time to make His move.

I'm sorry you're having such a hard time reading. God will provide, Jody, one way or another; we just don't know how…but He will. Job is definitely heavy, and as Job asks, "Why me?" I think the answer to that is Job had the faith to survive it and maintain that faith through the worst possible circumstances. We all go through those "Why me?" times in life. I see it all the time at Children's Hospital, and to be honest, I don't fully understand it, but it's not mine to understand. I need to trust the Lord is always right, and someday the answers will be made clear. You could certainly ask that same question, which you did in your last letter. Why did you have to wait until now to get in fellowship with God, and how different would your life have been had you opened the door to Him thirty-five years ago? I certainly don't have the answer to that, except to say now is the time and, without question, the right time.

I'm sure part of the reason God put us together is our desire and ability to work with kids. You're right; we did come from two different worlds but are now working in the same direction, and I'm convinced that those differences in our backgrounds will come together and form a powerful message to kids…He's always right! It is a blessing to represent God in working with kids, and I thank Him for it every day and ask Him to let me continue to do so. I truly believe my prayer was partially answered by Him bringing you into my life. You're right, Jody; He was always there and always will be.

Karen is a genuine blessing in my life. She, too, is a great Christian and is always interested and concerned about how you're doing. I hope it's okay that I let her read your letters because she is such a huge part of my life and my relationship with God. She finds all of this as amazing as we do. Yeah, that picture of us was at a celebration in Independence called Neewollah, which is Halloween spelled backward. It's the biggest festival in Kansas every year at, strangely enough, Halloween. Independence has a population of about 9,500 people, but during Neewollah it swells to over 50,000. They have several parades, and the final parade has over forty floats and another sixty bands and other parade entries. I had written a book about Independence, and in the year of that picture, they let me ride on my own float. It was beyond belief! As a matter of fact, Karen and I are going back again this year so I can do some book signings and check out all the festivities.

Karen and me on my own float…are you kidding?

Glad you got the money, and hope you get that digital clock. Your description of the prison was remarkable and helped me understand what you face daily. Jody, I can't imagine what you've been through and continue to go through week in and week out. Your faith and continued devotion to God are something I admire more than you know. You have truly become a warrior for our Lord!

Take care, my friend, and know you're in my prayers daily! God's blessings on you, Jody; you richly deserve them!

Your brother in Christ!

Jan

Revelation 3:20:

"Behold, I stand at the door and knock. If anyone hears My voice and opens the door, I will come in to him and dine with him, and he with Me."

Chapter 17

Matthew 1:1–17—in the first seventeen verses, we meet forty-six people whose lifetimes span 2,000 years. All were ancestors of Jesus, but they varied considerably in personality, spirituality, and experience. Some were heroes of faith; some had shady reputations, while many were ordinary, and others were evil. God's work in history is not limited by human failure or sins, and He works through ordinary people. Just as God used all kinds of people to bring His Son into the world, He uses all kinds today to accomplish his will, and God wants to use you.

* * * *

In most people's eyes, I would be placed in the evil category. What category do you think you'd be in? Does it matter? No, not really. As you can see, my life is an example of evil, and yet God now has me doing work to help others. Does it matter that I committed all those terrible crimes, or does it matter that I landed in prison and continued my destructive ways? Not at all because God has forgiven me and is now giving me a chance to help others. Do you have any idea how good that feels? Well, give it a try, and you'll soon find out. I guarantee if you do try it, your destructive behavior will fade away and be replaced with good feelings and a sense of accomplishment in God's name. It's a pretty awesome feeling!

9/4/18

Dear Jan,
How are you and your family? Hope all is well. Things here are okay. A lot of lockdowns lately. At times that is how it goes. There will be long

periods where we go on a lot of lockdowns, or one long one and other times no lockdowns for long periods. God keeps me company every day so I'm in great hands.

Now that you have switched churches, how are things coming along with the new group of kids? Have you had the opportunity to get acquainted with some of them? Funny how the kids are on my mind. Probably 'cause I've been writing a lot on this book, and I'm in the time frame of when I first started going to church and Sunday school. What would really be fascinating is if we could go back in time and go back to Sunday school. Well let me know what you think of the kids and how they reacted to meeting you.

I wanted to tell you about a dream I had the other night. I was being chased by people cloaked in shadows. I could tell when they got close to me that they resembled people I knew. They had pipes and sticks and other weapons. It was late at night in the dream and they were chasing me through the prison. I would find places to hide, but it was only temporary. Eventually they would find where I was and start to form a circle around me. I'd get up and take off running, barely making it through the small opening that seemed to always be there for me to get away. Then, no matter how fast I tried to go I was always stuck in slow motion and could hardly move. Have you ever had a dream like that where you're stuck in slow motion? I kept trying to go faster and was going nowhere fast. Then one of the shadow hands touched my shoulder. It was so cold it burned. I got so scared and ducked down and took off again. I was going around a corner and a door opened. A silhouette of a man was there saying, "Come in here and you will be safe." That's what I did. When I got inside the room it looked very clean and lit up really bright, but the man was gone. I sat there waiting for what seemed forever. I went to the door and opened it. It was daylight and no shadow men. That's how it ended, nothing more. Am sure it was God who saved me. They say that when something is really on your mind a lot and you focus a lot of time on something you have dreams that relate to your circumstance. God has been a critical part of my everyday routine. Being saved like that in my dream sort of feels like how God saved me in real life. Or maybe, because I was shown the true power of God when He pulled me back to Him and put you in my life, my faith has grown so strong that I related my dream to Him. Wanted to share that with you. For some reason that dream feels really significant to me. Do you have dreams like that? That's all for now. Will write

*more when I hear from you. Take care, and know you and your family are
in my prayers.*
                    You are my friend and brother in Christ!
                                                    Jody

9/10/18

Dear Jan,
    *Wow! We have passed a year already. I knew we were close, but hadn't
thought its been over a year. We have come a long way already, and it really
only feels like the beginning. God's love and grace has moved us both in ways
that are a little beyond my understanding, but His guidance can thoroughly
be seen. I have a really good feeling we are going to do some really good
things for others in His name. That's pretty exciting for sure!*
    *Reading in your letter about God having all this planned before we
even existed sounds plausible enough. I would've thought when we were
born. Then I look at all the people you wrote about who came to God, or
came back to God. Makes me think God's plans have been thought out long
before we were born. Reminds me of a movie writer honestly. He writes the
movie, then produces it. The story was there, but only known about later
after it was produced into a movie. The actors weren't even known yet for
the movie. So I can believe God has had this planned far in advance of our
existence. And you are so right. If you would've told me fifteen years ago I
would come back to God and go through a newspaper obituary to find a
church that would help me find somebody to help me through this journey—I
totally would've said that would never happen. Revelation 3:20, that you put
in your letter hit it right on. Sure took me a long time to open that door. I
ignored the knock for so long.*
    *Have been reading Job, and I must say that is some powerfully heavy
reading. His faith is outrageous and I'm not sure how many people, even
from back in those days would have kept their faith. I lost mine at a very,
very young age. You lost yours, or just walked away for your own reasons, as
have so many others throughout time. We've found our way back, but what if
we didn't? That would have not been good. One thing I have noticed this time
though, my faith is far more stronger and unwavering.*

111

I have absolutely no problem at all with Karen reading my letters. She is just as much a part of all this as we are. I'm very thankful for that. Don't believe God would have put us in touch if He didn't think we would all be a supportive group! He knew! And I'll be perfectly honest—I've shed some tears over all of this. Why? Well, because I don't think anybody but myself and God fully understand all the changes this all has had on my life in just this short time. Hard to explain it all because if you haven't lived this type of life you can only imagine—if even that—what a hard, rough, violent life this is. Then I come back to God and meet a husband and wife who are amazingly caring, kind, supportive, understanding and who accept me for me and who I'm trying to be. You don't hold my past, which is not such a good one, to say the least, against me. It's such a blessing for me it can't be put in words. You and Karen have been devoted Christians for a long time. Everything that's happening in all this is new to me. It really is a powerful message from God that His love isn't just for the few; it's for all! Psalm 147:5 says it all for us. Especially after reading the explanation of its meaning at the bottom of the page. I have to say the Bible you gave me is awesome. I'm so new to this, I have a hard time understanding a lot of it. The explanations are such a help. Thank you so much for that!

For now I will end this one. Please let me know how things are with the new group of kids. Very interested to know how that's going and how I can help.

You and your family are always in my prayers. Take care and be safe.

Your brother in Christ and good friend,

Jody

Psalm 147:5:

"Great is our Lord and mighty in power; his understanding has no limit."

Jody Mobley #60021
PO Box 777
Canon City, CO 81215

9/17/18

Dear Jody,

Got both of your letters—great, much to talk about. Wow, that was some dream, and I think you're right; it was God who opened the door to save you, not only in your dream but in your life now. As we know, Satan is always after us, and the closer we get to God, the more he attempts to distract us and pull us away. I know there are lots of people who think the Christian life is the easy path...not! It is without question the most difficult path! The easy thing to do in life is to make your own path and do what you want when you want and with whomever you want. We all go through that, even when we're walking God's path. Satan tells us he'll give us anything we want, as he did Jesus, and all we have to do is worship him. Your dream was probably a little indication of what we get when we follow Satan, darkness, shame, and eternal damnation. No thanks, I'll take the more difficult path and follow our Lord and Savior. Yes, I, too, have had dreams that, in retrospect, I now know were the great deceiver's attempts to mislead me. Mine always involved a wolf that was after me, and much like you, I was ducking and diving to get away from him. He never did catch me and never will!

That truly is amazing, isn't it? We've been corresponding for over a year now...astonishing, well, at least to us. When you think about it, it's far too complicated for us to comprehend, but nevertheless, here we are. Your comparison to a movie being made was perfect! One of my favorite pastors I record every Sunday once put it this way, "Our lives are like standing on a river bank and watching the water flow by. We know where we came from and where we are right now, but we don't know where we're going—only God knows that." Well, you certainly know where you came from and what you've been through and where you are right now, but only our Lord knows where and how this journey ends, and I could not be more confident or comfortable with that.

Yeah, Job is certainly the heaviest book in the Bible. You're right; his faith was beyond anything I can imagine. I suggested it, Jody, because I see a similarity in your lives. He lost everything in his life, as you did. His faith was tested, and he began to question, "Why me?" As I'm sure you have through your life. As you said in your letter, you lost your faith at a very young age and have now found your way back as Job did. As I've said before, God knows our hearts, and He knows the exact right time to knock on the door and step through into our lives. And maybe I'm like one of the three men who came to help Job, only hopefully more understanding than they were. Job's reward was far greater than he could have ever imagined, and so yours will be!

You're right, Jody; I can't remotely imagine what you've been through or are going through even now, but I can tell you your message to kids, young adults, and adults in general would not be taking place had you not gone through it. I can talk until I'm blue in the face to kids about tough times, and I'm sure they would look at me and say, "How would you know?" On the other hand, your story and message come from one who has been there and knows the dark and evil that awaits them. Your voice will resonate with them!

Now for some great and uplifting news about our continuing journey to serve the Lord. This coming Thursday, the 20th, I will be giving another talk about you and the miracle of what is happening. I think I told you I'd titled it "Have You Ever Seen a Miracle?" This is for a women's group called Sarah's Circle. Sarah's Circle is a refuge for women who are homeless or in need of a safe space. By providing life necessities, housing, case management, and clinical and social services, they encourage women to empower themselves by rebuilding both emotionally and physically, realizing their unique potential. The organization is named after Sarah in the Bible. You can read all about her in Genesis 16:3. She was barren but, through her eventual faith, gave birth. It's a remarkable story. Anyway, I'll be speaking before them about our journey. As for the kids at my new church, there are a bunch of them, and it's taking me a little time to make connections, but I'm having some success. I think I told you they have a Friday night group, which is all troubled kids, drugs, abuse, neglect, and abandonment. Last Wednesday night I had a good talk with the woman who runs it and told her about you and what we're doing. She was absolutely intrigued and wanted me to come and talk to the kids one Friday night. Day by day and step by step, God keeps leading us down His path. I am humbled and honored He is letting me do this!

Glad you're getting an alarm clock. How's the vision? Any progress there with regard to glasses? We will definitely take some pictures at the parade and festival, and I'll send some your way. That doesn't take place until the end of October, and maybe not long after that I can come down and see you. In the meantime stay strong in God's faith, Jody, as I know you will. Our journey continues and continues to amaze me as our Lord works in our lives.

Take care, Jody, and may God bless you and all you do. Your eternal friend in Christ!

Jan

* * * *

Jody suffered from constant nightmares over a catastrophic event involving his closest friend and for years would never discuss it, but here he's describing one of those nightmarish dreams and how God saves him. Initially, I thought Job might be hitting a little too close to home, but he seems to be able to look at Job and understand the amazing faith Job maintained through unbelievable suffering and how God rewarded him for his devotion.

Chapter 18

Luke 4:3—often we are tempted not through our weaknesses but through our strengths. The devil tempted Jesus when He was strong. Jesus had power over stones, the kingdoms of the world, and even angels, and Satan wanted Him to use that power without regard for His mission. When we give in to the devil and wrongly use our strengths, we become proud and self-reliant. Trusting in our own powers, we feel little need for God. To avoid this trap, we must realize that all our strengths are God's gifts to use, and we must dedicate those strengths to His service.

* * * *

I'm not sure what strengths I possessed at that time in my life, but I do know that since I was against God, the devil was free to step in and manipulate whatever strengths I had for his purpose instead of God's. It ended up costing me my life in prison. Back then, I used all I knew for wrong. Now that God is back in my life, He has me doing things and using my strengths for good. I hope this story of my life inspires you to turn to God more, pray more, and help others more.

9/23/18

Dear Jan,

Received your letter the other day. Always a great day when that happens. Never fails either, it makes me feel like a kid in a candy store. Can't wait to open the letter and see what you have to say. You're always so uplifting and inspiring with your word. God has certainly put my life on a great path. All aspects of my life have changed since opening my heart to God. You hear things like this happening to others but you never think it will happen to you. Then you give yourself to God, and all of a sudden your mind is filled with ideas. You reach out, and somebody's hand is guided to yours, and God clasps them together, and here we are. The changes He has made in my life—wow! As much as I praise Him and His guidance and love for all His children, there is also a lot of thanks and praise that is due you Jan. You're an extraordinary person full of kindness, very caring and sincere and you inspire me to be a better person. My thanks to you goes beyond the realm of understanding. For you, as well as Karen, to be a part of my life, goes beyond my realm of understanding. You will see why I say this when you begin reading my story. The deeper you read the more you will understand.

Oh—there is no doubt the deceiver is always tempting to get me to change course, but my renewed faith in our Lord and Savior will not be diminished. Satan's hold on me has been broken and will never disrupt my journey with God ever again!

There is some good news to share. Went to medical a few days ago and was given the news they will be starting me on hep C treatment, Harvoni. I go in next Wednesday for blood draw and lab work. Then a week or so after that, they will start the eighty-three-day treatment. It's one pill every day for eighty-three days. I've had hep C since late 2001. So am very curious to see how my body feels once it is free of the hep C. Just one more positive happening in my life.

The only difference between myself and Job is he kept his faith even with the three men who came to help him, whereas I lost mine in the time of disaster. Wonder what would have happened if somebody like you would've come into my life back then?

Today has been a long day of football and Bible study. That's my Sunday now. Well, let me say am certainly looking forward to the end of November. I will get a visiting form for you in November. Really looking forward to meeting you in person.

With that, I hope you've had a great weekend with all of God's blessings. Also hope Karen is well, as well as the rest of your family. You're always in my thoughts and prayers.

Your friend and brother in Christ!

Be safe,
Jody
Jody Mobley #60021
PO Box 777
Canon City, CO 81215

10/12/18

Dear Jody,

I, too, enjoy your letters and look forward to getting them. Here we are in two completely different circumstances, and yet we lift each other up through our relationship with God. I had a call from a man whose wife was at my last talk with Sarah's Circle. He wants me to talk at their Optimist Club meeting. I was supposed to talk to the troubled kids at Colorado Community tonight but came down with a stomach bug, so we're rescheduling. I'll tell you, Jody, God is truly at work here, lining up speaking engagements to talk about this miracle He has created simply because you opened the door to Him. Yes, I wish you could be there to tell your own story, and maybe someday you can. I try to do the best I can, but coming directly from you would be very powerful, and I think that's where the book will come in. As we've discussed, we don't know exactly where this is going or how soon we'll get there, but He does, and I'm sure when the time and circumstance is right, you'll be there. By the way, the Sarah's Circle talk went very well, and all the women told me they want to send you a Christmas card and that when the book comes out, they're all going to buy a copy.

My favorite pastor was telling a story Sunday about an earthquake that took place in 1984 in Armenia. Thousands were killed. A father whose son was attending school nearby immediately ran to the school. He had always told his son, "No matter what, I will always be there for you." The entire school had collapsed, so the father ran to where he knew his son's room would have been and started digging by hand. He dug for several hours, his hands bloodied and beaten. Other rescuers and the police told him it was no use. Nevertheless, he continued—six hours, ten hours, never letting up. Somewhere around thirty-five hours, he moved a large stone and heard noise. He yelled into the hole, "Arman, is that you?" "Yes, Father, it's me." He pulled his son out along with several other students. With a grin on his face, Arman said, "I told the other students we'd be safe because my father told me, 'No matter what, I'll always be there for you.'" Well, as the pastor said Sunday, our Father will always be there for us, no matter what, and rescue us from whatever circumstance we're in. I immediately thought of you, Jody. That's exactly what He's done for you.

Bible study and football—you can't beat that on Sunday. I, of course, am a big Broncos fan. I started going to their games when they first entered the old American Football League back in 1960. I really don't care about any other team, except when the Patriots lose, which I really enjoy. I don't think the Cowboys or the Broncos are going to have a lot of success this year.

I'm so glad your life has turned in such a positive way, Jody. It just shows you how wonderful things can change when our Lord and Savior is involved. Trust me—this wouldn't be happening if you didn't deserve it. You opened the door; He stepped in, and now you're walking the path He wants and has chosen for you. Yes, please send me the visitor paperwork, and as soon as I'm allowed to visit, I'm there. It will be an honor to meet the man who has so changed my life and brought me even closer to God! I pray for you and your well-being every day, and I know God is blessing you more and more all the time.

Your brother in Christ,

Jan

* * * *

You can see Jody really believes and is truly comfortable with God directing his life, and it's very humbling when he gives me credit for any of this when, in fact, I'm simply the conduit for God's message. I also love how Jody now feels like he has a life outside the prison where his story is being told, and he knows he's touching the lives of people who, up to this point, never knew he existed.

Chapter 19

Interlude

The following is a summary of Jody Mobley's life as told by Jody, the extent of which could easily be a book unto itself.

I'm in my fifties and have been in prison most of my life, and I'm currently serving a life sentence as a habitual criminal. My father was killed in a trucking accident when I was six, and that was the beginning of the end of my life as a child. I do have one memory of my dad and me that was good. I can remember us wrestling. Now whether that's a real memory or one my mind made up, I'm not sure.

I'm going to go with real since there are no other memories of us in my mind. I can picture it crystal clear. He was lying on the floor, and he was holding me as I sat on his stomach. We were both laughing and having fun. I wish there were more times I could remember, but I'm thankful for the one I have. I will always wonder, though, what my life would have been like if he hadn't been killed.

Following my father's death, my mother and her new boyfriend began years of abuse, which included whippings and beatings with belts, pig straps, horse whips, and eventually fists, which went along with constant verbal abuse, telling me how dumb and useless I was. I didn't see a lot of kids getting beaten like I did. As a child you begin to think there is something wrong with you, that you're not good enough, that you're worthless and no good.

I remember walking home from school kicking a beer bottle. It broke, and part of it went into my right ankle, where the scar still is to this day. I was bleeding pretty well, and when my mom asked me what happened, I was suddenly this complete idiot, something all kids want to hear about themselves, right? These adults were supposed to love me and protect me but forgot what it was like to be a kid. Instead of putting me down all the time, a little love and compassion might have been the one thing that could have changed my life, but love and compassion never showed up in our house.

Around this same time, Troy, my older brother, and I began to huff model glue, and we got caught a couple of times and got beaten for it. Terry, my mom's boyfriend, and my mom would make us take our pants and underwear off and then whip us with belts; it was pretty brutal, and it wasn't just one, two, three hits; it was over and over and over again. Sometimes, the skin would break, and we were left bleeding and bruised. It seemed like it was the only time we got any attention from our mom. If we weren't in trouble, we were pretty much ignored.

My friend Ralph and I were playing at his house one Saturday; I only know it was Saturday because the next day they went to church, which they did most Sundays. I'd spent the night over at Ralph's, and they asked me if I wanted to go to church with them Sunday morning. My mom said it was okay, so I started going to church with Ralph and his family. After going to their church for a while, I decided to go to a church closer to my house so I could walk. It was a Lutheran church, and I'd go by myself every week. I would sit with the congregation and listen to the sermon of the day, and afterward they'd serve donuts in the cafeteria, and all the kids would go to a Sunday school class. Looking back, I now see our good Lord planned for me to come back to Him one day. Sunday school was fun, and it was one of the things I looked forward to every week, but as time passed and home life kept getting worse, I began to question God's love toward His creation.

One afternoon we were at Terry's mom and dad's house. They were actually foster parents who had taken him in when he was a child and were really nice people, but things were not meant to be good that day. I saw a $20 bill in Terry's mom's purse, just sitting there saying, "Take me, Jody!" so I did. I have no idea what I was thinking because I was right where everybody could see me. I slipped the money into my pocket, but nobody said anything or made a move toward me, so I thought I might have gotten away with it. A little later I went to the bathroom, and as I was coming out, Terry was standing there. He told me to give him the money I'd stolen, and I said, "What money?" That got me a backhand across the face. It was the first time I'd been hit in the face. It split the inside of my cheek open, and I could taste the blood. I remember being extremely scared, and he said, "You better give me that f*****g money, or I'm gonna beat your ass right here!" I handed him the money and told him I was sorry. He told me when we got home I was going to be really sorry for what I'd done. I was petrified and didn't want to go home but knew I'd have to eventually. When we got home, Terry started talking to the man who was my mom's friend and rented the room downstairs. Corey, my younger brother, and I went to our room, and I told him what Terry had said to me—how he was going to beat me and I would be really sorry for taking the money. Suddenly, my mom came into our room and told Corey to go out and play. He left, and my mom told me to take all my clothes off. She was holding a thick leather strap. Man, I was scared. I'd gotten into a habit of wearing long shirts so when I got a beating, it would cushion the blows. She told me to take everything off, including the shirt. I remember shaking all over. Then I felt the first blow, and it hurt really bad. This wasn't a normal strap; it had a handle on it and was probably four to six inches wide and very thick. It hurt twice as bad as a regular belt. She didn't grab me or anything, just one hit after another, and it didn't seem to matter where she hit me; she just kept going. I remember thinking I was going to die. I was praying so hard, asking God to please make her stop, but it didn't happen. She finally stopped, and I couldn't even move. I was hurting so bad. Then Terry came in and said, "So you want to be a thief, huh?" and started hitting me all over again with the same strap. Over and over again while I was begging him to stop and asking God to please help me, but to no avail—Terry just kept hitting me. Finally, he stopped and just walked out of the room. I crawled into bed and asked God why this was happening. *Why would He let somebody do this to me? I'm just a kid.* While lying there hoping God would answer, the man who lived downstairs walked in holding the same strap. I lay there frozen, thinking this couldn't be happening. God would never let this happen unless He didn't love me. Then the first hit came, but I was too weak and in shock, so I just lay there as my body jerked with each hit. It was the worst day of my life, and God let it happen because I wasn't good enough for anybody to love...including Him.

As kids we learn as we go, but the problem for me was I was learning all the wrong things. My learning consisted of, "If I do this or that wrong, I will get attention from Mom," and it didn't matter that the attention was a beating here and a beating there; it was still attention. Looking back, I now understand a lot more about all the stuff that happened to me, but at the time all the childhood heartache that I went through was because God didn't like me. He'd made a person who was no good and not worthy of love or kindness and was just plain bad. Because of this, I went down a long, hard road. If I'd just talked to someone, maybe things would have gotten better, but I kept it all bottled up inside, and others had to pay for my misery.

This was in the 1970s, and I'd met Walt at school. We had coatrooms, where we could hang our coats, next to some of the classrooms. Well, one day I got to school to hang up my coat, and Walt had hung his coat on my hook, so I told him to move it; he said no, so I punched him in the side of the head and threw his coat on the floor. I felt bad later, so I apologized, mostly so I wouldn't get in trouble, and we began talking. He asked me if I wanted to come over to his house after school, so I did, and we became best friends, which lasted until 1986. We hung out all the time, and his parents were so nice and caring. Some of my best memories of our friendship were in the winter when we'd sled down Mason Drive. When I wasn't hanging out with Walt, I devised a way to make some money. It wasn't cool—what I was doing—because I was taking advantage of people's kindness. I would take a pail that I'd made a sign for, kind of like the Salvation Army, only mine said it was for the Cub Scouts, and I'd go door to door in this apartment building and ask for donations. At the time I had no feelings of being remorseful or feeling bad about what I was doing; that had all been beaten out of me, so I took advantage of being a kid and preyed on the kindness of adults. I collected a lot of money every weekend; it sort of became my Sunday school, like passing the collection plate at church.

I was getting high on weed at ten years old, and I didn't care if I got into trouble or got beaten anymore because nobody wanted me around anymore, including my relatives. My world became isolated, except for my friend Walt. If it wasn't for him and his family, my life would have been even worse. Ralph was still around, and one day during winter, I'd been kicked out of school for fighting, and I was just walking around and saw Ralph at this kid's house holding a rifle. I went into the house and began telling Ralph to shoot him. We got into a fight, and the whole time I was yelling at him to shoot the kid. Some neighbors heard us and fortunately stopped it, but that was all she wrote for me. I was cool with it and knew the belt was coming, but this time it wasn't a regular belt. My uncles worked at a slaughterhouse and had given my mom a pig strap. My mom had taken me to the slaughterhouse—I'd seen the strap used on pigs, and now it was going to be used on me. It was so wide; it covered a lot of skin, and this was a pretty bad beating, one of my worst. I hated my life; I hated my mom; I hated Terry, and I hated God. It was all their fault for putting me on earth.

Moving to Colorado from Iowa was a whole new chapter in my life, albeit a crazy one. We moved to an area called Deerfield Hills, which is a southeastern suburb of Colorado Springs. It was just my mom, Terry, Corey, and me because we left Troy behind in Iowa at a boy's ranch. There was a recreation center across the street from our house, which had a swimming pool outside and foosball, a pool table, and ping pong inside. I had a lot of fun there, and at first things weren't too bad. I met a kid whose dad was in the army, so we'd take army rations, go to the fort we'd built, start a fire, heat up some water, eat the rations, and act like we were in the army. One day we caught this kid going through our stuff at the fort, which made me mad, so I started hitting and kicking him. I chased him home and threw rocks at his house, and, of course, his parents caught me and took me home, and my mom whipped me for what seemed like forever. Terry was at work, but when he got home, he came into my room, grabbed me by the throat, and started punching me. It made me light-headed, and all I could see were tiny sparkling lights, but he just kept hitting me and yelling, "So you want to hit people, you little piece of crap! Well, this is what it feels like!" I guess it was pretty bad because Corey told my mom that the neighbors were asking if everything was okay. I wasn't allowed to go anywhere for a week or so, and my mom called the school and told them I was sick because she didn't want anyone to see all the marks and bruises on me. It was the first time Terry had beaten me with his fists. It wouldn't be the last.

One weekend toward the end of the year, Terry told me he was taking me hunting. I thought, *Yeah, we're going to finally do something cool, and he'll be nice to me.* We were dropped off up in the mountains by my mom, and I was given this big backpack to carry, but I didn't care; we were going to go camping and have some fun. We hiked into the mountains a long way and came to a small creek with cold water, which was clean and really tasted good. Terry made me gather up a bunch of wood for a fire, dig a shallow hole, and put rocks around it. He finally let me sit down; we got the fire going and had something to eat. The next morning we hiked into a valley where there was a bunch of cows grazing. Terry loaded his rifle and shot one of them in the head. He looked at me and told me I could never tell anyone or he'd kick my ass. He took out a big knife and started cutting the hind legs off the cow. When he was done, he took one leg and told me to carry the other leg. I could barely do it because it was so big, so I had to drag it, and then I knew he'd only brought me along to do a lot of the work. The next day I had to drag and carry the leg and my pack back to where my mom picked us up. When we got home, he and my mom threatened me again about telling anyone and what would happen to me if I did. I never said anything to anyone until now.

Things got worse and worse, and I remember wishing I was dead. Corey got into trouble for something, and Terry beat him pretty badly...he was only nine years old! He was locked in his room, and we all went out to dinner, but when we got back, he was nowhere to be found. The neighbors had come over while we were gone and took him out the window. I'm not sure what happened, but we all had to start going to Social Services for therapy. Mom and Terry threatened us and told us we couldn't say anything about what was going on. Life is unbearable when you're twelve and you walk around all day, every day, afraid. I began fighting more and not caring about anything or anybody except for my little brother.

I came home one day from school, and my mom had searched my room, which is something she and Terry did all the time. We had no problems with privacy because there was none. Now I'm in prison, where guards can come into your cell anytime they want and search through your property; well, that's what my childhood was like—a prisoner in my own home. You're supposed to be able to turn to your parents for love and protection, but not in my house; we were hostages. There was no trust, love, compassion, nothing! She had found some tobacco in a pocket of my shirt, and she went crazy. She locked me in my room, and when Terry got home, I could hear them talking. Then suddenly, my door flew open, and Terry came storming in and started pounding me with his fists again. He didn't care where he hit me—my face, back, stomach, anywhere he could land a blow. When he finished, I was lying on the floor, curled up in a ball, bleeding, battered, and bruised. This is the beating that broke me. It changed the outcome of my life for the rest of my life. There was no God or Son of God to save me.

That night my mind was made up; it was time to get away from the beatings, verbal abuse, and living in constant fear. The next morning I got up to get ready for school, but I wasn't going to school. Corey heard me get up and came out of his room to see what I was doing. Mom and Terry were still in bed, so I gave Corey a big hug and told him I was leaving. He thought I meant to school, but I was running away. He started crying and telling me I couldn't go, but I had no choice; I just turned and walked out the door. I was about to turn twelve years old, and I haven't been home since.

I went downtown to a place called Acacia Park and met a couple of people. We stole a radio to listen to, but I wound up stealing it from them and selling it for $10. I hid from them in a security building and fell asleep under some stairs. The security guard found me early the next morning and called the police, who took me to Zebulon Pike Juvenile Center. They called my mom, and she told them to keep me. So now, not only had God abandoned me—my own mom didn't even want me anymore.

One afternoon Corey, who I'd meet on the sly, and I were walking around with an old milk carton filled with gas. I was mad at a kid inside the rec center because he'd been giving Corey a hard time, and I took that very personally. We went to the rec center where the kid was attending a Cub Scout meeting, poured the gasoline all over the door, and set it on fire. I told Corey to go home before anyone saw him. Out they came with fire extinguishers and put the fire out. They caught me and took me back to Zeb Pike, where the police questioned me. One of the detectives asked me, "You were going to burn thirteen kids because you were mad at one of them?" I said, "Yeah, why not?" I was sent in for evaluation and diagnosed with depression and some other emotional problems and, at age twelve, committed to the Colorado Mental Health Institute in Pueblo, Colorado, where I was put in the juvenile cottages for treatment.

I was out of control, running away from the institute a lot and beating other kids up. I was pretty much lost. I didn't conform to anything positive because I was filled with hate and anger, and I didn't care about anything. Life was just no good for me; I continued to run away and cause problems. Then in the winter of 1980, I ran away to Carla and Curt's, a couple I knew, and told them I was going to Iowa to see my older brother, Troy. I can't believe they helped me and let me go, but they did. I had just turned thirteen; it was winter, and I was going to hitchhike from Colorado Springs, Colorado, to Fort Dodge, Iowa. I got a ride outside Colorado Springs to Denver and, from there, got a ride to Cheyenne, Wyoming. I was standing on an on-ramp for I-80 just east of Cheyenne when a Sheriff's car drove by. He saw this little kid with a backpack trying to hitchhike, so he turned around and came back and picked me up and took me to the sheriff's office and called the State Hospital in Pueblo. The hospital said they'd come get me in a couple of days. Well, I wasn't having any of it, so I told the sheriff to call them back and either come get me now or let me go. He called them back, and they said they weren't coming to get me, so he could let me go, so once again, nobody wanted me, which only made my convictions stronger. This seems absolutely crazy to me, but the sheriff drove me back to the interstate on-ramp, let me out, and drove off. Looking back, I can only wonder, "What was he thinking?" I stuck my thumb out and caught a ride, and after a couple of days, I was getting close to Fort Dodge. My last ride was from a lady who drove me to my friend Walt's house. I told his mom and dad what was going on and that I'd come all this way to see my brother Troy. They took care of it and brought Troy to see me. We kicked it for a couple of hours and got to have a good talk, but then he had to be back to the boy's ranch, so we said goodbye, and I hitchhiked my way back to Colorado Springs.

I was hanging around with my friend Dick, and we started talking to a guy named Jeff, who told us about this coin shop in the Rustic Hills Mall in the Springs that he wanted to rob in the middle of the night. I think it was Mother's Day weekend, 1980, when we broke in and robbed the place. We ran out and hid all the money and went to an IHOP restaurant across the street. We could see a line of cop cars speeding down Academy Boulevard with all their lights and sirens going, and when it was clear, we got on our bikes and went home. The next day we went back and got all the money and split it up. Here I was, thirteen years old, and we had just stolen over $250,000 in rare coins and bills. There were coins valued at over $2,000, and we were using them to play video games at 7-Eleven and the Citadel Mall. I had a stack of mint-condition $100 bills dated 1929, which I used to buy weed and shoes. The other kids involved all wanted to take off, but I told them I was staying, so they left. They got caught in Florida when the cops were looking through their suitcases and found some of the rare coins. When the cops asked them where they got them, they said Colorado, and that's what led to me being caught. That summer the police showed up and arrested me for the coin shop robbery.

After my arrest for the coin shop robbery, they sent me back to Zeb Pike, and my court hearings began. Dick and one of the other guys in the robbery testified against me, and they gave me two years in the Department of Institutions, which is what they called the juvenile camps. On November 19, three days after my fourteenth birthday, my two years began. I was sent to a facility called Lathrop Park Youth Camp in Walsenburg, Colorado, and my stay there would be very eventful.

I met a kid named Hank, and we hit it off right from the get-go and hung around together a lot until we decided to run away. A few days after we made this decision, we took off after dinner, and we got away and found a road, which we followed until a guy in a pickup truck picked us up. We eventually made our way to Canon City and went to some kid's house Hank knew where we got high. The next day began a week of burglaries all over Canon City. We were so bold when we saw someone working in their front yard we'd go in the back and take what we wanted. One house we robbed was a cop's house, and we got some billy clubs, a gun, and a couple of knives. Then armed, we went down an alley and in another back door where there was an older man in the kitchen watching TV. I took my knife out, and Hank had the club ready, but the man looked up and asked us if we were the paper boys; we said yes, so he wrote us a check, and we left.

The next part of my life, although new, was very much like what I'd lived before—the only difference being I was free, no more running from state custody. My old ways and habits were still there, though—drinking, drugs, and fighting, which I really enjoyed, even if I lost. Some people thought I was crazy, but I loved the thrill of it. I learned to drive, albeit without a license, and got a job delivering produce for a company in the Denargo Market warehouse area near downtown Denver. My friend Scott and I would drive one of their vans to make deliveries. One day a semi-truck almost hit us, so I began yelling at the driver, who started chasing us through downtown Denver—it was wild, and I loved it. This is also about the time I started shooting up drugs like coke. We'd stay up all night doing shot after shot; Scott wasn't really into needles, but it was the only way I'd do my drugs. Coke wasn't really my thing, though, so I got into speed really heavily and started bouncing from job to job.

A girl named Penny and I dated for a while. She had a new car, a green Mustang, and it was fast and pretty much mine while we went out, but one night coming back from Red Rocks and too much partying, the car slid sideways a little, and she told me a car just hit us, so I took off after the guy, and we got into a high-speed chase. I remember taking an off-ramp at about 95 mph. We caught up with the car, but the driver had taken off, so I got a crowbar out of the trunk and smashed all his windows, slashed the tires, and put holes in the hood of the car. Penny's dad was really upset, to say the least, since he didn't like me much anyway and told her she couldn't see me anymore, but that didn't stop us, and I ended up getting her hooked on shooting speed. Since I didn't have a job, I started doing burglaries again to pay my bills and pay my drug debts.

One day, when Corey was visiting, Penny got really bent out of shape and started yelling at me. Her parents were on vacation, so she went and got her dad's gun and started saying she should kill herself. I took the gun away from her, loaded it, threw it on the bed, and told her to do it. She was yelling how much she hated me, which I didn't respond to, but I did tell her if she wasn't going to use the gun, we needed to go so I could pay my dope man and get some more drugs.

Corey kept yelling at me how crazy I was and what if she shot me. I told him if she did, so be it; I didn't care.

Scott was living a couple of blocks away, but he stopped by one day, and I told him we needed to get high. I boiled some needles, but something went wrong because he got blood poisoning; luckily we caught it in time, and he was okay. I took all the needles and threw them away in the trash a block down the street. I would always bend the needles over and put the cap on so I knew they were used. One night I had some cocaine, but I couldn't find a needle, so I ran barefoot down to the trash and dug some out. I bent the needles back to an L shape and stuck them in my vein sideways. If they had broken off and gone into my blood, I could have easily died, but that's how important my dope was to me, so I took the risk.

A guy's name I can't remember was Jock's brother-in-law, who I knew stole some of his tools and pawned them and then said Corey had done it and then stole some of Jock's cocaine and blamed that on Corey as well. I came home one night, and they had Corey tied up and were beating him. I flipped out and went to get a gun, but they stopped me, so I grabbed Corey, and we took off. Corey and I then moved in with some drug dealers. I knew a retired ex-cop who was selling illegal guns, so I went to see him, and he let me borrow a gun because I was going to kill Jock's brother-in-law. I sat in an underground parking lot at Cinderella City for two days waiting for him before I found out he'd left town, so I took the gun back and told the guy if I needed it again, I'd be back. I later heard the guy died in California…I was glad.

We got evicted, so Scott and I got a place together, and we were doing pretty well. It was 1986, and I'd held my job for a while doing roofing. Corey was living with a woman named Trish and her three kids, and I was dating a girl named Rhonda, and Scott was dating a girl named Allison. The girls had decided to go shopping, so Scott and I stayed home and chilled out. It was December 20, 1986. We had taken a couple of hits of Orange Sunshine acid and were drinking beer, but we'd run out of beer, so I told Scott we needed to go get some more. He said he was too high to go, so I got a few bucks from him and took off. I used to love cruising on acid cause all the lights had trails behind them. I got the beer, and when I got home, Scott was sitting in the living room with a shotgun in his mouth. At first I thought it was a joke, but as I reached out to hand him a beer, he pulled the trigger. I got splattered with blood, brains, and bone fragments. I fell to my knees in shock and just stared at him; my mind stopped—everything stopped, and I must have stared at him for half an hour. I don't remember calling 911, but when I became coherent, cops were everywhere, and when Rhonda and Allison came home and wanted to know what was going on, I told them Scott was dead. That was the longest night of my life. Scott's family had taken me in and treated me like one of them, but when his mom showed up, it turned ugly. This was all my fault because I'd driven him to this, and if he hadn't known me, he'd still be alive. It was the worst verbal beating I ever got; they disowned me. Rhonda left me, and my life spiraled even more out of control after that day. The mental health facilities I've been in verified it wasn't my fault, but it sure felt like it was for the next thirty years. I was really torn apart and, of course, blamed God for creating such a worthless life. How dare He say He loves us and forgives us? If He was so forgiving, I sure couldn't tell. I know differently now, but at the time He was to blame for all my misery.

After Scott's death, things really went crazy. I got a hold of some really strong drugs and was getting higher than ever. Corey found me lying on the floor and took me to the hospital, where they put me on suicide watch, and when I got out, I started down a long, reckless road; whether it was in my car or a bike or my motorcycle, I would drive around in rich neighborhoods and notice the houses were a good distance apart. I'd pull into the driveway of one of them, knock on the front door, and if nobody answered, I'd walk around the house looking in the windows. If no one was home, I'd kick in a basement window, go in, get all I could carry, and start loading up my car like I lived there and was just moving some things. Then I'd sell or trade all the stuff for drugs or pawn it for money.

I moved into a drug dealer's house in Thornton, and my life continued to spiral out of control. I robbed a house and got a beautiful 357 magnum pistol, 2 lbs of weed, and $6,500 in cash. After the burglary, I got this crazy idea that I'd rob drug dealers; after all, my best friend had just killed himself in front of me and I had lost everyone I cared about, so I figured God had given me this crappy, no-good life and taken everybody away from me and was making me lose my mind. After that last robbery, I got my first motorcycle, a Honda Magna V45, and man, was it fast. I had sold some of the weed for $1,200, which is what I paid for the bike. I also got a quarter ounce of speed, which was ether-based, and when you did a shot, it took your breath away; I know because I took a shot, got on my bike, and cruised into the mountains. I was going to show God that since He'd taken everybody away from me and given me this worthless life, I was going to press the envelope and rob every dealer I knew and force God into having somebody kill me; after all, they all had guns and didn't play around.

It was the summer of 1987, and I had my 357, my dope kit, and my bike. I went to the residence of my victim around 9 p.m. and could see the guy and his wife were watching TV in the living room. I put on a mask and knocked on the door with my gun in my hand. He opened the door, and I pushed my way in, then made them sit on the couch, and I told him I wanted all his money and dope, and I'd give his old lady five minutes to get it all, or I'd shoot him. This was her chance to get a gun and get me first, but she didn't. Within a few minutes, I had 3 lbs of pot, half an ounce of cocaine, and over $3,500 in cash, which I put in my backpack and walked out. I'd left the keys in the ignition so I could make a quick getaway. I'm sure they could have gotten a gun and started firing at me, but they didn't. You'd be surprised at what people will do when their life is on the line. She could have easily gotten a gun and shot me, but she was too scared; I could see her trembling all over with fear. I ran to my bike, hit the starter, and was gone. That was the first time I robbed a dealer, and when I got far enough away, I pulled over to catch my breath because I was shaking with fear. I got home and started bagging up the coke into grams, which made thirteen grams, and I was going to use the rest. Now I wasn't big on coke, but I'd do it when I had it just to try it and see how potent it was. I went into the bathroom and took a pretty good shot, and it began to hit me as I was rinsing out the syringe, and then it really hit me. My arms started shaking uncontrollably, and then my whole body began to shake. I thought for sure my heart was going to explode, which is what happens if you do too much. If you overdose on coke, it's usually a heart attack because your heart can't stand the pressure. It was pretty intense, and when my body stopped shaking, I did a shot of speed, which I did when I used coke so I wouldn't die from the coke. I got all the weed and coke ready to sell or trade and then went riding for a while, which is what I did—shoot speed, ride, eat Häagen-Dazs ice cream, and drink orange juice.

I continued down my path of destruction, pulling off thefts and robberies. At one house I went through the back door and was greeted by four dogs; none of them appeared vicious, as far as I could tell, but then one of the bigger dogs jumped up and grabbed hold of my hand. I grabbed a broom and started hitting him in the nose until he let go. I still have the scars from that on my hand. I held the dogs off with the broom and walked further into the house. I went into a bedroom that led to a bathroom and another room. I got into the bedroom, then circled around so I could lock the dogs in the bedroom, then took everything I could to pawn or sell. My name was getting around to all the pawn shops, so I'd have to go from shop to shop to eventually get the best price. At night I was still driving around, breaking into vans and work sites and stealing all I could. I was getting way out of control, strung out on speed, pulling burglaries, robbing dealers, and getting paranoid I was going to go to jail. Then after being up for six or seven days straight, I walked into this dealer's house to rob him, but unfortunately for me, there were four or five big bikers there, and before I knew it, I was getting stomped out. One of the guy's girlfriends jumped in and saved me, but it was the worst beating I'd ever taken. I had broken ribs and a broken nose, and my face and body were black and blue from head to toe. I was barely able to drive home, and I missed my probation officer's appointment, so a warrant was put out on me since it was my third miss. Once I healed up, I started moving around and didn't leave my house for about a week and a half, staying high as a kite the whole time. This wasn't the plan—my plan was to push the envelope and have somebody step up and put me out of my misery.

In April of 1988, I pulled a burglary on my bike and then went to a pawnshop I'd dealt with from time to time; unfortunately one of the bracelets I was trying to pawn had a girl's name on it. I should have been more on my game, but the drugs had me so far gone I didn't realize the setup, and that was my downfall. The owner told me to come back in a while because he had to go to the bank and get some more money. I left, did a shot, got some food, and went back to the pawnshop, but when I walked in, two detectives grabbed me and asked me if I was Jody Mobley. I told them no, but they checked my ID, put me under arrest, and took me to the Denver County Jail. I called a dealer friend and made an arrangement with him, so I could bond out of jail before I got rolled up in Arapahoe County. It took a couple of days because I had to post bond on this case and the warrant for my arrest in Arapahoe County.

I could go on and on about all the bad things I've done to people, all the illegal activities and drugs, and that my life has been a pile of garbage, filled with crime, drugs, anger, violence, women, and alcohol, all the negativity you could ever want, but there were some good times; they were just a few and far between and were mostly filled with drugs, alcohol, and women. I couldn't hold a job for long, and I lived in so many places I can't even remember them all. At one point I slept in the back of a friend's truck during the winter, and no one ever knew. I spent time in the Arapahoe County Jail, and they had us working on building the new jail. I stole socks and shirts from the old jail, then smuggled them into the new jail and sold them for weed. That's the life I lived; it wasn't productive, positive, or very enjoyable, and throughout the years before I went to prison, everything in my life was negative, and it didn't stop after prison, which is another chapter of my reckless life.

So here I was, just a few months past my twenty-second birthday, and I'd landed in the big house with killers, rapists, assaulters, gang members—people that society had given up on. I was put in cell house five, which was a three-tier building with cells across from you, which meant there was absolutely no privacy; other prisoners could see everything you did. It held about 150 people but was double-bunked, so it was up around 300. You had a bunk bed made of steel, a stainless steel sink and toilet combo, a desk, and a couple of shelves shared by two people. The cells were twelve feet long and eight feet wide with no windows and no fresh air. You ate, slept, used the bathroom, washed up, wrote, read, and tried to work out all in this little box.

You got to go out in the yard once a day—three times a day in a less secured facility. It was surprisingly quiet in cell house five because there was an unwritten rule called ten to ten, which meant from 10 p.m. to 10 a.m. no one made a noise. If you did, there were severe consequences, which were usually violent. You might get a warning the first time, but if you did it again, you'd probably get beaten pretty badly. In prison, the slightest misstep will cost you dearly, again, usually violently. I spent about two weeks in cell house five, mostly doing tests like mental health, school level, and job skills. Once I was done with the tests, I was transported to cell house three, which is where the gas chamber was located.

As time went by, I kept wondering where they were going to send me next. There were places you wanted to go to and places you didn't. At that time the Ordway Correctional Facility was one you didn't want to go to. It was the roughest facility in Colorado at that time, so naturally on April 11, 1989, they transferred me to Ordway. When I got there, they had just had a riot and the inmates had torn the place up pretty badly. The facility was wide open at that time, so that first night, I went out walking around the yard by myself. You could walk between buildings and chill out on the grass. As I came around a corner by the buildings, I heard a noise between the units, and when I looked over, there were two guys stabbing another guy. My mind went crazy, and all I could think about was what I had gotten myself into, and no matter what, keep my mouth shut.

In July I was transferred to Four Mile Correctional Facility, which was a minimum restricted custody level facility. I was only at Four Mile for four months, and on my birthday, November 16, 1989, they sent me to a minimum security facility in Rifle, Colorado, called the Rifle Correctional Facility. I got drunk one day, and a guard started hassling me, and before I knew what happened, I'd assaulted him, so on July 20, 1990, they transferred me to the Buena

Vista Correctional Facility and put me in the hole. While I was in the hole, a guy started talking crap to me, so I waited for the next shower day, and when he passed by my cell, I jumped him and beat him all the way to the front of the unit. This was my second assault in two months, so they put me in the secure management unit. Everybody there was scheduled to be transferred to maximum security, and on October 5th, 1990, thirty-five prisoners, all with records of violent incidents, were put on a bus along with a SWAT team and transferred to maximum security at the Centennial Correctional Facility, where I spent the next ten months. The first few weeks were rough; the guards would come to our cells, pull us out, then take us to intake, make us strip, and then jump on us. If you had an assault on a guard, like I did, this happened at least once a week. They got me three or four times because of what I'd done; it was the price I had to pay. This was the life God had given me, and I despised Him for it. This life was not what I wanted, but I was stuck with it.

They opened up Fremont with Shadow Mountain, and a lot of us got moved to the Fremont side. My cellmate was a good friend I'd met while in the Rifle facility, and we had a good thing going. We'd steal meat, ice cream, eggs, cheese, and all kinds of stuff from the kitchen and then sell them to other prisoners. We made a lot of money, and then we'd get high. If you've ever watched the show *Locked Up*, you should know that's all staged because if you go on national television and tell all the secrets of what's going on in the facility, you're going to have the entire prison after you. I'm telling you things I've done, but not how they were done because I'd be putting my life at risk.

My stay at Fremont wasn't too bad. I arrived there on December 1, 1991, and stayed until January 5, 1993. I did get into a fight and had to do thirty days in seg, and when I got out, my cellmate got sent to the hole. When he got sent to the hole, they put a new guy in with me. He was a big guy but not in good shape, and I figured he wasn't good because he had a friend who was a child molester, and I really disliked anyone who did anything to children because of what happened to me. While he was moving in, they paged me to the office and told me that no matter what I thought, he could live there, and if anything happened to him or his property, they would put me under investigation. I went back to the cell and told his buddy to leave and that he couldn't come back to my cell for any reason. Not long after that, I was paged to the office again, and they told me his buddy could visit whenever he wanted to. That sealed it for me; he was telling on me, so at a lockdown for lunch count, I got out of my bunk, and I laid down how his life would be in my cell. I let him have one tiny corner shelf and told him whatever didn't fit on that shelf had to be stored under the bunks and he was not allowed to use my sink or toilet ever and wasn't allowed off his bunk at any time during counts or lockdowns. When the doors opened, he was to leave the cell and not come back until counts and lockdowns were over. I also told him if he went to the guards about it and squealed on me again, I'd stab him. He took it to heart because he slept in his clothes and left every day while the doors were open—his life was miserable. Then one day they came to his friend's cell, where he'd go to get away from me, and carted him off on a stretcher. The guards asked me what I'd done to him, and I told them nothing. Apparently, he'd had a mental breakdown, but they could never put it on me, and shortly after that, my friend got released from the hole and moved back in.

On January 5th, 1993, they transferred me to a pre-release facility, which was the most boring place I have ever spent time at, and it was almost my downfall. I had a visit with them, and when we were done, I was going to go get high, but right before I did, they called a bunch of us in for a UA test. It was perfect timing; I went and gave them a clean UA, then went back to my room to get lit. For the next two and a half weeks, I stayed high. Then, just when I thought everything was working out, I got hit with another bombshell. My mom called and told me my uncle had changed his mind, and I was no longer welcome—two weeks to go, and once more, my family abandoned me. I remember wondering how this could happen again. It had to be a sick, cruel God who was playing with me, or obviously there was no God, or He wouldn't be doing this to me. I got released and had to go to Adams County Jail, where the girlfriend of one of my buddies bailed me out. The girl that picked me up had a friend named Sherry, and I stayed with her. She had a young daughter who was really cool and liked it when I was around.

For the next three weeks, my life was back to the old, outrageous days I'd grown accustomed to—drinking, fighting, bar hopping, and robberies and burglaries. We had guns; other people had guns, and looking back, I'm amazed somebody didn't get killed, especially me. Part of the problem is that in prison, you don't let people disrespect you; if they do, there are always repercussions, and they're usually violent. Sadly, we took that to the street when we got out of jail. We were like wild animals.

A friend of mine came in from Nebraska, and our plan was to rob a store I'd seen. That morning Sherry dropped us off, and we went in the front door of the business, carrying our guns. My friend jumped over the counter and made the owner get on his knees with a gun to his head. As I walked by, it looked to me like the guy was trying to get a look at me, so I kicked him; we duct taped him up, and I dragged him into the back of the store, out of sight, and out the back door we went. We went back to Sherry's, got our stuff, and headed to Colorado Springs for a few days to stay with a friend I had there. While we were in the Springs, it was more fighting and drinking. Then it was back to Denver. I went and visited my brother Corey in a halfway house, and soon after that he went to jail for fighting, but for me, it was all about sex, drinking, and money.

One night Sherry's friend Penny asked me if I wanted to go out for a drink, so Sherry, Penny, and a friend of mine headed to a bar on West Colfax. We started playing pool for drinks, and Sherry and I kept winning. I was drinking beer and Long Island iced teas, and after a few more wins, I blacked out. When I woke up, I was in jail. I called Sherry and asked her what happened, and she said I'd gone to get some smokes, and the next thing she knew, I was in a fight. She said we left and went back to her place, where she dropped my friend and me off, then she and Penny went to get some food. When she got back, she stood outside and listened to us talking, but I was so drunk she couldn't understand what I was saying. Then at some point, I decided to leave. I do remember her asking me not to go, and I told her not to worry—I'd be back soon. When I finally came around, I was sitting naked in a cell in the Jefferson County Jail. A guard came to the door, opened the window, and asked me if I was ready to cooperate. I told him I would, so they gave me some clothes and moved me to a holding cell while they processed me into jail.

Once I was processed, an investigator pulled me out to ask me some questions. Everything he asked I answered with, "I don't know." I could tell he was getting mad, so I told him I had blacked out from drinking and I didn't really know what had happened. He got so frustrated he finally asked me if all I could say was, "I don't know," and of course, my answer was, "I don't know." That was the end of the questioning. I asked a guard what I was being charged with, and he told me aggravated robbery, a weapons charge, and crimes of violence. So apparently I was heading back to jail, but I wasn't really worried about it; I'd already spent time in prison and saw plenty of people go in and out with new cases, so there was no thought I'd be spending a long time in prison.

On April 7th, 1993, they transferred me to the Department of Corrections in Denver, and on April 22nd, they sent me to the Limon Correctional Facility in Limon, Colorado. I was going back and forth until my trial, and during this time of going to and from court, my drug use got out of hand. Heroin was a drug I'd never done much of, but now it had me hooked. The court wanted me to testify against my codefendant, but I told them I couldn't because I didn't remember what happened that night. They told me if I refused, they'd file the Habitual Criminal Act against me, which meant a sentence of forty years to life. I was in shock! All this time I'd watched people come and go with new charges, and now I was being threatened with life. My codefendant had bonded out and left the state, so I went to trial alone. They didn't have any real evidence against me and kept trying to get me to testify against the other guy, but that just wasn't an option, so I pled not guilty. They told me again if I didn't testify, I'd do life, so I told them, "Well, I guess I'll be doing life." They found me guilty, and I was sentenced to forty to life in the Department of Corrections in January of 1994.

I was still dealing drugs, and they arrested me off the unit and put me in dry cell. Dry cell is where they take all your clothes and give you an orange jumpsuit to wear. You get no blankets, sheets, or anything, and the lights are on all the time, and a guard sits in the open doorway of your cell, and they videotape you twenty-four hours a day. On February 10, 1997, they placed me in segregation in Limon, and on May 29, 1997, they transferred me to the Colorado State Prison, where they kept me until August 17, 2001. For four years I was in segregation with twenty-three hours a day in lockdown, so for over four years, I didn't get to go outside. Oh, I could look outside but not go outside. Then they sent me to the Buena Vista Correctional Facility in August of 2001, and I got to go outside again.

In February of 2002, on the way in from recreation, some of us got into it with some gang members. They put me in segregation again and told me I was getting written up for trafficking drugs. I have no idea where that came from because I never did that in Buena Vista, but that, coupled with the fight with the gang, sent me back to the Colorado State Penitentiary. That was in February of 2002, and for the next three years, I sat in segregation; then, one morning in January of 2005, I was told to pack all my stuff and send it home. I knew they were sending me out of state, and sure enough, they sent me to Wisconsin because I refused to renounce my gang ties or give up my leadership role from 2003 to 2005.

The Colorado penal system was hoping that a change of scenery would give me a chance to step down from my gang leadership role, but all it did was bring all my mental issues to the forefront. My time in Wisconsin didn't go well because I was in fights and in and out of the hole a lot. They sent me to a security facility called Portage Care Facility. Colorado wanted them to put me in a segregated facility, but the mental health doctor said I had too many mental health issues, such as major depressive disorder, PTSD, anger control problems, and suicidal tendencies. Even though these issues were affecting me, they decided to put me in segregation anyway, and I stayed there from September 2005 until the middle of 2008.

I stayed to myself, but the mental health staff was concerned because I was isolating myself from everyone. We continued to contact the Colorado DOC, letting them know I was declining psychologically, but they continued to deny my return. Wisconsin mental health sent me back to WRC, where I stayed for about twenty months. They even requested my records from Colorado concerning my trying to burn down a building because I was mad at one kid, and they wanted all the facts about Scott's death. They found out everything I'd told them about those events was true, so they ordered a complete psychological evaluation on me and were concerned because I'd told them God had put me on earth to suffer and death would be preferable to the life I was leading. My nightmares and depression were getting worse, and I was angry all the time. During the twenty months I was in WRC, they put me on suicide watch because of several attempts I'd made. I told them I wasn't going to live like this anymore; God had destroyed my life, and Colorado had sent me away from everyone I knew, so I'd rather be dead.

The holidays were coming up, and I was still struggling with the anniversary of Scott's suicide, but in January of 2014, I got word from Ben's lawyer that a motion would soon be filed to get me back to Colorado; however, because of all the time away from my friends and being all alone in Wisconsin I was weakening, and then one day I woke up and a voice in my head said, "It's time to go!" That's the only thought I had in my mind, so I decided to watch the Super Bowl between Denver and Seattle and knew after that I was going home. I watched the game and then set my alarm, and at 3 a.m., I got up, covered my window, and started to dismantle my cell. I took the toilet off and got some pipes to jam the door to my cell. I do remember the guards banging on the door, and I remember falling to the floor, but I don't remember anything else until I woke up strapped to a bed in the hospital. My psychologist and a captain from the facility came in to talk to me and asked me why I tried to commit suicide. I told her I didn't want to live anymore away from my family and friends and that I just wanted to go home. I asked her what was going to happen to me now, and she said I'd be going back to Portage eventually, so I told her if that was the case, they should prepare to ship me back to Colorado in a wooden box because one way or the other I was going home. The next day they moved me to their reception and diagnostic facility and put me in isolation. Not long after that, a couple of people from mental health and a couple of guys in suits

143

came in and asked me if I knew what was going on. I said, yeah, I was just waiting to go back to Portage, and they told me that was not going to happen, that I would be going back to Colorado very soon.

When I arrived in Wisconsin, they drove me out to the prison in a big dog cage, and I was chained and shackled. The ride took forever, with the metal cage door rattling the whole way—it was the worst ride of my life. When it was time for me to return to Colorado, it was like something out of the *Silence of the Lambs* movie. I was taken to a private airport with five guards who put me in handcuffs and shackles and shackled the handcuffs to the leg shackles. They put mittens on my hands and strapped them around me so I was hugging my waist, and then took a strap and hooked it to my right bicep and pulled it across my back and hooked it to my left bicep, which pulled my arms back so my elbows would touch behind me then put me on the plane and strapped me to the seat. When we got to Denver, they drove me to the DRDC and put me on observation in the medical infirmary in a cell where I had no clothes, sheets, or blankets for five days. I was behind two doors, but I could look out; I just couldn't talk to or hear anybody. After the fifth day, they moved me to an infirmary cell where I had a TV and a good bed.

Then on June 30, 2015, I was sent to Buena Vista Correctional Facility and got to see some friends I hadn't seen in several years. When I arrived, they took me to the intel and case manager's office and drilled me on my past and current activities and asked me if I was ready to lay down my flag. I told them I'd been waving the white flag for a while, to which the guy said, "You know what flag I'm talking about." I was telling him I knew they would never take my STG affiliation out of my file, but he assured me it could be done. I asked him how and he said I'd have to give him information on me and some other people, so I told him I wouldn't do it, and that was the end of our conversation. A couple of months later, I was called into the captain's office, and they asked me to keep the people I knew in line. I told them I wasn't telling anyone to do anything because that would make me an active participant, so the answer was no! They said if anything happened, they'd come for me first, so if I didn't want to end up in segregation all the time, I had to make sure everybody I knew stayed cool.

I ended up in trouble a few times after that, with the last being on January 20, 2016. We were playing basketball in the gym, which we called woodball because it was so rough. We played every week, and there were always guys getting hurt, being taken to medical in a wheelchair or on crutches for some kind of injury. We loved it because it was the only time we could really cut loose and have fun without getting in trouble. It was more like rugby than basketball, and everyone watched and enjoyed it, but on the 20th, a guy decided he wanted to take the court from us. It ended up being a free-for-all with about twenty-five guys involved. In the spring of 2016, I was transferred to the Colorado State Penitentiary, where mental health did an evaluation on me and sent me to the Centennial Care Facility to do a residential treatment program. I made it through the program, and then they sent me to the Sterling Correctional Facility in Sterling, Colorado, in March of 2017.

In August of 2017, they sent my best friend to Wyoming and put him in administrative segregation (isolation) like I was in Wisconsin. It has a very debilitating effect on your mental health; I know—I've spent over eleven years in isolation. My friend had some medical issues, and now he was away from his friends and loved ones, isolated in another state. It takes such a toll on you mentally. I'd tried to leave and move on to the next life, but God was looking after me; unfortunately, He wasn't there for my friend because they found him hanging in his cell the day after he arrived. This, coupled with the lingering memories of Scott's suicide and my older brother, Troy, hanging himself in January, just tore me apart, and I began getting reckless again.

After going to the hospital about my eyesight and then being released from segregation, my friends told me they needed me around and couldn't afford to lose me. I assured them I wasn't going anywhere; however, I did tell them if I lost my eyesight, I wanted one of them to step up to the plate and take me out. I was still dealing with my friend's death in Wyoming, and now with the possibility of going completely blind—well, if that happened, I wanted out of this life.

In late August of 2017, I was looking through a newspaper and came across the obituary section, and while going over it, I saw there had been a memorial service at Grace United Methodist Church in Denver, and for some reason, I got the urge to write to them. Why I picked that church I have no idea, but I wrote them a letter asking the pastor to post it along with my picture on a bulletin board in hopes that somebody would take the time to write me back. I wrote the letter on August 30th, and in the first part of September, I got a letter back from a guy named Jan. Apparently, the pastor had given it to his wife, who in turn gave it to Jan's wife, and we began corresponding. I explained in my letter how I had opened my heart to the Lord and was hoping to find a good Christian who would be supportive and help guide me on this new path. Jan was very receptive to helping me on my new journey with God, but I was still on a downward spiral. With my friend's suicide in Wyoming and my fear of going blind, I overdosed on heroin in November. My cellmate and two other guys found me and administered CPR for ten minutes, but it wasn't working, so they had to get help. I was then taken to the hospital in Sterling, and once again, God was working His will.

Ever since then, it's been one miracle after another. Jan and I began to grow close, and his wife, Karen, has also been so supportive on this journey we've begun, so I mentioned to Jan that I'd had thoughts of writing a book about my life, and in his next letter, he told me he thought that was a great idea and that he could help me with it, especially since he had written nine books himself. Now, what are the odds that out of all the churches I could have written to, I chose Grace, and Jan got my letter, who also just happened to be a published author? So here we are, having conversations about God's plans and how, in our minds, He had all this planned before either one of us was ever born. When I look back over my life, I realize God has been there the whole time, preparing me for this journey.

The purpose of this book is to show you that no matter who you are or no matter how bad your life has been or is now, God can change your life for the better in an instant—all you have to do is open your heart to Him. Now, that is certainly easier said than done, as many people don't want to give any of their life to God; some will give parts while those that can step across that difficult line of handing all of their heart and soul over to God will find there is nothing like it. That's certainly not to say you won't face adversity; you will, but when you do, He will be there to comfort and direct you if you let Him. Whether you're trying to find your faith or strengthen your faith or possibly help someone develop their faith, the Lord will be there with hope and love.

I've always wanted to help kids and young adults realize there is something better in life than what I've been through, and that's what prompted this book, and now I'm aware of God having been there guiding me and preparing me for this very thing. He has given me a direction, and He will do the same for you if you just allow Him into your heart. I'm using my life, even while I'm in prison, to try and help those who thirst for His glory and for those who may not know yet that God is in their future, just waiting for them to invite Him in. Trust me, I never expected to be a messenger for God, yet here I am spreading His glory!

In my life I always thought I knew what was best for me, even as a child. I really thought I knew more than the grownups, the counselors, criminal psychologists, or anyone who had authority over me, including God, but it's pretty obvious now that those thoughts were not accurate. I can actually chuckle about it now because it's something we all go through in life. We like to believe we know what's best for us when there are only two individuals who knew and know what's truly greatest for us, and they are God and our beloved Lord and Savior, Jesus Christ. God has certainly seen the worst in me, and yet He has given me a second chance to be the person He knew I could be, the person He saw before I was born. Our Lord gives us all a second chance if we're open to His presence.

I've shared with you a life of abuse, cruelty, and evil things that have been done to me or I've done to others, and still, I have been offered the grace of God and given a second chance. Because of all the terrible things I've done and the fact I've spent over half my life in prison, I assumed I was no good, an evil person, and that was certainly true at one time in my life, but before we judge anyone, including ourselves, it's advisable to look at prominent people in the Bible. For instance, look at Moses, who committed murder; Gideon, who let his nation get plundered as he hid and also set up an idol on the very spot where he was called to God; Sarah, who laughed at God's promises; David, who was an adulterer; and Eve, who disobeyed God's one crucial request. We all make mistakes and bad choices and stumble in our lives; some are more severe than others, but we all do it, whether on purpose or not, but God's love is so strong and powerful that He allows us to begin again…as I have.

The second chance He gives is not just for ourselves, but it also gives us a chance to help others in His name, which is the very reason I'm sharing my story. It has helped me understand all the things that have happened to me in my life, and I hope it can help you comprehend all the things that have happened to you in yours. I also hope my story will inspire you by letting you see firsthand the power and love of our heavenly Father, which is the most important part of all of this—that He forgives us when we have done wrong and hurt others. He has forgiven me for all the pain I've caused others and saved me from sure death as He did for Jonah, who He tasked with saving the Assyrians, but Jonah ran away, and yet God had him go back and make them repent, which he did, saving them from God's judgment. Through God's love and compassion, no one is beyond redemption, as God has done for me and will do for you because He uses us to spread the good news of His kingdom. He uses imperfect people like me to bring light to darkness; even though I cursed Him and blamed Him for my life, here I am, showing you His love and forgiveness and how He brought light into my life, even here in my prison cell.

You might be asking yourself, "Why would God waste His time on me?" I used to ask that same question; after all, there are thousands and thousands of people who are more deserving and more capable of delivering His message than me. Well, God doesn't look for the better person—He looks for the *right* person, someone He knows will serve Him with humility and grace. So even with all the hatred, cruelty, and arrogance I had, He chose me, and now I serve Him…it's awesome!

What has happened to me is the most exhilarating and glorious thing I've ever done, and it's certainly not because I'm the most deserving or better than the next person; it's because He has healed my bitterness toward Him and life in general. He has graced me with His forgiveness and love and blessed me with two kind, caring, and loving people, Jan and his wife, Karen, who have accepted me into their family. If our Lord can do this for me, He will do it for you; all you have to do is let Him in. I've gained so much just by renewing my faith in God, love, both giving and taking, peace, joy, patience, self-control, and kindness. For me it's an overwhelmingly good feeling to know I am helping spread God's love because I've often thought if I were God, I wouldn't have chosen me, but His decision to use me, to let me be His voice of inspiration, makes me both grateful and very humble.

To have the chance to be God's servant is something beyond words, and I only pray that my complete story will help you see and understand that our Lord is here for all of us. God is greater than our greatest challenges if you only believe in Him. Often, in spite of our defiance and doubt, God's mercy will allow us to have a second chance to serve Him. I am living proof of that!

God bless you all!

Jody Mobley
2021

Chapter 20

Genesis 18:15—Sarah lied because she was afraid of being discovered. Fear is the most common motive for lying. We are afraid that our inner thoughts and emotions will be exposed or our wrongdoing discovered. But lying causes greater complications than telling the truth and brings even more problems. You will be far better off telling the truth right from the start.

* * * *

This is exactly what I did. I didn't want Nancy (a former girl-friend) to find out I was in prison for life, or then I'd lose her, and that lie cost us our relationship in the end. Even before God came back into my life, I decided on two things: one, don't lie about my prison time, and two, I refused to ask anybody for help in any way, even if it was offered, because I didn't want to be alone. The quickest way to be alone in prison is to ask people for things. Even now I try not to, but I'm honest about things now regardless of whether people believe it or not or like it or not. In John 8:32, it says, "*The truth shall set you free,*" and it certainly does. Be true to yourself and God because they are the only two who truly need to believe.

10/8/18

Dear Jan,
Here is the first part of my life. If you want, look it over and ask any questions you need. Will do my best to remember stuff. A lot is blocked out from the trauma I suffered. It's unfortunate, but it could be worse. I'm just thankful God has pulled me back in and has shown me so much love!

Thank you my friend. Will write more when I hear from you. Read Matthew 10:32, which I know you have. The meaning of the verse is great! I keep you and your family in my prayers always.

Your brother in Christ,
Jody

Matthew 10:32:

"Whoever acknowledges me before others, I will also acknowledge before my Father in heaven."

Jody Mobley #60021
PO Box 777
Canon City, CO 81215

10/14/18

Dear Jody,

I got your letter about your childhood the same day I mailed my last letter to you.

I don't know what to say except what you wrote was disheartening and sad and explains a lot about how your life veered off into chaos and trouble. In reading it, I found myself asking, "Would I have fared any better?" and the resounding answer was no! I remember my mom, who was abused as a child, telling me, "If you keep telling a child they're stupid, pretty soon they're going to believe it." Well, in your case it was the whole nine yards, names, beatings, no show of love or caring, so you, as you said in your story, believed you weren't worthy of love or compassion, and my sense of it is you rebelled out of anger, frustration, and hopelessness…and who could blame you?

As the old saying goes, negative attention is better than no attention at all. I have no idea how you felt or feel now about your mom and forgive me if I step out of bounds, but I've always wondered about a parent who beats their child and never sees any change in behavior, except it probably gets worse. Is it they don't know what else to do, or are they repeating their upbringing, or are they taking out their anger with themselves on their child? I certainly don't have the answer to that, but the bottom line is many times, they create a clone of themselves. Again, I'm not trying to bash your mom because I certainly don't know anything about her. It's just my observation from what you wrote.

Yes, Matthew 10:29–31 is awe-inspiring and a great reminder of what we are to do. The part about the test of true value comes from how well something holds up under the wear, tear, and abuse of everyday life, and that certainly fits you, Jody. Through all that abuse and degradation, God has brought you out on the other side, into the glory of His presence, with a promise of what you lacked growing up: never-ending love, forgiveness, and understanding.

I want to read what you wrote a few more times and then get back to you with possible questions or maybe suggestions. By the way, I thought you did a great job of writing your story because I know it was painful, but it might have also been healing as well. I hope so.

I'll be getting back to you soon. Take care, Jody, and God bless you!

Your brother in Christ,

Jan

10/17/18

Dear Jan,

Received your letter the other day. As always I was excited to see what you had to say. Every day that goes by I find myself asking questions as to, "What does God have in store for us next?" At some point in time we will know. As far as being in two totally different worlds, and still, by God's hand, lifting each other up, is something that is more amazing than words can express. For example, you're out there going to different functions and talking about the miracle that's happening, and I'm in a place where just the other day I watched a guy get taken out of a pod with holes in him from a stabbing. Only a few days later in the pod next to that, I saw a guy get his face split open from a fight. And about three or four days before these incidents, I watched a couple of guys going after each other, and they shot through the tray slot at them four times with a non-lethal shotgun to get them to stop. Yet here we are we are working together to bring inspiration and a little ray of hope into people's lives all in the name of our Lord and Savior! Have never in my wildest dreams thought anything like this would be a part of my life.

153

Its moving at such a fast pace right now. Psalm 1:3 is a scripture I found that says a lot. Anything worthwhile we must have God's Word in our hearts. What we are doing is very worthwhile, and we are doing it with God's words in our hearts.

Yes, it's great news I'm getting the hep C treatment. It used to be Interferon they would give, but it made people sick, and honestly, I always denied any treatment because, in my mind, if the hep C took a hold it didn't matter. Life didn't matter. Still do have some thoughts like that due to the depression. At times I go down into the depths of the tunnel that depression can cause. My faith is tested to the limits at these times because I'm scared to the point of no return sometimes. You can't live in a prison system blind. No, I'm not going to give in to my urges. Even though I know it has a lot to do with my mental health situation, Satan also knows my weaknesses. Believe he puts his voice in the place of God's to test my will, the bad thing for him is God is running this show and my faith won't waver! Have seen too much in the last year with all that's happening to let evil dictate the future. Only God has that right. Still scares me a lot at times though. You know I've never admitted that before to anyone.

The story your pastor told was pretty cool. Stories like that really touch my heart. Kind of like some shows I watch. Will watch something and see the love and family bonds in the show. My thoughts right away turn to, Man, I wish I had a family like that, to be able to feel that love, loyalty and caring. Oh yeah, even at my age I still daydream of things like that. Something all kids deserve to have and feel.

Please let me know how all the speaking engagements turn out. Also am very interested to hear about how I might be helpful to the kids you will be working with. Take care and know my prayers include you and your family and their well being always.

Your friend and brother in Christ!

Jody

Jody Mobley #60021

PO Box 777

Canon City, CO 81215

11/1/18

Dear Jody,

I know we're kind of in between letters here, but I wanted to drop you a note and let you know I've started writing the book. I've enclosed the first few chapters so you can give me your opinion on them. I know you liked the title *Have You Ever Seen a Miracle?* but I also thought of another possibility, *Prisoner of Faith*. Let me know what you think and/or if you have a title you'd like.

Yes, it never ceases to amaze me how God has worked His plan through us. When I tell people what has happened and the transition you and I have gone through, and yet we've never met or talked in person, they're astounded. Although we are in such completely different worlds, we're exactly where we're supposed to be to carry out God's plan. I know you, and I feel exactly the same—that He has blessed us with a sacred trust to complete His mission. There are adults and kids out there right now who have no idea you and I exist, and yet at some point in their futures, your story will touch them, change them, and hopefully let them open their door to our Lord and Savior. How many people have that opportunity in their lifetime?

I used to do book signings at Coors Field with a dear older man named Joe Cullinane. I've coauthored his autobiography, and he was one of the dearest souls I've ever known. We'd set out on the concourse outside the retail store where everyone passing by could see us. One day he turned to me and said, "You know, Jan, this is embarrassing." We were sort of on display, and I think he found that uncomfortable, and sometimes it was; however, I turned to him and said, "Joe, how many people do you think are at the game today, 30,000, 40,000?" He said he didn't know, and I told him of all those thousands of people, how many of them had written a book, maybe two or three, maybe none. He smiled, and I told him he should be proud of what he'd done, not uncomfortable or embarrassed. Now I don't know how many people have written a book while in prison, but my guess is very few, and here you're doing it, and best of all, you're doing it for the Lord…it just doesn't get any better than that!

Jody, I can't remotely imagine the battle you must have with frustration and depression. I think about your circumstances often and marvel at how you've raised yourself up by trusting in the Lord and knowing He has a plan for you and your story. What you see and put up with daily is unimaginable to those of us out here, but you and I both know there are adults and kids out here who desperately need to hear what you have to say. You'll touch them in a way no one out here can or, sadly, too often are just not interested in helping. I'm seeing this firsthand at my new church. I've had kids open up to me about being gay, about attempting suicide, about their parents not caring, or about being bullied at school. Unfortunately, there are far too many of these kids around the world. Like I can't change your circumstances, you can't change theirs, but your story will show them God is the answer because He can change their heart and soul and give them hope and understanding of what it's like to walk with Him.

I know you have great fear over possibly going blind in prison, but as we've discussed, God's in charge here, and as we know, His ways are not our ways, but His ways are always right, so there's no doubt in my mind He has this already worked out.

Well, Jody, I'll close for now, but know you're always in my prayers. Let me know what you think of the first couple of chapters, as long as it's positive…I'm kidding. Be honest because you have to be comfortable with this; it's your life. Take care of yourself, and God bless you!

Brothers in Christ,
Jan

* * * *

As Jody began sending me his life story, it hit me how hard this must have been for him—to have to relive the horror of his childhood. It was just appalling to me that a mother would treat her son the way she did and, worse yet, not only allow her boyfriend to beat Jody but apparently encourage it. I don't think there is any conceivable way Jody could have recounted his childhood without God in his life.

Chapter 21

Ruth 2:20—though Ruth may not have always recognized God's guidance, He had been with her every step of the way. She went to glean and "just happened" to end up in the field with Boaz, who "just happened" to be a close relative. This was more than a mere coincidence. As you go about your daily tasks, God is working in your life in ways you may not even notice. We must not close the door on what God can do. Events do not occur by luck or coincidence. We should have faith in directing our lives for His purpose.

* * * *

Well, I certainly didn't know what God was working on in my life. However we see our lives, we really need to look closer at all the things happening in our lives. What things in your life can you say you made happen, and what things did God make happen? Obviously, we don't always know or see what He's doing, but you can be assured He is getting you prepared for whatever plans He has for you. Faith in the Lord and what He has in store for you is the key to living a more fulfilled life. God will not let you down, even if you think that He might. He never forgets any of His children, so don't make the mistake I did by not believing. I certainly regret a lot of things, but my biggest regret is I stopped believing in God!

11/1/18

Dear Jan,
    How are you my friend? I'm well. Was just moved to an MCU pod today. One step closer to moving out of this facility. There are three classifications

here. You have MCU high risk, MCU, and CCTU. MCU stands for management control unit. Just went from high risk to regular MCU. In January they should review me for CCTU which is the transition unit. The last step to leaving CSP (Colorado State Penitentiary). With the Lord's help and blessings I should go back to general population during the warmer months. That will be nice!

Your analysis was correct. There was no doubt I believed I was unworthy of love, kindness or compassion. That complete feeling of hopelessness turned to anger and frustration and it came out and was directed toward God until it got to the point religion and God meant nothing. Now that the Lord has shown His reasonings, or at least that's how I see it now, my faith and love for Him fills me with joy and happiness. Can't ask for more than that!

Listen Jan, you never have to worry about stepping out of bounds, or overstepping boundaries with me. Really want to hear whatever you have to say on anything. I've been brutally honest with you, and I want you to know me as who I was and the transformation into who I am today. The things you brought up about my mom are all legitimate questions. Have asked myself those questions and so many more now that I'm able to see things without the anger and frustration. Think it's a mixture of things as to why she was the way she was. Her upbringing, anger from that, my dad dying and leaving her to take care of three boys on her own. There could be more of course but this is just what I assume were the problems she dealt with.

Was reading scripture about value and being valuable. Have always wondered, as I've mentioned in previous letters, What value does my life have? We have found through our talks that it's to help and inspire people and work with kids. The other day I read in Luke something that amazed me, after I read the explanation of the verse. By looking up the verse on value, the verses before that are about worry, which has been what I've been doing on the value part. Luke 12:22–34. Was a wow moment for me because of how it all fit together, but the most amazing thing was the three parts to overcoming worry. Number three—a support team to help. Find some believers who will pray for you to find wisdom and strength to deal with your worries. That's very significant to me because you have been my support team. More importantly though, is you've become a true friend, and if that's not being blessed by our heavenly Father, then I obviously don't know Him very well.

Pretty close to finishing the next chapter of my life story. Then it will start going into some things I won't be too thrilled in re-living, but it has to be done for people to understand that no matter how low life may take you—with faith and belief in God you can overcome any and all obstacles that have been placed in your path. There really is no limit to what a person can accomplish, even in the worst of situations, when your faith and belief in God takes over!

Here is the next part I've written on my life. After going over the records of the state hospital I saw my dating was off. So it all just goes under the beginning of 1979 and the end of 1982. I also saw on one page I used to have headaches and blackouts. Now I understand why a lot of my anger problems I don't remember. It's been since 2012 since I really went over it. It's not fun to realize you have no real memory of things that have happened due to blackouts. Nothing like that has happened to me in years. Only during my childhood.

Will close now. You take care and know you, Karen and the family are always in my prayers.

God bless—your brother in Christ!

Jody

11/6/18

Dear Jan,

Hello my friend. How are you? Things are going well here. Got your letter the other day. As always, it was great to hear from you. Find myself wondering how you, Karen and your family are doing all the time. A very good feeling to know you are all well.

You'll be happy to know God has been working hard here. They moved me to E-2 last Thursday. Have been approved to move to a MCU pod since October 6th. There are others who were approved before me that haven't moved, but they will. My next review should be the first week of January. Our heavenly Father decided to move me first. It's really not any different from where I was, except for the classification of E-6 being MCUHR and this being MCU. Next step is CCTU and then to a general population facility.

Can't imagine how people truly believe in God's Word would react to the miracle of what is happening. There are a lot of people who think people who have committed crimes, and are in prison, cannot be saved. However, God's plans have been going forth from the beginning of time and He has allowed me, as well as so many others, to stray. When the time is right He brings us back to Him if we open the door to Him. John 3:8 talks of being spiritually reborn and I've latched on wholeheartedly. My door is wide open, and I really want to make a difference in people's lives with God and you Jan.

As for the start of the book? Wow! As I sit writing it, it does not register, with the impact it has on me, until I'm reading it. The craziest part of it all is, the letter and first part of the book arrived yesterday. Last night on World News at 5 p.m., they had a report on children being spanked and verbally abused and the effects it has on them. Serious anger, violence and your brain not fully developed. Read what you wrote of the book, then saw that report. A lot hit home after that.

On the book, I think it is great so far. Feel you will do a wonderful job on it if the rest is like the first part. I am scared to have my entire life put on full blast for everybody to read. Only because if I make a mistake with any of it, it could come back on me being here in prison. So when I get to the chapters of my prison life I won't be using anybody's name.

Oh, you are so right—what I see, or go through, or deal with daily in here can really blow your mind. Just in the last month I've seen two guys carted out of a pod next to me after being stabbed.

Well Jan I really hope all's well with you, Karen and family. Look forward to hearing from you. Take care and be safe. God bless you all. Oh, can you believe I'll be fifty-two on 11/16? Never thought I'd make it past fifty.

Your friend and brother in Christ!
Jody

Luke 12:22–34:

Then Jesus said to his disciples: "Therefore I tell you, do not worry about your life, what you will eat; or about your body, what you will wear. For life is more than food, and the body more than clothes. Consider the ravens: They do not sow or reap, they have no storeroom or barn; yet God feeds them. And

how much more valuable you are than birds! Who of
you by worrying can add a single hour to your life? Who of
Since you cannot do this very little thing, why do
you worry about the rest?

"Consider how the wild flowers grow. They do
not labor or spin. Yet I tell you, not even Solomon
in all his splendor was dressed like one of these. If
that is how God clothes the grass of the field, which
is here today, and tomorrow is thrown into the fire,
how much more will he clothe you—you of little
faith! And do not set your heart on what you will eat
or drink; do not worry about it. For the pagan world
runs after all such things, and your Father knows
that you need them. But seek his kingdom, and these
things will be given to you as well.

"Do not be afraid, little flock, for your Father
has been pleased to give you the kingdom. Sell your
possessions and give to the poor. Provide purses for
yourselves that will not wear out, a treasure in
heaven that will never fail, where no thief comes
near and no moth destroys. For where your treasure
is, there your heart will be also."

John 3:3–8:

Jesus replied, "Very truly I tell you, no one can see
the kingdom of God unless they are born again."

"How can someone be born when they are
old?" Nicodemus asked. "Surely they cannot enter a
second time into their mother's womb to be born!"

Jesus answered, "Very truly I tell you, no one
can enter the kingdom of God unless they are born of
water and the Spirit. Flesh gives birth to flesh, but
the Spirit gives birth to spirit. You should not be sur-
prised at my saying, 'You must be born again.' The
wind blows wherever it pleases. You hear its sound,

but you cannot tell where it comes from or where it
is going. So it is with everyone born of the Spirit."

Jody Mobley #60021
PO Box 777
Canon City, CO 81215

11/17/18

Dear Jody,

That's great news you got moved to MCU. The transition has begun from where you were to where you're going, not only in the prison system but in your walk with the Lord. It just never ceases to amaze me how all this happened and the long journey you've made in such a short time. When you hear the phrase, "God speed," that certainly applies here.

When you mention value and not feeling any when you were growing up—and we can certainly see why, given what you had to go through—sadly I'm seeing it in young people I deal with to greater and lesser degrees. There's one kid I see on Wednesday nights at the church I'm volunteering at who is definitely a lost soul. He's sixteen and always shows up dirty and is trying to hide his pain by acting cocky. We meet in small groups of four to five kids, and he always wants to mess around, make jokes, and be generally disruptive. Of course, I'm always attracted to those kids because they need the most help. Three weeks ago, when we got in our groups, he started his usual routine, so I took him aside, and we had a little talk. I asked him why he came to our meetings, to which he said he wasn't quite sure, so I asked him if he was getting anything out of them. Again he wasn't quite sure, so I told him that he could mess around all he wanted at home or at school or with his buddies, but he was in God's house, and he needed to show the Lord some respect and he could do that by paying attention, and maybe, he might get something out of it. I then quickly told him about you and the journey you're making. For the first time, he listened carefully, and when we went back to the group table, he was quiet and respectful. I got the flu bug and couldn't go two weeks ago or last week, so I don't know if he was there or not. I'm hoping to see him this week. I want him to know that God loves him and I'm there to help him in any way I can. If it's in God's plans, it will happen, and my suspicion is you and your story will be a big part of it.

I know I've told you I'm involved with a Christian organization called Respire Haiti. Having been to Haiti, I can tell you without question it is the most depressing, poverty-stricken place on this planet. They have over 100,000 slave kids on the island, and if they get sick or injured, they die. Respire has saved almost 600 of them and brought God into their lives, along with health care, food, and education. The other night we had a giant fundraiser for them here in Denver, trying to raise around $100,000 so they can build a second health care building. I contributed some of my books and some sports art for the silent auction. Karen and I aren't heavy hitters financially, but we try to help in other ways. I thought of you because the woman, Wendy, who coordinated the event, got up and told her story of going around the world on her own when she was in her early twenties. She had no money and had to live on the fly, immersing herself in whatever culture she was in. It was dangerous and chancy, but she survived and said it was that very experience that prepared her for her journey with God in helping the kids of Haiti through Respire—different people, different journey, same result. You and Wendy probably have nothing in common other than your faith in the Lord, but here you both are helping kids because of who you are and what you've been through. As a matter of fact, I've had lunch with Wendy, and I've told her about you, and she, too, believes this is a true miracle, and she is praying for you daily and always asks me how you're doing. Your Christian family is growing, Jody, and will continue to do so with each passing month, just another part of this heavenly miracle.

I know it's difficult for you to relive your life, but the reward for you and all those who get to hear it will be astounding. There were 400 people at the Respire event and Wendy, giving full credit to God, proudly spoke about how, even though she didn't know it at the time, the Lord was preparing her for what she's doing now. I just kept thinking as she spoke about how your name was all over it. The kids in Haiti have no idea what Wendy's story is and probably don't care because they are just trying to survive daily, but the kids you've touched and will continue to touch will care because they can relate to your trials and difficulties. I think your impact will be even greater because many of them are trying to overcome things you went through.

I'm glad you liked the first few chapters of the book. Keep in mind that's just the initial shot at it, and it will need more refining and adjusting, but that's all part of the fun of it. It will be a lot of work but worth every minute spent. I told Karen you wanted her to pick a name out of the hat, which she said she'd do, but she really likes the name *Prisoner of Faith*, as do I, but as I told you, this is your story, so you pick. . .as long as you pick *Prisoner of Faith*—kidding. You have to be sold on the title, Jody.

Well, I'm still working on the book, sorting through what you've sent me and breaking it into what I hope are logical chapters. In the meantime keep writing away, Jody, knowing God has this all planned out and did when you were six years old. We sent you a birthday card, which I hope you've received, so again, happy birthday and happy Thanksgiving! I always ask people I speak to, individually or in groups, to pray for you, so you've got a lot of folks sending messages to God on your behalf. . .is that awesome or what? I'll close for now, but as soon as I get a few more chapters done, I'll wing them your way. Take care, my brother in Christ, and God bless you!

Jan

* * * *

You can see how Jody has apparently handed over virtually all phases of his life to God, and that's only happening because he's trusting God and seeing real results.

Chapter 22

John 5:6—after thirty-eight years, this man's problems had become a way of life. No one ever helped him. He had no hope of ever being healed. The man's situation looked hopeless. But no matter how trapped you feel in your infirmities, God can minister to your deepest needs. Don't let a problem or hardship cause you to lose hope. God may have special work for you to do in spite of your condition or even because of it. Many have ministered effectively to hurting people because they have triumphed over their own hurts.

* * * *

What other passage could be more appropriate at this point? This puts it all in perspective. My problems were a way of life for me and may be for you as well. Where was the help—where was the hope? All of our situations can seem hopeless, but we can overcome adversity and learn that God has something special for all of us to do. Because of what I've been through, God has chosen me, the most unlikely soul, to pass a message on to you. Have faith, believe, and never lose hope because at some point all will be made clear, and you will see, as I have, just how great and powerful we can be in the glory of God. My prayers and good wishes go out to you all!

11/18/18

Dear Jan,

Just a short note to thank you and Karen for the (birthday) card. Can't begin to tell you what a great feeling it was to receive. God has certainly blessed me with more than just His love, but for Him to put you and Karen in my life? It just blows my mind.

Was just writing the worst part of my story. It's so unbelievable how difficult it was to write. Now I will be starting on the aftermath of that day. I'm okay, but it's hard. It feel like I am disrespecting him and his family by telling the world about that day, but God has made it all a lot easier. With His help we will get this done.

This note is really just to wish you, Karen and your entire family happy Thanksgiving. Hope your day is filled with love and joy. Personally I will be giving thanks for my renewed faith in our heavenly Father and our Lord Jesus Christ, you, Karen and the good we are going to do. All that goes on in my mind is how I want my story to help just one person. Am positive about that because this is all for Him!

Happy Thanksgiving and God bless!

Your brother in Christ,
Jody

11/25/18

Dear Jan,

Received your letter and as always was excited to see how things were going with you. Sorry to hear of your recent medical problems. Well my friend, don't feel alone. Seems we both have had a little bad luck. As I've mentioned to you in a previous letter, my old ties and position in the gang would be a thorn in my side for whatever time. There was an incident at Sterling Correctional Facility not long ago that put four guards in the hospital. Then sometime during the week of my birthday something went on at the Limon Correctional Facility with a guard getting attacked by an individual. The SCG incident was with the group I used to be with. The incident at LCF was supposedly a gang member. Well on the 16th we came out for day hall. After we were locked down they came around and told everybody who is in the computer as a gang member we were being locked down due to the incident at LCF. So I've been on lockdown since around 1 or 2 p.m. on my birthday. Today is the 25th. They say we may come off by Tuesday the 27th. Even though my birthday went from good to bad, I've taken it in stride and have gotten a lot of writing done. I've got one more section to do. The time from the day I got to prison up to now.

Yes, it was pretty difficult to re-hash Scott's death in this last part. To this day I have nightmares still, loud bangs take me to a high level of anger in less than a split second and triggers flashbacks. Definitely not a lot of fun. It's been a little easier with the Lord's help but still a problem. The worst part of the book is done.

Was reading a little of Deuteronomy about the forty years wandering through the desert on the way to the promised land and Moses' speech to Israel. The story is pretty good so far. They didn't listen to God's warning in the first part and went up the hill to battle. The more I read the Bible, I had no idea they had all these battles. I know back in those days tribes all over battled all the time, but I didn't think God lead Himself into any battles. But it said he told them to wait and follow Him and He would fight for them. Have to read all the meanings behind it all, but if I don't I don't really understand it that much. How many times do you think you have read the Bible? This study Bible you gave me is probably the best Bible I've ever seen.

I will send a visiting form to you after the 28ᵗʰ. Really hope they approve it this time. It would, and will be great to talk in person. Will get the information and times of visits this week. You won't be able to bring anything in or nothing like that. On contact visits you can bring a debit card they let you buy for food and drinks. My visits will be short non-contact visits for a little while. Then as long as I've had no trouble we can put in for a contact visit. I'm excited!

Any new offers for you to go speak to any more groups? I enjoy hearing about them. Liked the story of Wendy. We have a lot in common. Never in my wildest dreams did I ever see all this happening to me, or you. With that in mind I'll close this for now. Hope you had a wonderful Thanksgiving. God bless and be safe.

Always—your brother in Christ!

Jody
Jody Mobley #60021
PO Box 777
Canon City, CO 81215

12/1/18

Dear Jody,

Got your thank you letter, and you're more than welcome, and thanks for the Thanksgiving well wishes. I'm looking forward to getting the visitation forms, and, as you say, hopefully it all goes through. I'm certainly praying for it.

I'm sorry about all the lingering gang affiliation stuff you're still putting up with. Who knows if it will ever fully go away? But you and I know God will deal with it in His way. You know Paul in 2 Corinthians 12:7–8 talks about the thorn in the flesh, which never goes away, and no one really knows what it was, but he asked God to remove it, and God refused. Whatever it was, it kept Paul humble and reminded him of his need for constant contact with God and benefited those around him as they saw God at work in his life. It sounds like the past gang connection could well be your thorn. As you know, Paul dealt with it and wrote over half of the New Testament. He changed millions of lives just as you're going to change the lives of young people!

As for the book, I've enclosed the initial writing of chapters 4, 5, 6, and yes, you're doing a great job of putting your life to paper. It's difficult to read, so I can't even imagine how difficult it must be to write. But, as we've discussed, I hope it's cathartic and it does give you a chance to forgive all those who have hurt you. I know that's easier said than done, but we all have to forgive so God can forgive us. I spent many years not forgiving myself for my part in the split between my dad and me, but once I realized, with God's help, that I had to forgive him and me, I was able to move on; however, I will always have a hole in my heart because of our separation.

So, at least for now, it sounds like the title will be *Prisoner of Faith*, which by the way, Karen and I think is perfect! I'll be honest with you, Jody. I'm not a big Old Testament guy. There's just too much judgment, war, and darkness for me. I've certainly read the New Testament, and I love and try to follow all the parables told by Jesus. I have never found a problem in life He doesn't cover in one of his parables. You're exactly right. If you choose God and Jesus, you can't miss!

I'm so glad you're doing well and putting on some good weight. In a little over a year, you've gone from the bottom of the barrel to feeling wanted and loved, having purpose, and walking the Lord's well-lit path. God has certainly taken you into His embrace and provided guidance and grace in your life, but you and you alone opened the door and let Him in. Here's to you, Jody; you've become a soldier for God!

Well, keep at it, my friend, as our journey continues. This will never cease to amaze and inspire me. Thanks, Jody!

Your brother in Christ!
Jan

Second Corinthians 12:7–10:

> *Or because of these surpassingly great revelations. Therefore, in order to keep me from becoming conceited, I was given a thorn in my flesh, a messenger of Satan, to torment me. Three times I pleaded with the Lord to take it away from me. But he said to me, "My grace is sufficient for you, for my power is made perfect in weakness." Therefore I will boast all the more gladly about my weaknesses, so that Christ's power may rest on me. That is why, for Christ's sake, I delight in weaknesses, in insults, in hardships, in persecutions, in difficulties. For when I am weak, then I am strong.*

* * * *

You can see Jody is trying to balance his current circumstances of giving his life over to the Lord and the undertaking of helping others while still dealing with his past of gang affiliation and Scott's suicide. My admiration for him grows with each passing month and letter because he must deal with all of this trapped in a twelve-by-eight-foot cell with little to distract him.

Chapter 23

Second Samuel 12:20–24—David did not continue to dwell on his sin. He returned to God, and God forgave him, opening the way to life anew. When we return to God, accept His forgiveness, and change our ways, He gives us a fresh start. To feel as David did, admit your sins to God and turn to Him for forgiveness and then move ahead with a new and fresh approach to life.

* * * *

Every time you feel like you're straying from God, He forgives you. When your faith falters as mine has from time to time—God has always showed me a sign, and my faith was restored. As long as we understand that there will be times when we struggle, our Lord will always forgive us. Don't be discouraged or beat yourself up over having those struggles. Think of all the good things God brings to all our lives, and let your faith grow stronger.

12/9/18

Dear Jan,

Here is the next part of my story. Wish I could write better, but I'm doing my best. Here is something I want to put in the book. Either in the beginning or in the end.

The two most important days of your life are the day you were born and the day you found out why.

I found out why I was born when we met. What a glorious day that was!

Your brother in Christ,

Jody

12/18/18

Dear Jan,

Greetings my friend. Has been a while since you've written, but I am sure with the upcoming holidays, and other things in life, this time of year can be pretty hectic. Personally I'm not feeling as festive as I'd like. December 20th is upon us and it's a difficult time for me. Have had some very strange dreams lately of days where me and Scott are hanging out and all of a sudden he disappears. All the while I am searching for him, but am unable to find him. In one dream, while dealing with the daily grind of DOC it was my birthday and there was some trouble. A voice in my dream said, "Everything will be fine, and you will be okay." It actually woke me up. Saying it was God talking to me could be a far stretch of the imagination. However there were certain things that came up on and around my birthday this year that could've been disasterous for me. Yes somehow I managed to get through it all with no trouble. Needless to say, somebody was looking out for me at a bad time. Seems like every time I feel a slight separation from God, something happens that makes my faith stronger. There's a pulling, and my mind starts replaying all the positives that have happened since opening the door for our Lord. Sort of hard to really put into words. Have you ever gone through any of this?

Want to thank you for the funds you've sent for the holiday canteen. Am going to make a couple of Fat Bastards on the 20th to celebrate Scott and make it a positive this year instead of a negative.

Just wanted to wish you, Karen and your family a very merry Christmas. Let the kids at church know the same. Know that you all are in my prayers and thoughts always. Check out Ecclesiastes 4:9–12 and the meaning of it. So many things in the Bible have such powerful meanings. I was once so isolated, now I have God, Jesus, you, Karen and a purpose in which to spread the Word and help people in need.

God bless you all, my friend.

Your brother in Christ,
Jody

Ecclesiastes 4:9–12:

> *Two are better than one,*
> *because they have a good return for their labor:*
> *If either of them falls down,*
> *one can help the other up.*
> *But pity anyone who falls*
> *and has no one to help them up.*
> *Also, if two lie down together, they will keep warm.*
> *But how can one keep warm alone?*
> *Though one may be overpowered,*
> *two can defend themselves.*
> *A cord of three strands is not quickly broken.*

Jody Mobley #60021
PO Box 777
Canon City, CO 81215

12/27/18

Dear Jody,

I got your two letters, the note (which was amazing) about the two most important days of your life and your last writings about your life. You should have our Christmas card and chapters 4, 5, 6 by now. I hope they are what you're striving for. Enclosed you'll find chapters 7, 8, 9. The further I go with your life, the more amazing, disturbing, and now inspirational it is. You've had a life no one would want or can understand, but I don't care who you are; there is no way around the fact that God kept you close, and through all the heartbreak, sadness, and cruelty, He knew where you were going and, although painful and brutal, He had a special purpose for you. Every time I talk to anyone about you and our journey with God, I'm still astounded at how all this came about and that I'm a part of it.

I read about Scott. I can't in my wildest dreams imagine what that was like, and I know it's something you can never forget or not see in your mind. You mentioned your nightmares about it and how you felt God was talking to you about it, assuring you everything would be fine. There is *absolutely* no

173

doubt in my mind that was God taking care of you, Jody…that's what He does and will always do when we let Him.

Glad you got the extra funds so you could make some Fat Bastards and maybe have some other stuff you don't normally have access to. Our Christmas was great, with all the grandkids and family. Karen and I go over to my youngest daughter's house, and there are around eighteen of us, so you can imagine the chaos. My entire family knows about you and what we're doing and always asks me how you're doing and wants you to know they're praying for you. I was blessed with a wonderful family, and now you can consider them your family.

I'm going to speak to the entire Colorado Community Church youth group in January, so I'll let you know how it goes. I've read your latest writings, and a couple of times you've said you wish you could write better, so I mean this in the kindest way…knock it off! You're doing a great job, and I know this is extremely hard for you—reliving all these events in your life. You just keep putting them down, and I'll take it from there.

Well, that's it for now; I'm going to start working on the next chapters, and some of that is going to be difficult to write about, but we're in God's hands, and He'll bring us home. Take care, Jody, and thanks for the kind words about the day you were born and the day we met. *Yes*, that was a glorious day!

God bless you, Jody—my brother in Christ!

Jan

* * * *

I can't put into words how powerful and touching it was for me to read that note from Jody about the two most important days of his life. This coming from a man whom I'd never met or talked to on the phone up to this point, only communicated via letter…overwhelming! Truly, God at work!

Chapter 24

Matthew 12:46–50—Jesus was not denying His responsibility to His earthly family. On the contrary, He had earlier criticized the religious leaders for not following the Old Testament command to honor their parents. He provided for His mother's security as He hung on the cross. His mother and brothers were present in the upper room at Pentecost. Instead, Jesus was pointing out that spiritual relationships are as binding as physical ones, and He was paving the way for a new community of believers, our spiritual family.

* * * *

I chose this scripture because I am part of the new community of believers. It took years to come to this point in my life. I want to let people know that no matter how long it takes, you can always become a believer in God and Jesus. When I decided to become part of the believers, my world changed. Positive outcomes became more common instead of negatives, which were the norm in my life. Hopefully, good, positive things will be a daily occurrence in your life as it has been in mine. It's amazing what believing can bring into your life.

1/7/19

Dear Jan,

Received your letter and the chapters of the book. It's harder for me to read it than it is to write it. Think it's because when I write, it is a little at a time, but when I read it, it's all at once. In any case, it was great to hear from you as always.

There are some questions I'm curious about. Obviously our main goal is to help and inspire, but how does this book deal work? How do we go about getting it published? What are the legal details, and of course I have no idea who gets what as far as sales. One thing I want is to make sure I'm able to pay you back for all you and Karen are doing for me, as well as be able to support myself for years to come. I am also thinking, if there is enough profit on my end, maybe you and Karen can help me do some type of sponsor or mentor deal, where I can help a kid or two in need. Not going to lie, most definitely want to make money, but at the same time I want to use some of it to give back and help somebody have a better life. I want to mentor and help a kid. To show them that even with my very difficult life, you can still do good in God's name in prison or wherever. God will give you all you need if you just open the door to Him. Guess it would be like a pay it forward. Maybe I'm thinking too big and we won't make anything like I think, but it's a good idea if it's ever possible.

There is no doubt Scott's death was something that really got deep into my head. Especially when his family blamed me. That really hurt more than anything. I have a hard time not blaming myself for what happened. The nightmares are bad at times. The one I told you about where the voice was so loud in my dream it woke me up. I've never had anything like that happen before, and it was so authoritative it could only be one person. God spoke and told me all will be okay.

Tell your family thank you for their prayers and accepting me. You have no idea how good that makes me feel. There are no words to express the feeling it gives me. There are far too many good things happening and it's a lot to take in. My hopes are high, and yet I've got to remind myself to not get my hopes up so high. It's a defensive mechanism. If my hopes don't get high, I can't be let down or hurt. God is breaking my walls down, and even with my renewed belief and faith in Him, it can be a little unsettling. I mean this is my life story, and even though it's being done in God's name, and for good reasons, to have your hardships, struggles and bad deeds put out for the world to see, its pretty scary because its personal. However my commitment to God and what we are doing is 110% plus!

The picture of the Christmas tree was nice. The decorations people put up each year are really nice to look at. I see on TV the full house and yard decorations are wild. A lot of people go crazy with that stuff. There are some that are really nice, but when you overdo it like the Griswalds—it can be overbearing.

Have you sent in the visiting form? Am curious because I haven't heard anything. If you are denied they would send me a slip, but I'm hoping you sent it in and all's well. Would really be nice to talk face to face.

With that I'll close for now. Take care and be safe. My prayers are with you.

God bless you, my friend.

Your brother in Christ!
Jody
Jody Mobley #60021
PO Box 777
Canon City, CO 81215

1/16/19

Dear Jody,

First, thank you for the wonderful card and message. We, too, are thrilled to have you be part of our fantastic and outrageous family. Hopefully, someday you'll get to meet them.

Lots to discuss. I sent my request for visitation in on 12/13 and had not heard back, so yesterday, 1/11, I called the prison to find out what was going on. I talked to a guy in visitation, and he said he had no record of my request. So neither one of us know what happened to it. He told me to resend it with attention—visiting, so I did yesterday. I'll stay on them, and maybe something good will happen in February. I'll keep you posted.

This past Wednesday night, I spoke to a group of high school students at Colorado Community Church, where I'm volunteering. My talk was about you and your life and how God has changed your heart and soul and guided you toward helping young people. It was, for the most part, the same speech I've given to adult groups, but I altered it some to fit that age group. I've been there for other sermons and talks for these kids, but I've never seen them so gripped by what was being said, and believe me, it wasn't me or my presentation; it was your story that had them paying absolute attention. Every time I looked up, they were all, probably about twenty of them, staring at me like, "Are you kidding?" I guaranteed them I wasn't and at the end told them that if any of them wanted to write you a letter, they were free to do so through me. You never know who or how many might do it, and maybe this coming Wednesday night there might be some carry-over questions. As we've said, if one kid is touched or made to reconsider his/her choices, your life will have made a difference.

Okay, about the book. Getting a book from where we are, first writings, into a bookstore or on Amazon is a long, laborious process. Once the manuscript is finally done, and this usually requires several writings and editing, I'll go about finding a Christian publisher, and when one of them accepts it, then they'll publish and distribute it. As far as the money goes, it depends on the price of the book, but let's say it's $20. The publisher will take their share, and that varies, but let's say 15 percent; the bookstores get 45 to 50 percent, and we get the rest. That means we'd get maybe $3 to 4 bucks a book. The only way to make money selling books is to sell lots of them, and hopefully we can do that. Given our intent is to help kids—and since God is in control, I have no doubt this will be as successful as He wants it to be. You mentioned prospering from the book, and that would certainly be nice and may well happen, but look how much we've prospered already just from knowing each other and having our faith grow daily. What you're feeling and what I'm feeling are truly the riches of heaven, and think of the legacy you're going to leave, Jody—not of a prisoner but of a warrior for God who did, in fact, change people's hearts and souls and ultimately their lives, all in the name of the Lord! Hallelujah, my brother!

The part of your life with Scott was very difficult to read and tough to write, so I can't remotely imagine what it was like for you to live it. As for your hopes being high, I think that's a great thing. From what I'm reading about you, you've never had any reason in your life to have hope at all, let alone high hopes, so hope away because whatever comes of this is going to be more glorious than anything you've experienced before, and it will be in the name of God, and it just can't get better than that. I'm enclosing chapters 10, 11, 12. Take care, Jody, and God bless you!

Your brother in Christ,
Jan

* * * *

Jody had spent most of his life hating his past, trying to forget all the garbage, agony, and resentment, and now here he is writing about it, and although painful, he's able to do it. I can't imagine how hard this was for him, but he sees a brighter future, one with hope, purpose, and God's guiding light.

Chapter 25

Second Kings 19:31—as long as a tiny spark remains a fire, it can be rekindled and fanned into a roaring blaze. Similarly, if just the smallest remnant of true believers retain the spark of faith, God can rebuild it into a strong nation. And if only a glimmer of faith remains in a heart, God can use it to restore blazing faith in that believer.

* * * *

Throughout my life I've gone down the wrong path, not knowing that in the end my life would end up like it did. When I abandoned God years ago and blamed Him for all my troubles, He still left an ember in me. When I came to my senses and opened the door to let Him into my life, it was the ember He left in me, and it began to grow. Now I find myself doing the Lord's work, trying to spread inspiration to those who struggle with hard times and rough lives. God has forgiven me and sparked that ember into an inferno. He can do the same for you; just give Him a chance to show you a brighter future as He has done for me. None of us are unworthy of His love and forgiveness. We all have that spark—let it blaze!

1/21/19

Dear Jan,

Just a quick note. Things are okay here. Continuing to read and study the Bible as well as sign language. Always thought sign language was universal, but have found out that there is a lot of words that are made that are very different, depending on the book you're using. If you look at Acts 6:1ff, it talks about the language barrier that was most likely the problem between peoples. Sign language can be a big help to break down barriers for the hearing impaired. I get a lot of ideas from the Bible on things to do that would be beneficial in our time. Will write more later when I hear from you. Until then here is some more material on the book.

You know, the more I write the more I see just how out of control and uncaring I was. Not only is it a shock to relive my past it's a shock to see just how cold I'd become towards the world and to God. It's a chilling look at myself. Now you get to see it. Yeah—that doesn't feel too good. Then the world. Sure hope I'm doing the right thing and it helps a lot of people keep their faith. Not that I doubt what we are doing or God's path; it's just a gut check on how I was. An ugly sight for me! In any case here it is, and am working on the finale, from the time I got sentenced up until we met, and my life changed. Tell Karen and the family I said hello and I keep you all in my prayers. God Bless!

Your brother in Christ,
Jody

1/29/19

Dear Jan,

Hi! Hope this finds you both in great health and spirits. Am glad you liked the card. It was offered and I thought it would be nice to send.

As for me, am doing well. My spirits are good and I've noticed lately how my behavior has been changing. Even with my renewed faith in our Lord, there are times I find myself struggling to change. My behavior has been a learned behavior for so long its difficult at times not to resort to my old ways. It is a constant struggle. One that is getting easier. Have to credit the Lord for giving me the strength to overcome the bad habits. There have been a couple of incidents where at one time I would just get mad, and cuss and whatnot. Lately I've noticed that during these times, I've managed to just walk away and let it go. The rewards of being able to do that are so much greater than causing a scene and getting into trouble. God is working wonders in my life that I never thought would be possible. If I even ever thought about the things that are changing, which to be perfectly honest, I probably haven't thought on such things until last of 2017. God has really opened my eyes!

As for the book, it's great so far. Here's something you may find odd. Have let the guy next to me read all you have written so far on the book. He thinks it's really good. He told he has read the book "The Shack"; are you familiar with it? He told me that although "The Shack" was a good book, what we have done so far is more interesting. That's good news!

Scott's part of the story was probably the worst part to relive. That's the one thing in life I have yet to conquer as far as guilt that's on my shoulders over that. That may be the one thing in life that is beyond conquering.

Thank you for your phone number. I will turn it in and it should be on within three to four weeks. You and Karen and family are in my prayers always.

Take care and God bless you!

Jody
Jody Mobley #60021
PO Box 777
Canon City, CO 81215

2/9/19

Dear Jody,

I got your two letters and your writings for the book. By the way I think that's way cool—you're learning sign language. I always wanted to do that but just never did, so you're one up on me.

Given where you are now, I'm sure looking back at your life and all the things you did must not only be painful and difficult but probably somewhat hard to believe now that you have God front and center in your life. I'll be very honest with you, Jody; this is by far the hardest thing I've ever had to write because I know it's true—because I know you, and I know you had to live through it. As you said, you were very uncaring and cold, but given where you came from and what you had to endure, how in the world could you have been any different? I know this sounds strange, and we have talked about this before, but had you changed your path and gone the straight and narrow when you were a young man, chances are we wouldn't have met, and there would be no book. That being said, I know that doesn't make it any easier to write your life story and to have to relive all the negative you had to go through, but that is behind you, and now through our Lord you are getting to actually make a difference in others lives, and how many people get to do that? The shock and brutality of your story are what make it so powerful and meaningful. I can tell you for a fact when I speak about it with a group or individuals, they are profoundly moved. Your life is already making a difference, Jody!

Isn't it interesting how God can change our behavior, sometimes when we're not even aware of it until we're confronted with situations that fire up our old habits? I loved how you said when situations come up now, rather than return to your old ways, you can turn and walk away. God's power and influence are truly beyond understanding. You lived for over fifty years operating one way: anger, frustration, and retaliation, with little or no remorse about what you did or to whom. Now you're a different man because you're living in Christ...and He's living in you. Believe me, Jody, we all struggle at times to stay the course with God, and I think He expects and understands that. Jesus was man and God, and on the cross He cried out, *"My God, My God, why have you forsaken me?"* (Mark 15:34). I have heard it discussed that this was the human part of Him crying out. Since we're all human, without question, we are going to struggle and backslide occasionally. As you said in an earlier letter, God picks you up and leads you to greener pastures as He does for all of us who believe in Him.

I know I mentioned to you a kid named James in my Wednesday night group at Colorado Community Church. He has a rough life and covers it up by being a mess around, smart comments, not paying attention, etc. Sadly, he wasn't there for my talk about you, but I had mentioned you to him earlier in a one-on-one. The next week after my talk, he was there, and when we broke into groups, some kids asked me about you, which let me talk about it again. He sat quietly and listened and then, out of nowhere, started telling us about his life. He has no dad and said his mom is an alcoholic and drug addict, and he hangs on the streets a lot. This change was earth-shattering, given all his previous behavior. He then told us about a homeless veteran he'd befriended who did some painting on the street. He bought a piece of art from the homeless man and then told us that right before Christmas someone had loaned this guy a car so he could go to Nebraska to see some friends, but on the way he had a seizure and crashed the car and was killed. It truly touched this young man as well as the rest of us. The next week he came and was serious once again as we talked about God's love and how He can change lives. When we got up to leave, I asked him to hang back because I wanted to talk to him.

He sat down, and I said, "You know, kids will listen to you. I happen to think you're a pretty smart kid with a lot going for you, and I think you could be a great warrior for God. However, you have to make that decision, but if you let God in, He'll change you and use you to spread the good news, just like He's done with Jody. I'm just putting it out there. Why don't you pray about it and see what happens?" He sort of looked at me and said, "Okay, I will." It's going to be very interesting to see where this goes, but you and I both know if he opens that door, God will come in and change his life, and maybe that will lead to him changing other lives as you have his.

That's cool you're letting the guy next to you read what's been written so far. I'm glad he likes it. Yes, I am familiar with *The Shack*, which was a great book and movie. If he thinks this is more interesting, that's a great sign. It never ceases to amaze me how God finds different avenues to spread His good news. In Exodus 3:2 He spoke to Moses through a burning bush, and now He's speaking to who knows how many people using your life. As it says in Exodus 3:2—He uses unexpected sources, whether it's people, thoughts, or experiences, and we need to investigate and be open to His wonders.

Jody, I know writing about Scott had to be agonizing for you. I can't remotely imagine having to do that, and I know that guilt is with you all the time, but I honestly believe God can overcome that. If you haven't read them already, here are three great scriptures to help you: Philippians 3:13–14, 1 Timothy 1:12–17, and 1 John 3:19–20. I know I've told you I have great regret and guilt about my dad, nothing to compare with yours regarding Scott, but I have prayed and prayed about it, and God has brought me comfort and understanding, and I know I will see my dad again in heaven, and all will be forgiven as it will for you and Scott. It's God's way!

The fact that Karen and I are part of your life never ceases to astonish me, and what a wonderful blessing that you and I can share our lives together and, best of all, help others in their quest to find a more meaningful life with our Lord and Savior, Jesus Christ! I know hope has not been in your life before now, but boy, has that turned around. Speaking of hope, Karen volunteers at a homeless shelter called the Network Coffee House. She does this several times a week, and I've gone with her a few times. She was telling my youngest granddaughter, Gracie—age eight—about it at Thanksgiving, and there was a man there named Mark who had put a small Christmas tree on his shopping cart. I pick Gracie up from school every Monday, and we get Starbucks, and then I take her home, and we mess around until her mom, my daughter, comes home. Well, the next Monday after Thanksgiving, she took me into her bedroom and took some ornaments off a small Christmas tree she had and asked me to give them to Karen so she could give them to Mark. Then all on her own, she went to her third-grade teacher and asked if all the kids in her class could make Christmas cards for the homeless people at the shelter. Her teacher agreed, so on Thursday, December 20th, I took her down to the Coffee House, and she handed out all twenty-eight Christmas cards. Channel 9 came and filmed it, and, Jody, I can't tell you how touching it was. They filmed her giving one to Mark, who began to cry and said, "She made this just for me." It was something to see and a memory I will always treasure. Gracie is a special little girl and has a huge heart. I think she will wind up doing good work for the Lord. I've sat and talked to some of these folks at the shelter, and even though they apparently have nothing, they all have the Lord and are so thankful they do…is that something or what? So yes, Jody, we have hope through our Lord, and it's the only and the very best kind of hope! Amen, my brother!

Well, I'll close now, but as always, know you're in our prayers and thoughts daily and God is blessing you with each passing hour. God bless you, Jody!

Jan

Philippians 3:13–14:

> *"Brothers and sisters, I do not consider myself yet to have taken hold of it. But one thing I do: Forgetting what is behind and straining toward what is ahead, I press on toward the goal to win the prize for which God has called me heavenward in Christ Jesus."*

First Timothy 1:12–14:

> *The Lord's Grace to Paul*
> *I thank Christ Jesus our Lord, who has given me strength, that he considered me trustworthy, appointing me to his service. Even though I was once a blasphemer and a persecutor and a violent man, I*

186

was shown mercy because I acted in ignorance and unbelief. The grace of our Lord was poured out on me abundantly, along with the faith and love that are in Christ Jesus.

First John 3:19–20:

"This is how we know that we belong to the truth and how we set our hearts at rest in his presence: If our hearts condemn us, we know that God is greater than our hearts, and he knows everything."

* * * *

As Jody says, writing his life story has been a real gut check for him, and I'm sure it's the first time he's looked at his life objectively, which helps him realize just how far he's come in a relatively short time by trusting God.

Chapter 26

Joshua 5:11–12—God had miraculously supplied manna to the hungry Israelites during their forty years in the wilderness. In the bountiful promised land, they no longer needed this daily food supply because the land was ready for planting and harvesting. God had miraculously provided food for the Israelites while they were in the wilderness; here he provided food from the land itself. Prayer is not an alternative to preparation, and faith is not a substitute for hard work. God can and does provide miraculously for His people as needed, but He also expects them to use their God-given talents and resources to provide for themselves.

* * * *

In life we want things that, a lot of the times, are out of reach. One of the things that has eluded me in life is having or belonging to a real family. God granted me that when I decided to let the Lord in my life. He provided not only a great friend in Jan but a family as well. I was provided, by the Lord, a spot in the Sumner family. When you feel something is out of reach, turn to God and ask Him for guidance and help. When I did that, He planted the seed for me to write Grace Church, miraculously out of the obituaries in the newspaper. You just have to have faith. Ask God for guidance and help and listen. His answers may seem pretty far-fetched, but trust me, you will find an answer from Him as I did. The obituary made me understand His answers can be wonderful. I've never been happier, thanks to God providing for me.

2/19/19

Dear Jan,

Received your letter and the new chapters of the book. It is coming along great. The last part is coming around. Yes, there is a lot of bad, and not a lot of good. Have decided to not give some things a lot of detail, like the suicide attempts. Would rather not get into details on those. So please be careful with that part. Regardless of whether I'm a retired member, you still are held accountable for your actions. Besides that I didn't really think of how writing this book would affect me, or any others. Truth is, writing all of it really hurts. When people go through life it is in pieces. You can look back and remember this or that, but when you put it all in one lump and can see it all at one time, it's quite different. Now if it was a good life with good memories, fun times and good people it wouldn't be bad at all. A negative, violent, out of control life with few good memories can be quite shocking. Even to the individual who lived it. God's love and guidance is making it a little easier to take, but it does hurt. Not sure I could do it without Him that's for sure! Plus I have you and Karen. Believe me, that helps more than you will ever know. Our Father knew what He was doing by connecting us.

I do have some good news. You have been approved to visit. Now all I'm waiting on is for the phone list to come back, and all will be right as rain in my life. Where did that saying—right as rain—originate, do you know?

When you talk about making a difference in people's lives now, and if I would've went down the straight and narrow I wouldn't be writing this book, or making a difference, I won't lie, the book is good for several reasons, but I'm not sure this life would've been preferable over having God with me and never losing my faith. On the other hand what I have now is pretty special to me. God is my Lord and His Word and love is guiding me to better things in my life. As well, I now have a real family, that despite my history and all I've done, have let me join them. For me there is no greater gift that God could have given, or bestowed upon me, than that. Every time that dream has been close at hand, it was snatched away. His miracles never cease to amaze me. The way things have been progressing in here has been okay. As I've mentioned there are still times that resorting to old ways would be so easy, that's the true test for me. Being bad is easy. Following the Lord is the hard part because of the life I've lead. All good things come in time though.

I read the scripture you sent, 1 Timothy 1:12–17 was one of the most powerful scriptures I've read! Wow! God and our Lord Jesus are filled with more power than my mind can fathom. When you read something like that it can blow your mind if you're me. Think that is a great powerful scripture to put in the book.

The story you told me of your granddaughter is something special indeed. Little things like that means more to some than most can even imagine. Until you go through some hard times like that you'll never really comprehend it. Gracie gives me hope, believe it or not. Kids like her are what's gonna make the future of our country great.

My prayers are with you, Karen and family. Take care—God bless you all!

Love,
Jody
Jody Mobley #60021
PO Box 777
Canon City, CO 81215

2/26/19

Dear Jody,

I received your latest letter—always good to get—and I'm glad you think the book is coming along well. Remember this is just a first draft, so there will probably be lots of changes with rewrites and editing, but I think you and the Lord will be pleased when it's all said and done. I love that scripture, 1 Timothy 1:12–17; you're right, it is powerful and oh so true, and I thought it would mean a lot to you. My plan is to start each chapter with an appropriate piece of scripture. I haven't done it yet because that's down the pathways and will take a lot of research and study. As you read what I've written about your life, I'd love to have you suggest scripture you think is appropriate; after all, this is your story.

I know writing all you've been through is far more painful than I can imagine and certainly with regard to all those you encountered in your life. You know, Jody, we certainly have the choice of using fake names in the book rather than the actual names. If you feel that might be a little safer for all involved, we can do that. I'll leave that up to you. Yes, a negative, violent, out-of-control life with very few good memories is quite shocking, and your life has certainly been that, but to me the most shocking part of your life is what you're living right now, and I can tell you without reservation that everyone I talk to about you feels exactly the same way. Your new path with God and Jesus Christ is beyond shocking, and that's shocking in the very best possible way! Here's to you, Jody, a new man in Christ!

Here's some more great news about the spreading of the Jody Mobley story. I know I've told you Karen volunteers at a homeless shelter on Thursdays and I've gone with her a few times; it's where Gracie handed out the Christmas cards. So this past Sunday, Karen and I went to the shelter for their Sunday worship service, taking along a couple of dozen donuts. I had the entire group say a prayer for you, and after the service one of the other volunteers, a homeless man named Rick, and I gathered and said a special prayer for you and your continuous journey with the Lord…it was awesome! Rick is a Black man and has been homeless for a long time, but his faith in God is unsurpassed. He sleeps on the streets but has a deep and abiding peace and joy, which come from his relationship with God. I'm going to talk to him about writing you a letter. He's a special man and another wonderful brother in Christ. Another great scripture that certainly fits your situation and Rick's and the homeless is Philippians 4:12–14—it basically says, *"I, Paul, have learned to be content in all circumstances whether with everything or nothing."*

Okay, so here it is. I'm planning my first visit on Sunday, March 10. I talked to the visiting office, and I'd already read all the rules and regs, so unless there's a massive blizzard, I'll meet you on the 10th at the second session for an hour and a half, non-contact. At last, the two brothers in Christ will meet face to face…how amazing is that! Well, I'll wrap it up, but Karen and the entire clan say hello, and God bless you, as do I!

All our love and prayers are with you, Jody!

Jan

First Timothy 1:12–14:

> *I thank Christ Jesus our Lord, who has given me strength, that he considered me trustworthy, appointing me to his service. Even though I was once a blasphemer and a persecutor and a violent man, I*

was shown mercy because I acted in ignorance and unbelief. The grace of our Lord was poured out on me abundantly, along with the faith and love that are in Christ Jesus.

Philippians 4:12–14:

I know what it is to be in need, and I know what it is to have plenty. I have learned the secret of being content in any and every situation, whether well fed or hungry, whether living in plenty or in want. I can do all this through him who gives me strength. Yet it was good of you to share in my troubles.

Chapter 27

Deuteronomy 30:19–20—Moses challenged Israel to choose to obey God and, therefore, continue to experience His blessings. God doesn't force His will on anyone. He lets us decide whether to follow Him or reject Him. This decision, however, is a life-or-death matter. God wants us to realize this, for He would like us all to choose life.

* * * *

Choosing this path to follow God has been a challenge for me. As a child growing up and during my years in prison, I've lost so many people in my life. So by writing this story, I'm hoping to help others understand that God will bestow upon you His blessings and guide you through the hardships of loss. We all depend on others as we grow up, and in prison we have to depend on others for luxuries most people take for granted. However, God's blessings can give you motivation to make the right choices in life so you don't lose relationships with people. By giving myself to the Lord I chose life. By choosing God and following Him, your life can only get better. I am living proof of that. Whether people believe it or not, we can choose to go with God and continue to have people in our lives.

3/4/19

Hi, Jan and Karen,

May this find you both and family in great spirits and health. Our Lord has blessed us all! It was so awesome to talk to you both on Sunday. It's a bummer the calls are only twenty minutes, but any time is better than no time. Am so excited about the upcoming visit. The timing is so crazy because ot moved to the transition unit, and our visit will be a contact one now. No talking behind a glass window. God is certainly showing me, in every way possible, that my decision to let Him into my heart was the best, and most important decision in my life. He is making everything so wonderful. I'm happy! Wow—been a long time since I could say that, and actually mean it.*

The cell I moved into is a corner cell. That means I have two outside walls instead of one, which makes it pretty darn cold when it's really cold outside. Has been in single digits at night and below freezing during the day. Been having to wear a sweatshirt in the cell. When it gets warmer out or the sun shines, it's not bad. My window faces the west so the sun hits my wall. The pod is okay. A lot of time out of our cells. Two hours in the morning, two in the afternoon, and two in the evening. I know six hours out of our cells sounds good, but when you have nothing to do, it can seem like an eternity. Besides that, when we come out, it's all sixteen of us at once. Can get pretty loud, as you heard. At some point I will begin the class you have to complete before moving back to a general population facility. This is considered general population, but what I'm talking about is being able to go outside every day. Going outside is what means the most for me. A lot of people have different reasons on why they want to be in a GP facility, but for me, I love being able to go outside. Doesn't matter how cold or hot, I want to be outside. It's something most people in society take for granted. Nobody ever thinks for a second they won't be able to go outside when they want to.

Think putting a scripture at the beginning of each chapter of my story is a really good idea. Once I send the last part I will start searching for the appropriate scripture for each chapter. That's pretty awesome about the prayers at the homeless shelter. Thank you and all involved. Have to pinch myself from time to time to know this is all real and happening to us. Philippians 4:12–14 is something I've been through and still learning from. Being content with, or without, is new as far as feeling good with either or. We all desire to have everything we want or need. That's why people go to work every day. For me, it's nice to go to my box when I'm hungry and pull out some chips or a cake (Little Debbie) or have a cup of coffee in the morning. I've experienced both sides of the spectrum. Lived with nothing for long periods and during others I've had all I needed. Now, I just accept what God's love allows me to have.

196

Well it is now 12:07 a.m., and am getting tired. Just know my prayers are with you.

With love and God's blessings,
Jody
Jody Mobley #60021
PO Box 777
Canon City, CO 81225

3/11/19

Hey, Jody,

It sure has been great to talk on the phone. After over a year and a half writing letters, it seems a little bit surreal finally getting to hear each other's voice. When we spoke last Thursday, I was battling the flu, and sadly I'm still at it. I'm hoping for a little bit of God's intervention so that I can make it down to see you next Sunday, the 17th.

I'll tell you, Jody, to hear you say on the phone how happy you are and that you have a big grin on your face, and in your letters, how opening the door to our Lord was the best thing that you've ever done and again, how happy you are is astounding, given where you came from. I know I've told you this before, but the progression from your first letters to now is what this miracle is all about.

In our first letters, we talked about how God couldn't change your environment but could change your heart and soul, and as always, we underestimated His power and grace. I know you're still in prison, but it sounds like it's much better than when we started communicating, and after you take this class, you'll be in the general population, which will offer more benefits like getting outside every day, which is so important to you. Plus, now we can have a contact visit, which is going to be so much better than the behind-the-glass visit.

I'm glad you liked the idea of scripture quotes before each chapter. I just finished reading an amazing book called *Under the Overpass: A Journey of Faith on the Streets of America* by a guy named Mike Yankoski. I'll tell you about it when we have our face to face, but he used biblical quotes and various other quotes about faith at the beginning of each chapter. In the last book I wrote, *Independence, Mantle and Miss Able*, I did the same thing at the beginning of each chapter, and people loved it, so that's something we can work on. As for the use of the actual names in the book, I figured you'd want to stick with them because, as you say, they could be the first names of anybody. God has certainly tested you in your life, and I'm sure everything surrounding the suicide attempts is maybe the biggest test of all, but now you're seeing that you have come through with unquestionable resolve and faith in Him, and He has and will continue to reward you for your devotion.

Well, here's hoping the flu bug departs and I can see you next Sunday. I look forward to hearing from you Thursday night, and I'll certainly know by then how I'm fairing. I'll close for now. Karen says hi, and know you're always in our prayers, and we feel blessed to have you in our lives!

All our love and God's blessing to you, Jody!

Jan

* * * *

It seemed so strange in this day and age to only be able to communicate by mail, so I was really looking forward to our first phone conversation. It's somewhat inconvenient because Jody never knows exactly when he can call, so I'm always sort of at the ready. The first time was in the early evening, and you had to listen to a long DOC message and then choose to accept the call. Even though we had exchanged numerous letters, I think Jody was still a little apprehensive about actually talking, so after I agreed to the call, I heard, "Hello?" Trying to put him at ease, I answered, "Jody, you beast, how are you?" That seemed to break the ice, and we were off and running. It was so great to get to put a voice to the picture and all the letters.

Chapter 28

Psalm 17:13–15—we deceive ourselves when we measure our happiness or contentment in life by the amount of wealth we possess. When we put riches at the top of our value system, their power, pleasure, and security overshadow the eternal value of our relationship with God. We think we will be happy or content when we get riches, only to discover that they don't really satisfy, and the pleasures fade away. The true measurement of happiness or contentment is found in God's love and in doing His will. You will find true happiness if you put your relationship with God above earthly riches.

* * * *

It has not been that long since I opened my heart and life to God, but in this short time, I've come to understand the happiness I feel. Life can be hard, and we as human beings can be ruthless, greedy, and hateful. Since letting God into my heart and life, those issues are not something that is overwhelming me anymore. The happiness and joy I feel now are something I want to continue. If you're feeling lost, angry, hateful, or any other negative feeling, know that God can and will bring happiness, joy, and love into your life. Turn to Him and see what changes it can bring to you. Experience something more than those negative feelings and outcomes in your life. Have faith, my friends, and watch the changes from negative to positive. God loves us all no matter what!

3/20/19

Dear Jan,

Received your letter. God has set an amazing task for us. One that is not your normal everyday ordeal but one that is full of great possibilities.

Yes, it is great to be able to talk to you now. You didn't sound well at all a couple of weeks ago, and last week you sounded better. Hoping by now you have gotten that nasty bug conquered and are feeling like a normal Jan again! Yes, it is so nice to feel better as far as myself. Without the Lord I was pretty lost, angry and mad. Feeling happy and more at ease is something that is not familiar to me. My mental health stuff still affects me, but it's been so long since I've felt happy. Now I get to experience it. I like it. To know people care about you and are there for you is something that is absolutely wonderful for me. Not struggling in here has relieved a lot of frustration and stress. There is no doubt that at the beginning of this journey there was never a thought in my mind that things would be as they are. Yes, things are certainly better now than when we first began this journey.

Am waiting to be put in a class they have us do in order to leave this facility. If I'm lucky they will put me in medium custody and end up sending me straight to a facility. Either way will be okay with me. You're so right about the contact visits being better. Contact visits allow you to have a soda, play a game or something while talking. Feels more normal, too, instead of making a person feel like they aren't able to control themselves. Makes a person feel like an animal.

As far as some people who will think or believe what's happening is not possible, I really don't care. People can believe it or not believe, whatever they want. We don't have to answer to anybody except one person. He is the only person that needs to know we are doing our best for Him!

Thank you for the picture of your grandkids. Now I can put a face to the names. Of course Gracie would be right in front. She looks like somebody who would try to make others feel good. Let Karen and the family know I said hi and they are all in my prayers daily, as are you my friend!

With love and God's blessings,

Jody

Jody Mobley #60021

PO Box 777

Canon City, CO 81225

3/31/19

Dear Jody,

I got your letter. I didn't go to Seattle with Karen; this bug just keeps on keeping on. I've been to the doctor twice, and they tell me it's a virus and I'll just have to wait it out, which I've been doing for the past month. I'm okay one day and then not so much the next day. I probably won't be down this week, not until I can get three or four days in a row where I feel good, but it will happen!

I certainly have enjoyed our conversations and look forward to more, along with a visit soon. You'll have to tell me more about this class that will enable you to leave your current facility. You know if God wants that to happen, it will, and if for some reason it doesn't, then He has a reason for that. My guess is it will happen.

You know, I think today people in general and, sadly, kids in particular are so self-absorbed with Facebook, Instagram, selfies, etc., that making room in their lives for God is all the more difficult. In any and all circumstances, turning your life over to God is challenging but in today's world even more so. You couple that with the fact the attention span of people today, on average, is less than a minute—we'll have quite the challenge to reach them. That being said, there is no doubt in my mind that there are adults and kids out there who will be touched by your story and God already probably knows who they are. As we have discussed, if there's just one kid who sees the light because of what you've been through, then this will all be worth it. You spent over fifty years living to survive, and not only that, blaming God for it, and now you have flipped 180 degrees and know the Lord is the answer. There's no way that doesn't impact people! As we've said several times, who in the world other than God knew that what's happening would happen? Well, you know there are people out there right now who have no idea what's going to happen and that your story will play a part in it. How incredible is that!

I'm glad you were comfortable with the questions I sent; there will probably be a few more, but I think it's important to cut to the chase on a few things that people can pick out and not have to search through a chapter to find. There may be some specific things a kid or parent is looking for and can quickly find them there.

Yeah, the grandkids are a hoot. Once a month I take Gracie and Mylee shopping, and we have a ball. We have lunch, and then they hit all the stores they care about. I couldn't possibly enjoy them more. They all call me Gampy Jan except Brody, who only wants to call me Jan. Every time I see him, I'll say, "Hey, Brody," and he always responds with, "Hello, Jan." It's an absolute hoot. You're right—they're quite a handful, but then I don't have to take care of them every day. Everybody always wants to know how you're doing and sends their best. You're always in our prayers and thoughts. Well, I'll close now, but I know we'll talk soon. Take care, and God bless you, Jody!

All our love and blessings to you!

Jan

* * * *

With each phone conversation Jody got more and more comfortable. I like to kid around and mess with people, and he started giving it back to me. Our conversations began to get more relaxed and good-humored.

Chapter 29

Luke 9:62—what does Jesus want from us? Total dedication, not halfhearted commitment. We can't pick and choose among Jesus' ideas and follow Him selectively; we have to accept the cross along with the crown—judgment as well as mercy. We must count the cost and be willing to abandon everything else that has given us security. With our focus on Jesus, we should allow nothing to distract us from the manner of living that He calls good and true.

* * * *

People today forget to spend time with God and Jesus. They get so caught up in text messaging, playing on the computer, and in video games. I've had the luxury of not being distracted by all that. I get to put aside time to study and read the Bible. Set some time aside each day to spend time with our Lord and study, even if it's just thirty minutes a day. The closer you get to God, the easier it is to let all the distractions go. Faith, like intelligence, takes dedication and work, which is something I've come to find out. It's not an easy task to pull yourself away from all the fun and exciting things in the world, but as in everything in life, faith grows with knowledge. Take the time to gain that knowledge. It's helped me tremendously, as it will you.

* * * *

On Saturday, April 20th, I made my way down to the Colorado State Penitentiary to visit a man I'd never met in person. I checked into the visitor's center a little before noon with our visit scheduled from noon to two thirty. You have to leave everything in your car except your car keys, which they keep in the visitor's center. You have to fill out several forms, provide ID, go through a scanner and get frisked, and then get taken to one of two prisons on the grounds. I was the only one on the bus going to CSP, and when I got there, a woman guard was waiting for me. We had to go through several gates before going inside the prison. On the way in, she told me he was waiting for me and seemed anxious because he had never had visitors. We took an elevator up to the second level, and there at the back of the visitors' room was Jody, all alone at a table. There were probably eight tables in the room, all occupied by prisoners and their families. The prisoners are not allowed to leave the table during a visit, so as I approached the table, he stood up and held out his hand. I grabbed his hand, then pulled him into me and said, "God bless you!" I don't know if that was allowed, but I did it anyway, and no one said anything. Jody was wearing some dark protective glasses, and after a few minutes, I asked him if I could see them. He took them off and handed them to me. I looked through them and set them down on the table. In retrospect I think he was a little more nervous meeting me than I was meeting him, and rightfully so. The more we talked, the more relaxed he became, and toward the end of the visit, he said, "You know, Jan, I read an article about a prisoner who wrote a book about his life in prison, and it said he made $300,000 on it." I said, "Wow, that's amazing! I'll tell you, Jody, if we make $300,000 on a book about your life, you won't see this face again because I'll be living in Maui." He looked at me for a second and then threw his head back and laughed; I guess he thought I was kidding, which of course, I was. It was a great way to end our first visit, and I think it laid the groundwork for a more stress-free and trusting relationship.

* * * *

Jody Mobley #60021
PO Box 777
Canon City, CO 81225

4/21/19

Dear Jody,

Just a note to let you know what a great pleasure it was to finally meet you after all this time. For the most part, all this still seems surreal to me, and I'm sure it is for you as well. I have to say you seemed very relaxed and at peace, given your circumstances. I'm glad we could discuss things about the book, your life, and what the future may hold. It always helps when you can sit down with the person being written about. It puts a face with everything that came before. I hope you enjoyed it as much as I did. There will be more, God willing!

I'm going to go through all your questions and start the chapter on Q&A, and from that I'll probably come up with some more questions for you. As we discussed, if you want to address Troy and Corey, your brothers, and give them some closure in the book, that would be great. You address that as you see fit.

The trip home was a lot less exciting, and that was fine with me. Next time should go a lot smoother now that I've been through the process once. Again, it was great to meet you. I'm looking forward to our next get-together. Take care, and God bless you, Jody!

Jan

* * * *

4/21/19

Dear Jan,

Just a quick note to let you know it was great to see you, and I enjoyed the visit. Look forward to our next meeting. I will talk to you soon and write more when I hear from you on my last letter. Our Lord is so grand and special. Letting Him into my life has been the best thing that has ever happened to me. You and Karen and the family are the second best thing to happen in my life!

You asked me at the end of the visit if I could do it over what would I want to do. The question was unexpected and I answered without really thinking. Now granted I really would like to go back and be an electri-

*cian, however as much as I would like that, I think, if I knew back then
what I know now, I'd study for a degree in some type of counselor who
works with young people who are struggling to live their lives and enjoy
those years. Believe God would have me want to help and show younger
people there is a lot to celebrate in life. Would love to do that, to give
somebody they could trust and confide in. Give them that place where
they could feel safe and be themselves. That's what I'd really like to do, as
well as an electrician.*

*You, Karen and the family are in my prayers always. Take care and be
safe.*

Sent with love and God's blessing!

Jody

Jody Mobley #60021
PO Box 777
Canon City, CO 81225

5/2/19

Dear Jody,

I'll probably be talking to you tonight, but I wanted to let you know that
the letter you sent me dated 4/21 wasn't postmarked until 4/29, and I got it
last night, 5/1. Ah, the postal service—you can't beat it. I'm enclosing the final
chapter of the book, the Q&A, with you. I'll tell you, you did one fantastic job
of answering those questions, and I know some of that was not easy. Take a
look at them and let me know what you think. Karen and I went to the shelter
church service last Sunday and then went out to breakfast with Kevin and his
wife and a couple of homeless men from the shelter. We all had a good discussion about you and your remarkable journey with the Lord. Last night at
the kids' meeting at CCC, I got to talk to three of the kids who had heard my
speech about you. They asked some questions and were genuinely concerned
about how you're doing. When we finished, one of them, who's kind of a
mess-around kid, said to me, "That's so amazing and interesting and in such
a good way!" As you said in your last letter, if you could do it over, you'd be a
counselor who works with kids; well, that's exactly what you're doing. Maybe
not exactly the way you'd like to, but nevertheless, you are, in fact, providing
guidance and direction for kids, and, given your answers to those questions,

that should just get bigger and bigger. I'll keep you posted on how soon Karen can come with me, but however long that is, I'll try and get down to see you this month. Take care, Jody, and God bless you!

All our love and blessings!

Jan

Chapter 30

Judges 9:2–5—Israel's king was to be the Lord and not a man, but Abimelech wanted to usurp the position reserved for God alone. In his selfish quest, he killed all but one of his seventy half brothers. People with selfish desires often seek to fulfill them in ruthless ways. Examine your ambitions to see if they are self-centered or God-centered. Be sure you always seek to fulfill your desires in ways that God would approve.

* * * *

Prison is a violent and unforgiving place to live your life. The same can be said of society. However, in society you can go someplace to remove yourself from any negative actions going on. Prison doesn't allow you to do that. You probably ask, "Would Jody turn to violence if it came to him, now that he's a Christian?" Unfortunately, yes, I would. The difference now is I'm not so self-centered that I would seek that result out. With God by my side, I try my best to do things in ways He would approve of. You may think it's easier to take the low road, and I agree it is, but that's what makes us better Christians—when we look for alternative ways that God will approve of. We all need to quell the urge to take the easy way out. God will make your life easier if you just give Him a chance. I have, and the results are and have been amazing. Take the steps necessary to be better, and let our Lord guide you.

5/14/19

Dear Jan,

Greetings my friend. Hope this find you, Karen and the family doing well. Have spent a lot of time with God this week. I've read so much of His Word from the Bible this week. At first I thought it would be fairly easy to find scripture for each chapter of the book. Am now finding out it isn't as simply, or easy, as I thought. Maybe I'm just trying too hard to find the right one.

We've been on lockdown for over a week now. We went on lockdown on Monday morning, the 6th, and it's already the 14th. They've been skipping around shaking down units. Am all for a lockdown from time to time, but the extended ones get old pretty fast. We only get to shower every third day. The rest of the time, we are locked down. We never know when it will end. You ask, and the only answer we get is, "I don't know."

Had a strange dream the other day. It was about me going to see some principals, pastors and coaches, trying to set up something to where I could talk to and mentor some kids. It's been a long time since I've been in the principal's office—ha-ha.

As far as my two brothers disappearing from my story? That's because that's pretty much what happened. The last time I seen Troy was for his wedding in 1985. Before that was when I ran away from Colorado State Hospital and hitchhiked to Iowa just to see him. That was the end of 1979. From 1979 to 1985 we had no contact. After deciding to go to his wedding in 1985 we had no further contact. Then he hung himself in 2003—January. He doesn't play a very big part in my life because I don't ever really remember him with us after he went to the boy's ranch. The only time I really remember him being around is when we went to the lake and he slammed the glass door on me, and when my mom made us fight each other. He was never really in my life. Corey was in my life up until I first came to prison. He was around here and there after that. Then he came to prison. He came to visit a few times and wrote a few letters, but I haven't heard from him in over fourteen years. He chose to go his own way a long time ago. He was afraid of who and what I was in those days. I know you're asking yourself what was he afraid of. Understand that the programs you see about prisons on television are not how it really is. There are things you don't ever talk about or give information on ever. The people you see in those programs are all more than likely looking behind them every time their cell doors open wondering if they are going to get jumped or killed for being on those programs. Living in prison is not much of a life to begin with, but to live inside a prison inside a prison, is not a life I want to live. So there are subjects and other things I will not get into. Prison has taken everybody I've loved or cared for from me. It's something I have to live with. Things have changed for me ever since I let our heavenly Father back into my life, and life is much better for me with Him by my side, but this is still prison and it doesn't matter who you are, or if you're a man of faith in God or not, violence lives next door and you still have to abide by the rules of this world I'm in, just as you have to live by the rules in your world. God has made life so much better for me, and I never want to let Him down. It would be a shame if I did something now to halt His path for me, so I will accept the reasons why Corey is not in my life, and rejoice in the fact he is free and living life. No matter what you think of me, or what you choose to believe about me, this is God's will. It's not about me—this is about God and what He can do for you if you let Him into your life.

Ephesians 3:14–17:

"If you are 1000 steps from God, He will take 999 steps in your direction. Then He will wait for you to open your heart and ask Him into your life."
That's about all for now. You, Karen, and the family take care. Let everybody know I said hello.

I send my love and blessings to you all!

Jody
Jody Mobley #60021
PO Box 777
Canon City, CO 81225

5/19/19

Dear Jody,

I received your latest letter and Scripture quotes yesterday. You, my friend, are becoming a true biblical scholar. Given your journey over the last year and a half, it's beyond miraculous.

With regard to your brothers, as I think I mentioned when I was there, you need to handle that as you see fit. I know Troy was in your life only briefly, and we can reintroduce that in the story. We can also talk about Corey as you did in this last letter and leave it at that, but I must tell you that I found him but did not contact him and wouldn't think of doing it without your permission. I'm going to be really honest with you, Jody. I know I have no idea what all happened between you and Corey, but there's a part of me that keeps thinking he would want to know what a changed man you are in Christ. As you said in your letter, he was afraid of who and what you were back then and decided to remove himself from that fear, but now he could love you as a brother and maybe find God through your example if he hasn't already. You are reaching out to kids and adults of all ages; maybe your brother could be one of them. Okay, that's the last time I'll bring Corey up unless you do. I certainly didn't mean to get out of bounds.

So as you know, Karen and I have been working with the homeless near downtown Denver—she far more than I. The other day a guy around thirty walked up and handed her a note. Karen did talk to him after she got the note but didn't feel like she got very far. She believes it has to do with his sister, who now lives in Florida. So it got me thinking about all the people who could benefit from your story and your redemption. I have talked to several of the homeless men at the shelter about you, and they are always intrigued by what you went through and how despite all that, you are now a man of Christ reaching out to help others. I know up until now our focus has been kids and their related adults, but you know better than I there are homeless of all ages, and you could reach them because you went through it. There's a lot to think about here, and probably the best way to handle it initially is to talk about it when I come down next Saturday. If you'd like to write this man a letter, please feel free, and Karen or I can give it to him. He sounds desperate for help, and who better than you, Jody!

Well, that should do it for now—hope we get to talk Thursday night, and I hope there's no lockdown next Saturday. God bless you, Jody, and all you're doing. Looking forward to seeing you Saturday!

Jan

* * * *

As you can see, Jody still has to deal with the reality of where he is and all that goes with that, but I think he's also recognizing how God has, in fact, changed him and is there for him in these dire circumstances no matter what. I can't remotely imagine what he has to go through day after day, but having been to the prison and reading all of Jody's writings, my admiration for him grows daily as I see his walk with the Lord continue to flourish. With regard to the letter from the homeless man, Jody wrote a wonderful response that Karen gave to him. He looked at it and said, "I've heard all this before," then walked off, and it was never brought up again. Forgiveness is so difficult, especially forgiving yourself.

Chapter 31

*Romans 12:19–21—forgiveness involves both attitudes and actions. If
you find it hard to feel forgiving toward someone who has hurt you, try
and act forgiving. If appropriate, tell this person you would like to heal
your relationship. Give him a helping hand, send him a gift, smile at
him. Many times you will discover that right actions lead to right feelings.*

* * * *

Forgiveness can be a difficult ordeal. There are people in my
life—or were in my life—that I really have to work at forgiving. The
wrongs that were done to me, however, are, for me, sometimes unfor-
givable. That doesn't mean it has to be that hard for you. We all just
have to work on things like that. Believe me, it's been a hard road for
me, but I'm learning to forgive; even though it's not easy for me, I'm
learning. You can, too, just give yourself the opportunity to do so.
Whatever God's plans are, He will show you in time. Work on bettering yourself with His guidance. If I can do it, anybody can.

5/28/19

Dear Jan,
    *Received your letter with the photocopied note in it. This is quite a
difficult situation. I will try and respond to the best of my ability. The whole
ordeal is really something that God is playing a part in. Here we have been
on a path to help and inspire and all of a sudden Karen is given a note from
somebody seeking help. Am kind of at a loss here because I never expected all
this to be transpiring. It really is something!*

Okay, so nobody came to see me Saturday, but I was able to find out what the ordeal was. I guess my mom scheduled a visit, but did not show up. Was kind of shocked to find out it was her. Been over three years since I've seen her. Some weird thing's going on in my life right now. Not real sure how I'm supposed to take all this in, or how I'm supposed to feel about it all. A lot of questions running through my mind. The biggest one being, What is God trying to tell me, or show me? I guess in time He will reveal His plans, for now I'm stumped.

Here are some more chapters I've finished. I try to do at least one a day, but sometimes I get caught up in my studies and miss a day here and there. You know I've never read the Bible much before, now I read numerous scriptures and meanings almost every day. The actual scripture is hard to understand, but reading the meaning of them is totally awesome. Am glad I'm able to spend the time reading and writing all the scripture. Am really excited about getting it all done and seeing the finished product.

Received a thing from visiting today, Karen has been approved to visit. That's awesome! As far as Corey goes, I believe for now I am going to let things be as they are. I have too much on my plate right now. Maybe sometime in the future I will reach out, but for now it's fine the way it is.

Well, I hope to see you Saturday, and am looking forward to the day I get to meet Karen. Give her my best and know you both are in my prayers.

Take care, and God bless!

Jody
Jody Mobley #60021
PO Box 777
Canon City, CO 81225

6/2/19

Dear Jody,

I got your letter and new chapter scriptures. I know this is a lot of work, but I think you'll see it's well worth it. I've enclosed chapters 1–7 with the scriptures and a rewrite of the chapters. I think they look great and hope you feel the same. So I have a question for you: Do you want me to always use your scriptures, or do you want me to choose what I think is the best between yours and mine? I have certainly found some scriptures I think are right on the money, but it is ultimately your choice.

Wow, it was your mom that was supposed to visit. On the surface that is somewhat strange, but the more I thought about it, the more I thought—and this is just my opinion—she might be feeling guilty over everything that happened and isn't quite sure what to do about it. I think most everyone, as they get older, looks back and asks themselves, "What was my life about, and did I accomplish anything?" Obviously I don't know what's going through her mind, but that may be part of it, and she's struggling with how to deal with it. Either way, I can't even imagine how difficult this would be for you, but you know, Jody, if you haven't already, you have to forgive her, and maybe God wants you to do it face to face. This is just a supposition on my part, but I do know, should that take place, it would be life-altering for both of you, and there would be a weight lifted from you that is unimaginable. Again, this is all just guesswork on my part.

For somebody who didn't quite know what to say, your letter to the homeless man was awesome. Karen will probably see him this coming Thursday and give it to him, along with some info about you and your story. As we discussed last Thursday, you may well need a secretary in the future because, as we know, there are thousands of people hurting and in need of structure and guidance, and who better than somebody like you, Jody, who has been down those same dark streets they're going down right now? It just shows you how powerful and far-reaching your message can be!

Well, I'll close for now, but Karen and I are planning on coming to see you next Saturday, and hopefully we can chat next Thursday evening. Take care, and God bless you, Jody.

All our love,
Jan

Chapter 32

Esther 4:13–14—after the decree to kill the Jews was given, Mordecai and Esther could have despaired, decided to save only themselves, or just waited for God's intervention. Instead, they saw God had placed them in their positions for a purpose, so they seized the moment and acted. When it is within our reach to save others, we must do so. In a life-threatening situation, don't withdraw, behave selfishly, wallow in despair, or wait for God to fix everything. Instead, ask God for His direction, and act. God may have placed you where you are for such a time as this.

* * * *

God places us all in situations and spots that can help us in life. We just have to make sure we see His signs and take control. God has placed me in a unique situation. Now I've written my story, and I'm trying to help others. Nobody would believe everything that's happened to me over the past couple of years or that it would have ever happened. Some still won't, but that's no reason for despair. You just continue on and do what God has asked of you, and it will change your life. He will change your life as He has done for me. Trust in Him and have faith that where you are now is where God has placed you and make the best of it.

6/10/19

Dear Jan and Karen,

How is everything? Hope your trip to Canon and back was not too bad. Was totally thrilled to see you both and am definitely looking forward to our next visit. I had a great time and Karen is a real hoot. You had me laughing for sure Karen. On a scale of one to ten, I'd rate the day a ten!

This morning we went out to rec. A little overcast and very windy. We did our workout, then sat up against the wall near the vent system. It blows out warm air, so it was a nice spot out of the wind. Tonight is Fear of the Walking Dead and the TV premiere of Logan (Wolverine) on the X-Men trilogy. So a little something to keep me occupied on a Sunday evening. Did some Bible study this morning as well. So a pretty productive day. Now I sit here with God and write my letter. Can't beat that!

Okay, only three more chapters to go, but feel free to change some if you find scripture that's fitting better. Then I will write my thoughts on them. Enclosed with this letter are the ones I have done. At first it was a big chore, but the farther I got and the more I learned, I wanted to read more. Have had opportunities to read the Bible on several occasions, but never as much until I turned my life to the Lord, and really got into it this time—it's amazing!

On that, I hope this finds you both smiling and well, along with the rest of the family. God bless you all!

All my love,
Jody
Jody Mobley #60021
PO Box 777
Canon City, CO 81225

6/18/19

Dear Jody,

I got your latest letter and scriptures for the chapters 11 through 18. I'm going to send you those same chapters, which I've rewritten, along with the list of scriptures I found and the ones you've listed. You pick what you feel is best suited for each chapter, along with what they mean to you, and I'll go back and put them at the beginning of those chapters. As you said, this is a lot of work but will certainly be worth it in the end.

Karen and I certainly enjoyed our visit and will come see you in early July. I'm reading *Barking to the Choir* by Gregory Boyle, which I told you about on the phone. He founded Homeboys Industries, which is the biggest gang rehab and reentry program in the world. It's very interesting and certainly gives another perspective on faith and how it affects people from all facets of life. Some of what he says I'm not sure about, but it will be interesting to see your take on it. He says in the book that he changed the names of all those he talks about, and the more I think about it, maybe we should do the same thing. I know we're just using first names, but those people might recognize themselves and not be thrilled with what's said. My suggestion is we change all the names; let me know what you think. I'll order you the book, and we can talk about it later.

God bless you, my brother!

Jan

7/1/19

Dear Jan and Karen,

How are you both? Hope this finds you filled with the Lord's love and blessings! As for me—I am doing well. Some lockdowns here and there but nothing that has anything to do with this unit. It's not usually this unit that's in trouble. Which is a good thing. There are times when everybody wants a lockdown so they can sleep in.

I've went over all the scripture that you sent and picked up four of them that I believe would work good in the book. The rest I'd like to keep. However—the ones I have picked for the other chapters, I would like you and Karen to have the final choice in the ones I've sent. The book you ordered for me has my interests peaked. Am looking forward to reading it. As far as the other book you mentioned please don't order it until I'm done with the one that's coming. The reason being we are only allowed five books in CSP. Every time we get one we have to turn one in.

Wow—today we had a heck of a thunderstorm. The wind was extremely strong and two people in Canon City were struck by lightning. Now that's something you don't hear about every day. Lightning even hit the facility's lightning rods. It made the power go out, but only briefly.

Well—tomorrow is the big day. It's the day we finish the "Why Try" class. After that it's just a waiting game. Could take anywhere from a couple of weeks to a couple of months to go to another facility. Am certainly looking forward to moving along. I like the single cell and time alone, but it can get old not going outside every day and doing some activity outdoors.

You know I find having renewed faith in our Lord extremely uplifting. Sometimes I just sit here going over all the things that have changed in my life, and all the good things that have happened since that day. Just faith itself is so refreshing when you can actually see the things that it changes. It makes me wonder why God had me wait so long, but then it makes me think about how much he knew a family meant to me, and if it wouldn't have been his perfect timing I wouldn't have met you and Karen. And for me, I think it's great what we are doing and it's a big big deal to reach people with the power of our Lord, but God knew being welcomed into a loving family who cares was something I needed in order to further my path with him. And that's what He did. As great as our work for Him is, it's you and Karen being in my life that is the greatest gift God has blessed me with. Besides His love and forgiveness.

Have you got any plans for the 4ᵗʰ of July with your kids and grandkids? I remember when I was young and we went to the stock car races on the 4ᵗʰ and watched all the fireworks. I hope you all have a great 4ᵗʰ and have fun. I will be thinking of you all and keeping you all in my prayers.

Your brother in Christ always!

Love,
Jody
Jody Mobley #60021
PO Box 777
Canon City, CO 81225

7/20/19

Dear Jody,

Well, doggone it, I missed your call Thursday night because Karen and I were out to eat with her son, daughter-in-law, and granddaughter, along with some other people, and apparently you called the exact time I went to the restroom; what are the odds? Sorry, I was planning on taking your call, but it was overshadowed by nature's call. Karen and I will be in Telluride from 7/22–26, but feel free to call that Thursday night. I'll take the phone with me into the restroom! What are the odds they're having a baseball festival in Telluride while we're there, so the one bookstore in town is having me do book signings with four of my baseball books that Wednesday? Wish me luck because book signings are always fun, unpredictable, and not always profitable, but I'll be there slugging it out.

Okay, I just finished the second rewrite of the manuscript, and when I get back, I'll send you a copy. I think it's outstanding, and I have all the readers lined up and will get them copies when I get back. Here's God at work again. I know I've told you I went to Haiti in 2017 for a Christian mission there called Respire Haiti. The girl who started it, Megan Boudreaux, wrote a book called *Miracle on VoDoo Mountain*. She and her husband, Josh, are on Facebook with me, and several days ago she posted a picture of them at the publisher Harper Collins—Christian Publishing and talked about the great team there who helped her publish the book. Now, who knows what will come of it? But I'm going to contact her and get all the info about who I should talk to there about publishing *Prisoner of Faith*. It could be a dead end, or it could be God arranging things as He has certainly done with you and me. Either way, it's exciting and hopefully promising. The book right now is about 40,000 words and somewhere between 140–150 pages, which would make it a short story, but that's fine because I have a couple of books that same length and Megan's book is around that size. Books are generally classified as short stories, novellas, and novels. You have to be over 100,000 words to become a novel, and that's not what we're after anyway.

I hope you're enjoying Boyle's book as I did. I'm reading his first book, *Tattoos on the Heart*, which he wrote seven years before the *Barking* book. He says in there he never names gangs because he does not want to give them any additional publicity and/or cause any repercussions. I think that's probably a great idea, so I wanted to talk to you about removing the names and just calling them gangs and nothing more. Let me know what you think.

Well, over and out for now; Karen says hi and hopes you're doing well, and she will come with me next month when I head down, assuming you're still at CSP. Take care, Jody, and by the way, my two daughters Jackie and Danni said to tell you hi and send their good wishes. I may well talk to you before you receive this letter, but that's fine; we can't cover all this in our twenty minutes of sporadic connection.

God bless you, my brother!

Jan

Chapter 33

Second Corinthians 11:6—Paul, a brilliant thinker, was not a spell-binding speaker. Although his ministry was effective, he was not trained in the Greek schools or oratory and speechmaking as many of the false teachers probably had been. Paul believed in a simple presentation of the gospel, and some people thought this showed simple-mindedness. Thus, Paul's speaking performance was often used against him by false teachers. In all our teaching and preaching, content is far more important than the presentation. A simple, clear presentation that helps listeners understand is of great value.

* * * *

Hopefully, the message we are trying to send to people is understandable and easy to see. The message is: Believe and have faith in our Lord in order for all of us to live a more faithful and better life. God's Word and your faith can and will make a huge difference in your life.

7/18/19

Dear Jan and Karen,

How are you two youngsters doing? Hope all is good with lots of smiles, happiness, laughter. Things are fine here. Our Lord keeps me on the straight and narrow. Pretty funny sometimes—I will find myself randomly talking to Him from time to time throughout the day. He certainly is good company.

Well it shouldn't be long before I leave here if what they've told me is true. Am definitely ready for a change. This place isn't too bad, but the privileges you get as far as rec and some other small things would be really nice. Will miss being in a single cell, but have to give up something to gain other

225

things. I really don't have a lot of problems with other prisoners. That is one good thing that comes from my past. I've gained my respect over the years and I mind my own business. Nobody really bothers me. So that's good.

That's great—the second re-write is done! Really am excited to see what people have to say that you have lined up to read it. Sure hope the message is clear and people respond to it in a positive way. Am close to finishing up the book you sent me. I love the message that Mr. Boyle is putting out. The short stories are great also of all the Homies. Would love to meet him and some of the Homies. That would be pretty cool. Am real curious to know how he got all the facilities to work with him. If God ever puts freedom outside of these walls and fences in my future, I'd really like to try and work with the juvenile institutions and be something like a big brother or mentor of some sort. People forget that the younger generation is our future leaders and care-takers. They aren't bad people, they just made bad choices.

I hope your trip to Telluride went well and you had a great time. Sounds like a really nice place to visit. Maybe one day I'll have the opportunity to go there. My studies are going well, I spend time on reading the Bible, study books and of course sign language. Am almost up to over 300 words in my sign vocabulary.

On that note I will get this in the mail. Let Jackie and Danni know I say hi and wish the best for them every day. Send the same to you and Karen. Take care and I'll talk to you soon.

God bless my brother!

Jody
Jody Mobley #60021
PO Box 777
Canon City, CO 81225

8/11/19

Hey, Jody!

I just got your letter, and we're all good here as I hope you are. I've held off writing thinking you'd be moving soon and not knowing if they'd forward your mail to your new location. I am, however, finishing up the final touch-up on the manuscript, and by the end of the week will start getting it to the readers. Once I get the results back, we can proceed with fixing up what might need fixing or doing some clarification, and then I'll start approaching publishers. We've come a long way with this, Jody, and it just gets more exciting all the time.

I'm going back to Grace to teach the middle/high school kids starting next month. We have a new pastor, and she went with Karen and me to see Father Boyle speak last Thursday night. He brought two homeboys with him, and it was quite an evening. He is one dynamic speaker. Prior to his speech, I told our new pastor all about you and what we are doing. She was beyond interested and wants to meet with me and hear more about it. I also met Father Boyle after the talk and briefly told him about you and what we were doing. You may still be in prison, Jody, but your story certainly isn't.

Well, I'll close for now. Everyone says hi and hopes you're doing well. Take care, and God bless you, my brother!

Jan

* * * *

I think Jody has come to a sincere realization about himself and his past when he says kids in trouble aren't bad people—they've just made bad decisions. For most of his life, he thought he not only made bad choices but that he was, in fact, a mistake, and now he's beginning to recognize that wasn't true and he does have worth and can contribute to the well-being of others, especially those who are going through what he went through.

Chapter 34

Exodus 11:7—Moses told Pharaoh that God made a distinction between the Hebrews and the Egyptians. At this time the distinction was very clear in God's mind. He knew the Hebrews would become His chosen people. The distinction was taking shape in Moses' mind also. But the Hebrews still saw the distinction only in terms of slave and free. Later, when they were in the desert, God would teach them the laws, principles, and values that would make them distinct as His people. Remember that God sees us in terms of what we will become and not just what we are right now.

* * * *

In the beginning, when I went totally against God, He knew where I would end up. Most of the time, we don't know where we will end up in life, and that's okay. God knows your path, and He will bring you along as He sees fit. Eventually, our paths are laid open for us when we are ready. God puts us on paths that we don't ever imagine. I just wrote this story to help inspire people to have faith and believe in God. Imagine that…from someone like me. It just goes to show you God doesn't forget about us.

8/19/19

Jan and Karen,

Hello! Hope this finds you both well, as well as the rest of the family! Am good on this end. Sitting here in Fremont. A&O actually, which is the admissions and orientation unit. They said I should be going to unit 1 today. That is the closed custody unit. Was told to do six months there without any trouble and they would review me for medium. That would be good. Was in this facility back in 1991–93. Quite a bit different back then of course, and so was I.

By now you probably have passed out a few copies of the manuscript to some readers. Really hope we get good positive feedback. How could we not though—this is all God's work—sure can't go wrong there huh? Am anxious to hear others' thoughts on it, and if they see the message throughout the whole book. We've certainly come a long ways in two years. The best part of it all for me is being filled with God's love and you, Karen and the rest of the family allowing me to be part of that family. There's no greater feeling in the world than the ones I'm experiencing!

Yes, my sleep problems can be a real pain sometimes. It's something that has been a problem for many years. More likely than not it will always be somewhat of a problem. The sleeping part you get used to, but the nightmares you never do. A nice soft real bed one day might do wonders also. Ya never know! We know miracles happen all the time. We are living proof of that.

We had to go sign some stuff in medical the other night and it was nice to be out at night. The lawns are real nice and green and a few rabbits in the grass. They weren't scared at all. They sat there doing whatever only a step or two from us as we walked by. They probably get fed pretty good by the other prisoners who get out and about. Makes you feel almost normal seeing that stuff.

That's great you're going back to teach at Grace. That is awesome for the kids. You'll have to keep me up to date with that. Glad you got to meet Father Boyle. I bet it was exciting.

So are you ready for the Bronco games? My boys seem to be having issues getting everybody to camp. Am sure they will be all right though. I mean they are America's team!

That's about all at this point. Not sure how things are here until I get to the living unit. Then I will get the rundown on how things are. Let everyone know I say hi! Take care, smile and be safe!

God bless and love, my brother!

Jody

Jody Mobley #60021

FCF Unit 1

PO Box 999

Canon City, CO 81215

8/23/19

Dear Jody,

I just got your letter of 8/19 and wanted to drop you a note. I'm glad you're doing well in your new environment. I'll come visit as soon as they let me. I called for two straight days and only got a recording that said I could not leave a message about setting up a visit...go figure!

The manuscript is complete, and I've given it out to four readers so far with several more to follow. As you say, it will be interesting to get their take on it, but whatever that is, it will only make it better. I have a complete copy for you and was just waiting for your new address. I think it looks great and hope you do as well. I can't imagine what it will be like for you to sit down holding your life story in your hands. Positively unbelievable, isn't it! You have come farther in the past two years than you did in the previous fifty; glory be to God!

More outside time is going to be great for you, and you deserve it! Yeah, it's back to Grace, but that's as God's planned it. I'll have a new batch of mostly middle school kids, and as we know, that will certainly be a challenge. You will undoubtedly be a topic of conversation as you were in the previous class. I only have one holdover from that last class who wrote you a note two years ago. Yes, I'll keep you posted.

Well, Jody, take care; hope to hear from you soon via the tele. I also hope you get this letter given your move. Had a long talk with my daughter Jackie last night, and she asked about you. They all say hi and send their best. We'll talk soon, my brother, and hopefully I can get down and see you before your next birthday!

God bless you, Jody! Your brother in Christ,

Jan

Jody Mobley #60021
FCF Unit 1
PO Box 999
Canon City, CO 81215

8/28/19

Dear Jody,

Great talking to you this morning, albeit pretty early…kidding. You call whenever you can, and I'll be ready. I was telling Karen how I always know it's you; I don't know why—I just do. Probably God at work once again in our lives.

So I've enclosed the manuscript, the same one I'm handing out to the readers. I think it looks great, and I hope you feel the same. I've also enclosed a batch of questions I came up with that just might pop up during a Q&A. I know some might be a little personal for you, but we both know there are some people out there who would get off asking them. Feel free to respond in any way you choose, and worse case, I can double-talk my way through some of them.

I'll be handing out the final three copies of the manuscript this coming week, so then we can sit back and see what we get back. Jack's response was fantastic, and I think exactly what we were hoping for. I've attached it here so you can reread it anytime you want: "Hey, Jan, just got done reading the manuscript. I read it from cover to cover and could not put it down. It started out kind of slow, but wow, it really picked up and had me riveted to his story and to see what happens next. I feel bad for him and what he went through, but the payoff made it all worth it. Thanks so much for letting me read this beautiful story. I wish you nothing but success. I know this book will be a big hit and hopefully influence lots of kids' lives."

Well, my brother, I'll close for now, but we'll be talking soon. Take care, and God bless you, Jody!

Your brother in Christ!

Jan

Chapter 35

Mark 1:2–3—hundreds of years earlier, the prophet Isaiah had predicted that John the Baptist and Jesus would come. How did he know? God promised Isaiah that a Deliverer would come to Israel and that a voice crying in the wilderness would prepare the way for him. Isaiah's words comforted many people as they looked forward to the Messiah, and knowing that God keeps His promises can comfort you too.

* * * *

When I started this story, I had no idea what an amazing situation for me it would turn out to be. I've been able to re-establish my relationship with God as well as share my story of hope and faith. We all have rocky times, and we need to understand that God is who we should always turn to for guidance and strength. He will lead us to a far better life. I'm a perfect example of what believing in God can do for one person. Look for God's guidance, love, and forgiveness no matter the circumstances. He can always show us the right way, and then our circumstances can change. Be faithful and live a life better than the one yesterday. The changes I've gone through the past couple of years are amazing, and God can do the same for you.

9/10/19

Jan,

Howdy, my brother! Hope this finds you and Karen doing well and in great spirits. Am doing fine here. Reading the Bible, getting some outside rec, and getting to go to the chow hall. Not too shabby. God certainly has blessed me with good things in life. Not to mention my Cowboys looked absolutely awesome this week. Life just doesn't get much better than that!

I love the way the manuscript came out. Am looking forward to hearing what everybody has to say about it. Yes, it is very strange to be holding my life in my hands. So many memories. Some good, most bad. Still in awe of it all. Hard to believe I actually am having a book published about it. Wow! The past two years has certainly been overwhelming at times, but all in all the greatest time in my fifty-two or so years on earth. Who can complain about that huh?

There is a possibility I could get a job in the library. That would be pretty cool. It would only be for an hour or so a day, four days a week, but it's something. I found out I'm on the top of the list for the job when it does come open. Keep your fingers crossed.

My celly and I get along pretty well. He says he is a Christian and we have some good conversations. I set the manuscript out for him to read, but he hasn't looked at it yet. He reads a lot of books his girlfriend sends him. If I ever decide to read a book that doesn't consist of studying it is fantasy novels that I like. I've went through phases where I've been into war books of Viet Nam, post apocalypse, horror, westerns, romance, stuff like Clan of Cave Bear series and fantasy, which I'm really into. Right now I'm on a study phase. It will change to something else from time to time, but I always have study time.

Tell Jackie and everybody I keep them in my prayers also—hope everybody is doing well. Will write more soon.

Take care, and God bless!

Love
Jody
Jody Mobley #60021
PO Box 999
Canon City, CO 81215

9/21/19

Hey, Jody,

Got your letter of 9/10, and it was great, as always, talking to you the other morning. Glad you and your celly get along; I know that's important.

Haven't heard from any of the other readers, but I told them to take their time, so maybe in the next couple of weeks. I can't tell you how great it is to hear you say the past two years have been the best years of your life. It just goes to show what God can do in one person's life no matter their circumstances or history.

Well, I just wanted to drop you a note. I'll call on the 23rd and hope to see you on the 28th, and maybe we can get a picture of two absolutely staggeringly handsome dudes. I don't know if society is really ready for this, but whatever!

Take care, my brother; your family out here is praying for you every day! God bless you, Jody!

Jan
Jody Mobley #60021
PO Box 999
Canon City, CO 81215

10/12/19

Dear Jody,

I'm writing this on Saturday the 12th even though I was supposed to be visiting you. I'm sorry, my brother, but this gut thing just won't go away. I think I told you I was diagnosed with IBS (irritable bowel syndrome), and right now it's having at me. They don't know what causes it, and there is no cure for it…great! It has to be controlled with diet, and they can give you an antibiotic that negates many of the symptoms. My doc is waiting for my blood results, and if they come back negative, she'll prescribe the antibiotic, and that can't come any time soon. I'm sorry I've had to bail on the last two visits, but right now, getting too far from home is…well, not good. Let's just keep chatting on the phone, and when I have this under control, I'll head south and see you.

I'm enclosing the comments I've told you about from three of the readers. The first one is from my dear friend Larry, the retired professor in Indiana; the second is from a dear friend at our church, Karen, who is a lifelong Christian, and the third is from my buddy Jack, who is a strong Christian. It's an interesting group with definite differences, but all loved your story and have great admiration for you.

Larry:

I finished reading *Prisoner of Faith*. Wow! What an amazing (yet stressful) story! Since it begins with his dad's death, followed by physical abuse as well as the neglect and emotional trauma he experienced and had to tolerate as a child, I kept thinking Jody's life can't get worse, but it does, then gets worse still. And then—it gets better because of:

- Faith

It's hard to imagine that one could still have (or actually find) faith after all the pain, suffering, and horror that Jody experienced and that he inflicted on many others. It's hard to believe that he is still alive when any one of many "incidents" could have ended tragically for him. And—to believe that his survival and his calling were in the cards all along. Incredible!

- Friendship

After decades of being a lost and lonely soul, he finally found someone who he could talk to and who would listen and understand without judging or labeling or casting him out to join the hopeless losers. Other than John Van Pelt (I believe that was this name), you and Karen gave him that person (those people). Fortunately for him, you listened, cared, acted, and expressed genuine compassion and didn't simply view him as another insincere beggar or con man out to get (or steal) something. And he recognized that; he was *ready* to recognize it and appreciate it.

- Forgiveness

It seems like it would be as difficult to forgive himself as it would be to forgive those who abused and tormented him and who refused to see a worthy human in that life. Indeed, he did not live (shall we say) an exemplary life, but he has forgiven himself for (most of) his transgressions and cruelty to begin making a better life for himself as well as for others who he can share his story with. It takes a strong person to forgive those who caused or facilitated his trip down a tragic path—albeit a trip that he himself executed.

- Future

Despite his past, he now envisions a useful future with a positive role to play instead of being an agent of destruction—personal and global destruction. Hopefully, there are listeners (and learners) out there!

Karen:

I read it that first week. Very, very powerful. I *loved* how you and Jody interspersed the story with positive words. It made the horror of Jody's story more palpable and more moving because you know he came out "the other side."

And I loved how you started with meaningful scripture and shared what it meant to Jody.

It wasn't as horrifying as I anticipated. Not because the things that happened to him weren't awful but because I have seen and heard stories about students through the years; this, unfortunately, is not an isolated case. What is so uplifting is how his life turned around when it easily could have been the opposite.

Jack:

Hey, Jan, just got done reading the manuscript. I read it from cover to cover and could not put it down. It started out kind of slow, but wow, it really picked up and had me riveted to his story and to see what happens next. I feel bad for him and what he went through, but the payoff made it all worth it. Thanks so much for letting me read this beautiful story. I wish you nothing but success; yes, I know this book will be a big hit and hopefully influence lots of kids' lives.

Well, I'll close for now, but I know we'll be talking soon, maybe tonight, and can catch up. Glad you're doing well and hope your new celly works out. Karen and the whole family send their love and prayers—God bless you, my brother!

Jan

Chapter 36

Acts 2:44—recognizing the other believers as brothers and sisters in the family of God, the Christians in Jerusalem shared all they had so that all could benefit from God's gifts. It is tempting, especially if we have material wealth, to cut ourselves off from one another, concerning ourselves with only our interests and enjoying our own little piece of the world. But as part of God's spiritual family, we have a responsibility to help one another in every way possible. God's family works best when its members work together.

* * * *

My story is being shared with all of you because we are all brothers and sisters in God's eyes. This whole ordeal has been overwhelming for me. Realizing what hurt and pain I've caused others is excruciating, but I'm sharing to show you the power of God. He wanted me to share my story, and hopefully by sharing, it will bring others to understand that no matter what you've gone through in life, share it with your brothers and sisters. I thank the Lord every day for letting me do His work and share for the betterment of all who follow and believe in Him.

10/20/19

Dear Jan and Karen,

Greetings with a big smile! Hope you both are well and getting better. Yes, I was saddened we didn't get to visit, but sometimes things happen that are beyond our control. It's kind of a good thing you didn't get to come. Why? Well they had unit 1 on lockdown and canceled all visits for unit 1 prisoners. We were told they were contacting everybody whose family or friends had scheduled a visit to let them know they had been canceled. Obviously they did not contact you. Which means you would've drove down here and then told visits for unit 1 had been canceled. That would not have been good, but these people do not care whether our friends or families are inconvenienced. I'm sorry you were sick but I'm glad you didn't drive all the way down here for nothing. Because of this I will suggest that you call right before leaving and ask if any visits have been canceled. Better to be safe than sorry.

The feedback on the book was phenomenal. My outlook for it to do well and reach a lot of people is very positive. We are doing a great thing in God's name. What could be better than that? My life has come full circle, and I've gotten to share that with you and Karen. I thank God every day for His love, kindness, and putting us in touch with one another.

Okay—I will have to disagree with you on the knowing of the Bible better than you. You are far more versed in the Good Book than I am. Of course I am learning and loving the time I spend getting closer to God. So much wisdom and knowledge in that one book. It covers any and all aspects of life and situations. Pretty cool. Sometimes I will try to think of a situation the Good Book doesn't cover, but as of yet—no matter what you can think of it is covered by God. Pretty smart fella to know all that He does.

All right! My Cowboys are in first place in their division. That's great. I also actually rooted for Denver this week. Kind of wanted them to win. There were some good games this week. Can you believe San Fran is undefeated? They are doing really good.

These past two years have really gone by fairly quick. Can't believe it's already my birthday month. I will be talking with God daily to keep me stable during the next few months. I seem to have this hard time when it gets close to the anniversary of Scott's death. Ever since turning back to God it has been getting easier to get through this time of year. You and Karen have played a huge part in my getting through these months also. Love and caring sure does play a bigger part than I ever expected. Thank you both for being there! And on that note I will close for now. But before I go here are a couple of things I've found during my reading and study from books in the library. There are a few things out of John C. Maxwell's "Today Matters." The scripture I told you about in Philippians 4:8:

"That there is hope even when you have the hardest beginnings, and there are good people in the world."
This makes me think of my story and meeting you and Karen. The next is from King Solomon—makes me think of all we are doing:

> *[King Solomon] The world of the generous gets larger and larger*
> *The world of the stingy gets smaller and smaller*
> *The one who blesses others is abundantly blessed*
> *Those who help others are helped.*

Proverbs 11:24–25

How true all of that is. As you can see, I take a lot of notes when I study. Things have real meaning to me now. A lot of this stuff would never have registered to me if God was not in my life. So not only do I get to study—God opens my eyes to things that mean something real. God is great and letting Him into my heart and life was the biggest reward in my life, as well as you, Karen, and the entire Sumner family. I'm a pretty happy man Jan. You and Karen take care and be safe. My love and prayers go out to you both. God bless you my brother!

Just me,
Jody
Jody Mobley #60021
PO Box 999
Canon City, CO 81215

11/23/19

Dear Jody,

I wanted to drop you a note to let you know how sorry I am for not being able to get down and see you. I've never really had anything like this gut issue. I'm good for a day or two and then not. I felt pretty good this past Wednesday, Thursday, and Friday until late Friday night, and then it hit again, and I was up at four in the morning with my usual problem. It is not only frustrating, but I'm also really having to fight off depression, something you

241

would know about. It just makes planning things almost impossible because I never know when things might go south. I'm doing everything the doctor has asked me to do, and yet it still comes and goes. I'm at a loss to explain it other than to say I'm sorry for not getting down there. Eventually, with God's help, it will work out, and when it does, I'll head south to see my brother in Christ. Thank the Lord we can still talk on the phone and keep up with what's going on. Anyway, I just wanted to let you know the circumstances and why I was a no-show on Saturday. Take care, and God bless you, my brother. I look forward to talking on the phone this week.

Brothers in Christ,

Jan

* * * *

It continues to amaze me how excited Jody has become about his life and the path he's on. I love how he's found that no matter what situation you're in, there is an answer in the Bible for whatever you're going through. I also look on in joyful astonishment that being part of my family, albeit from prison, means so much to him. It shows how important having a family can be, even if it's a surrogate family, and I'm very proud to say he is part of ours!

Chapter 37

Genesis 18:2–5—in Abraham's day a person's reputation was largely connected to his hospitality: the sharing of home and food. Even strangers were to be treated as highly-honored guests. Meeting another's need for food and shelter was and still is one of the most immediate and practical ways to obey God. It is also a time-honored relationship builder.

Hebrews 13–2 suggests that we, like Abraham, might actually entertain angels. This thought should be on our minds the next time we have the opportunity to meet a stranger's needs.

* * * *

When I was growing up, there were people in my life who, if I had let them into my life, might have changed my whole world, but I was stubborn and did stuff my own way. A lot of my past relationships are gone now due to ignorance, but now with God, I have a newfound outlook on relationships. The one I have with God has shown me how to forgive and let others in also. We all need somebody in our lives to make them complete. Look in places you normally wouldn't, and you will find you have more to offer than you realize. Keep your relationships strong. Of course, the one with our Lord is the most important. I hope and pray that all of you get the opportunity to have a fulfilling life with God in it—it's wonderful!

11/25/19

Dear Jan and Karen,

Boy, howdy—we are sure having a go of it on getting a visit—whew! Well, the Lord will see it through when it's time. I'm sure it was a med-

ical problem that held it up. I pray you will get through all of this and get to where things don't bother you anymore. So my prayers and best wishes go out to you all. May God bless your days with positive outcomes every day!

Besides that not a lot going on in the concrete jungle. That's what this is—all concrete and steel. Pretty cold place without our Lord and Savior around. It's one of the things I've found very pleasant since turning back to God—He certainly brightens everything and every part of my days in here. Have to thank Him every day for being my guiding light. It's pretty great as you already know.

We are supposed to have a snowstorm come through this part of Colorado today and tomorrow. The heating system is still not working completely correct here. One day it will be fine—then nothing but cold air coming from the vent. Oh, and Friday we were on lockdown and they came through and did a unit shakedown. The people doing the shakedowns ended up taking people's blankets. That was pretty strange—and they haven't brought them back—very odd.

Here is a little bit of stuff that I've written on good positive things that have happened in my life. Is this the type of stuff you're looking for? Hope so. Should show a lighter side.

Well I'm hoping to talk to you tomorrow. Until then, it's me, God, my Bible, and prayers for all. Take care and I hope you, Karen and family are all well. Certainly all in my prayers!

With love and God's blessings,
Jody

PS. Happy Thanksgiving!

I asked Jody to think back to some positive people he had in his life and talk about them because we didn't want anyone to think he only had negative influences in his life. There certainly weren't many encouraging individuals, but here is what he wrote.

Yes, these are some of the people who were shining stars in my life. The first person I can remember that could've been a big part of my life was the guy from the Big Brother program. I don't remember his name, but he was more like a father figure and actually did things with me that a father would do with his son. One tiny change in my path and he may have been around for a long time. Wish I could remember his name. Later on in life, much later, it would have been Rich Van Pelt. Now if I had my choice in life, he would have been my dad. His impact on my life was huge even though I didn't understand it at the time. When CDOC sent me out of state to Wisconsin I was in the mental health facility and a clinician that worked with me on my problems was somebody I really admired. She truly cared and she wasn't afraid to show she cared. Her name was Tiffany Dorst. She went out of her way to make sure the people she worked with were doing good. To find somebody that truly cares about people in a place like that doesn't happen as often as one would think. My foster mom would have been a great mom to have. If I would have turned down this road, or took a step down a different path these people could have been real significant people in my life. Now I can add Jan and Karen. God has shown me through them what a true friend is as well as a brother and sister. Knowing this I wouldn't have wanted to change too much in my journey or I wouldn't be doing God's work with my brother Jan and sister Karen. God has made this part of my life almost perfect. Last but not least—how could I leave God out of the mix? Who isn't inspired by Him—who doesn't want to be like Him or as good as Him? Yep—God is the biggest inspirational person in my life. My paths in life have come to this point where He is the greatest individual to ever be in my life and who I admire with every ounce of my being.

I want to thank Jan and Karen for being there for me and showing me what a true family is. They have been a blessing in my life and have walked beside me the whole time. God bless you all and I pray your days will be filled with good things to remember for the rest of your lives.

My prayers are with you.

Jody Mobley #60021
Colorado Department of Corrections
Jody Mobley #60021
PO Box 999
Canon City, CO 81215

12/7/19

Dear Jody,

I wanted to let you know I'm thinking about you and praying for you, as I know this is a very difficult time of the year for you. I do know one thing for sure—that Scott would be very proud of the man you've become through our Lord and Savior, Jesus Christ. My guess is Scott's right there with the Lord, cheering you on every step of the way, knowing you are using your story, of which he's a big part, to encourage and inspire others and, as we've discussed, change just one person's life by being a servant for God…well, it just doesn't get any better than that!

I found a great scripture you should take a look at: Acts 2:2–14. It talks about no matter how great our sins, God forgives us and makes us useful to His kingdom. Boy, does that sound familiar because you're living it! God, Scott, and all of us are so very proud of you and what you've done with your life, and I think the best is still yet to come.

I think I'm starting to get this whole weird diet thing worked out, so I'm planning on coming down on Sunday the 15th at noon time. I'm sure we'll talk before then, but I just wanted to let you know we're all thinking about you and praying for you, my brother!

God bless you, Jody!

Jan

Chapter 38

Matthew 27:24—in making no decision, Pilate made the decision to let the crowds crucify Jesus. Although he washed his hands, the guilt remained. Washing your hands of a tough situation doesn't cancel your guilt. It merely gives you a false sense of peace. Don't make excuses—take responsibility for the decisions you make.

* * * *

When we look at the things we've done in the past, do we like what we see? Not all the time. Like my situation every year when I have to face my best friend's suicide, which I feel responsible for. God has been there for me for the past few years, and my guilt isn't as strong. Trying to wash your hands of a bad situation doesn't relieve you from it. However, God will forgive any sins we make. I'm still on this earth because of God, so no matter how bleak things are or feel, God gives us the strength to press on. Don't give up on life—go with God and let Him show you things aren't as bad as we sometimes think. We all can have a better way of life with God. I'm still alive because of God, and my life, even in prison, is better off now than it has been most of my life. Thank God for His forgiveness and love. He can do the same for you.

12/23/19

Dear Jan and Karen,
*   How is everything? Hope all's well and you both enjoyed the holidays! My prayers and thoughts are with you always. Here it's been a rough go, but with God's help I've managed to get through the worst part. Should be smooth*

sailing from here. I did go see mental health the other day and discussed some of the problems. I was dealing with—such as grief, fault and retribution. That's one of the main issues I deal with is feeling as if I have to pay a price for Scott's death. That's what brought on the suicidal issues. Colorado sent me out of state, which moved me away from everybody I knew. Being away from everybody I knew and all alone in a foreign state made my feelings of retribution a hundred times stronger and I went on a suicide mission. I figured one way or another—dead or alive—I was coming home. At least being home and near people I know, the urge for death subsided. I did have a relapse at Sterling, but since I've coped fairly well. Thanks a lot to God and His forgiveness for that.

Not sure what's going on with getting a job. I've been trying and as of yet no luck. Guess all their talk of actually giving me some type of opportunity was just talk. They have no reason to deny me a chance at having a job, but so far no go. One of those things that are out of my control, so no sense in worrying about it too much.

Here are some other pages I had written. It started getting kind of hectic with the memories so it wasn't as much as I'd have liked, but people should get the idea in any case. If you think we need a bit more please let me know.

On that I will ship this out with love and prayers of good wishes for you all. Happy holidays!

With God's love and blessings,
Jody
Jody Mobley #60021
PO Box 999
Canon City, CO 81215

1/4/20

Dear Jody,

I hope you're hanging in and looking forward to the new year. It's always exciting to see what God has in store for us, and in our case I think it will be great! I'm sorry about not getting down to see you, but I've never dealt with anything like this bug I've got. I do think the meds are working, but some of the side effects are, well, shall we say, inconvenient. Nevertheless, I do feel better but still need to stay close to my porcelain facility. The meds run out on

Friday the 10th, so we'll see where I go from there. Hopefully I'm done with this.

I haven't had a chance to start writing on our new version of the book but will start kicking it around next week. I dug out my copy of *In Cold Blood,* and it's almost 400 pages long. I started going through it, and to be honest I don't think it will help us, at least not from what we are trying to do. There are two versions of Capote's life I'm going to watch because they center around his dealings with the two guys who committed the murders. That should give me a good idea of how to proceed.

I know December was a tough month for you, and I certainly didn't know you before the last two years, but as I've told you, Jody, you are now a man of God, and the difference I've seen over the past year is just another part of this miracle. I can't really put into words the transformation I've witnessed, so let's just leave it at awesome! Only God's power, grace, forgiveness, and understanding could pull this off, and He has.

Sorry they haven't stepped up to offer you the job, but if God teaches us nothing else, it's patience, which is something I've never been very good at, but He's showing me it's the way it has to be. You're right when you say the job thing is out of your control but not His. Hang in, my brother!

Sorry about your Cowboys, at least for you. You know I was bummed when they didn't make it, and I'm sure you're right; there will be a coaching change. Ah, the constant coaching carousel of the NFL. I'd love to have a job where I could fail and still pick up a mill or two. Maybe in the next life.

Well, I just wanted to drop you a line; sorry it's taken so long. Karen and the whole fam say hi and wish you a great New Year. Our prayers and thought are always with you, Jody. Take care, and I'm sure we'll be chatting soon. God bless you, my brother!

Jan

Chapter 39

Mark 5:19–20—this man had been demon-possessed but now was a living example of Jesus' power. He wanted to go with Jesus, but Jesus told him to go home and share his story with his friends. If you have experienced Jesus' power in your life, are you, like this man, enthusiastic about sharing the good news with those around you? Just as we would tell others about a doctor who cured a physical disease, we should tell about Christ, who cures our sin.

* * * *

My life hasn't been the most positive one throughout the years. I'm sure you all have negative times and it's hard to grasp any positive outcomes. When things like that happen in life, I now turn to God for inspiration. I know a lot of what I've written on my thoughts is repetitive, but that's how we learn, repetition. My story and message of inner peace with God is inspired by God. We all need inspiration, and if I, through God, can inspire you to have a better life, then I feel like I've done God's work. You are not alone; a lot of us struggle, but when we find that inspiration, we need to take hold and do what we can to bring inspiration to others through our faith and belief in God and Jesus Christ.

1/22/20

Jan,

Greetings, my brother—how are you and Karen? Hopefully upon receiving this you both are doing great, as well as the rest of the family! We are well into the new year now, and I feel God has big things in store for all of us. My only New Year's resolution this year was to grow closer to God and inspire people through my story. It's truly going to be a great year!

Am concerned that you've not been doing so well for this long. My prayers have you in them daily and I'm hoping they have found something out by now. Pretty sure you're ready to be done with this situation for good. Hang in there my brother—things have to get better.

There were a few people I thought of that impacted my life in a good way. Thought there would be a lot more, but it seems I was too much of a loner and didn't really get close to anybody for fear of abandonment. Thinking on it made me realize a very important weakness in me. The chances to get close to people and not taking it has left some serious gaps in my being able to interact, but I can see the past still holds on to me in ways that I wasn't really looking at.

No luck on a job yet. I've tried and tried, but for some reason they haven't looked at me for anything as of yet. The library wouldn't have been nice but am not sure why they wouldn't pick me.

Maybe God has other plans for me. I'm sure He does. He will tell me in His own time. Guess it's another lesson in patience for me. It's a vital part of our day in here. Patience is something we have to use every day, all day!

Well Jan—I really hope they can get this medical stuff cleared up soon and you're back in action. Being cooped up is no fun at all. I pray for you daily as well as the rest of the family. Take care and God bless you my brother. You take care too Karen.

With love and prayers,
Jody
Jody Mobley #60021
PO Box 999
Canon City, CO 81215

1/19/20

Dear Jody,

I hope this finds you well. I'm so sorry I haven't been able to get down and see you, but maybe this week the doctor will nail down what's wrong, and I can start treating it. In the meantime I'm pretty much homebound; can't wait to have that end! I'm thinking you guys are probably in lockdown since the two guys escaped in Custer County. Call when you can. I always look forward to our talks.

I don't think I've mentioned that I'm still friends with Clint Hurdle, who used to manage the Rockies and just finished up a long stint managing the Pirates. When I first met Clint in 1997, he was a party guy, which shortened his career in the big leagues. In 1998 he met who is now his wife, Carla, who just so happened to be a very strong Christian. Long story short, God, with Carla's help, turned him around, and he is now a big-time Christian. He opened his heart to God, and just like you, he's now a huge warrior for the Lord. He sends out daily inspirational messages, and I'm enclosing a few I think you'll enjoy and find encouraging. I haven't talked to him in a while, but when I do, you and your story will be front and center in our discussion. He's a man who will appreciate and understand what happened and what's happening now because of the Lord.

Well, Jody, my brother, I'll wrap it up for now, but I know we'll be talking soon. The whole fam sends their love and prayers to you, especially Karen and me. God bless you, my brother—all our love!

Jan

Chapter 40

First Samuel 1:7—part of God's plan for Hannah involved postponing her years of childbearing. While Peninnah and Elkanah looked at Hannah's outward circumstances, God was moving ahead with His plan. Can you think of others who are struggling with the way God is working in their lives and who need your support? By supporting those who are struggling, you may help them remain obedient to God and confident in His timing to bring fulfillment to their lives.

* * * *

The writing of my story is so people who have struggled can see that by letting God into their life, their life can change for the better. It is also being written because I want to make a difference in someone's life out there. I want to help them remain strong in their faith and belief in God and our Savior, Jesus Christ. Be patient and let God work His magic. The story of my life is a work in His name, and I hope and pray I have done His name justice. We have to make decisions in life to do the best we can under God, so please let my story be a reminder of God's power. He has placed me in a unique situation where I can hopefully help others. I pray I've done a good job. If I only reach one person, I've accomplished more through my story than I have in the rest of my life.

2/6/20

Dear Jan and Karen,

To start I send my best wishes to you both on full blast! After talking to you today Jan—I looked at my communicational verbiage and how different *it is in some cases. People have such large differences in lingo all over. Even in the US you can go to one state and then another and have a different style of verbiage that all means the same thing—just different words to express it. Excuse my French—but in here the language is a more gutter type of communication. Every other word if you didn't already know is f***. People say that word two to three times in just one sentence. I used to be pretty bad myself. However, in the past few years—two really—I've focused very hard to change the way I talk or communicate. I don't like cussing but still find myself from time to time saying things. I thought that by having God in my life again my language would be better but God doesn't always work in ways that seem best to us. I got that from Exodus 13:17–18. Basically what I get from those passages is God knows we are working on a particular goal and He doesn't lead us to betterment on our wishings. He does it in His own way. He knows the end result already and leads us down a path that is best suited for our individual learning capabilities. It's little things like this that show me that no matter what issue—goal or self betterment task we take on or go through—there is always several passages throughout the Bible that covers what we do.*

As for the book—the actual work wasn't too hard. The hardest part for me was going through it all in my mind. Very difficult but worth every second because I truly believe the book is going to do good. I believe God is going to show us this was not a wasted effort. In the beginning I wasn't sure about all of this. With your support, God's guidance, and our hard work—now I just want to make a difference in somebody's life. I want to be an inspiration to those who are struggling. To those who have doubt. I want to be a good Christian who is positive and not the negative person I was before God shined His spotlight on me. I've been blessed by God and things couldn't be looking better.

They gave me a porter job. I have to sweep and mop the tiers and floors in the pod. It's actually good because it gets cleaned. That's where most of the dirt—dust and whatever else—gets tracked into your cell. Also nice because I can use the phone without fighting for it all the time. Took a while to get the job but that's okay. Really would've liked the library but it's better this way in the long run. The Lord knew something wasn't right and got me into a better situation. One—I could've gotten into trouble the way they treat you in the library. The other—I accomplish helping others from tracking dirt and whatnot into their cells and I can use the phone to call you without the hassles. So the Lord knew the porter job was best for me.

Karen I hope all is well at the coffee house and good things are happening for you. Awaiting foot surgery and that's all. Went to see the eye doctor and all's well. No changes or new damage. Definitely happy about that.

Tell everybody my prayers and thoughts are with them. Take care and God bless.

Your brother in Christ!
Jody
Jody Mobley #60021
PO Box 999
Canon City, CO 81215

2/14/2020

Dear Jody,

I got your letter of 2/6, and right back at you with best wishes and our love. You mentioned your verbiage, and I know where you are it's just the way people talk, but believe me, that's the way it is in sports, locker rooms, in business, and just in general anymore. A couple of years ago, when I was doing my Sunday school class with the high school kids, they wanted to show me a video of a Christian comedian they thought was funny. So this guy is in some arena with a good size crowd, and the basic premise was Christian, but all of a sudden, he starts F-ing this and F-ing that, and I made them turn it off. I asked them if they thought that was funny, and they said yes. I asked them if they thought it would have been just as funny without the F-ing stuff, and they thought it probably would. It did lead to a good discussion about words and how we use them. I also asked them if they knew where the F word came from and what it meant. They had no idea. It started in England, and when they would bury prostitutes, they'd put that on their grave marker. It meant For Unlawful Carnal Knowledge, so everyone just started using the first letters. I explained that to the kids, and it never came up again, at least not during class. Anyway, don't worry about it because that's just the way it is.

Yes, rewriting the book is going to be a big challenge, but it's going to be so worth it. I'm sure you have the book on Ron Lyle by now, so have at it and imagine that approach with your story.

Glad you got the new job and, more importantly, that you like it, and, as you said, God always knows what's best. I think we've figured out what was wrong with my gut, and for the past two weeks, things have been back to normal, so my plan is to come down and see you on the 22nd, God willing. I know we'll be talking before then, so I can keep you updated. Well, got to go for now, but God bless you, my brother. All our love and thoughts are with you every day!

Your brother in Christ,
Jan
Jody Mobley #60021
PO Box 999
Canon City, CO 81215

3/27/20

Hey, Jody!
Wanted to drop you a line to let you know we're thinking about you and praying for you every day. Last time we talked, you had food poisoning and I had my usual. Hope you've gotten better and are on the mend. I'm better since I started using peppermint oil for my gut. This having to stay home except to shop is weird, but sadly I know you're used to this. I have no idea when they're going to allow visitors again, but when they do, I'll be heading your way.

I've restarted the book in a whole new way...I'm using your letters. I'll explain when we talk on the phone, but I can tell you this way is absolutely the best. Call when you can and feel better and stay close to the Lord!

All our love and prayers, my brother!

Jan

* * * *

Jody Mobley #60021
PO Box 999
Canon City, CO 81215

4/6/2020

Dear Jody,

I wanted to drop you a line and let you know we're thinking about you and praying for you every day. My guess is you're in a quarantined lockdown and can't make any phone calls.

They're asking us to only go to the store if we have to, and we have to wear masks when we go outside. It seems unbelievable, but it's the only way we can overcome this.

I also wanted to let you know I'm through chapter 12 on the rewrite of *Prisoner of Faith*, putting your letters and my response in each chapter. I hadn't looked at those letters from the beginning back in 2017, and it has been absolutely amazing to see the transformation in you from then to now. Jody, what you've done in the name of the Lord has been truly inspirational and remarkable. God bless you, my brother, for taking us on this journey. When I get more of them done and can go back over them, I'll send them your way. There is no doubt in my mind this is the absolute best way to do this book.

Take care, my brother. Stay safe and healthy, and as Jesus said, "And this too shall pass." Call when you can, and know we love you and pray for you every day! God bless you, Jody!

Jan

* * * *

The initial writing of the book had been Jody telling his story, and I would then do some paraphrasing, arranging, and sequencing. Once I finished it, I gave it to seven people to read, both Christian and non-Christian. I thought this would give us a good take on his life and transformation. To be honest I was a little concerned the message of redemption might get overshadowed by the horror and darkness of Jody's life, and once all the results were in, that was, for the most part, the general consensus.

I decided we needed to take a different approach, and I knew Truman Capote had trouble developing the lives of the two killers in his book *In Cold Blood*. The movie *Infamous*, starring Toby Jones as Capote, dealt with this in a very insightful way. Having known Jody for over two years, worked with the homeless for several years, counseled troubled youth, and studied the lives of gang members through books by Jesuit priest Gregory Boyle, I realized that, on the whole, most people look at prisoners as just that, prisoners, and homeless people as troubled, lazy bums and gang members as violent, no-good criminals. I can tell you without reservation that is true in some cases, but certainly not all. There are good people in all segments of life, and that includes those living in the margins. With that in mind, I knew I needed to make Jody three-dimensional because he is way more than just a prisoner. I restarted the book with this in mind and quickly determined this was going to be a major challenge, mostly because Jody and I couldn't just sit down and talk for hours on end. We could only have twenty-minute conversations on the phone every week, and the rest of our communication was all through letters. At the end of February, we had our good friends Sandra and Ray over for dinner. She brought me a great book called *Last Days of Summer* about a young boy communicating with a Major League player via letters, and here I had well over fifty letters from Jody, and as I went back through them, it became apparent his letters and my responses told the entire story in the most coherent and significant way possible. The transformation of this man from hating God to completely giving his life to Him is totally embodied in this collection of letters, which is how *Prisoner of Faith* finally came into existence.

Chapter 41

Genesis 29:20–28—people often wonder if waiting a long time for something they desire is worth it. Jacob waited seven years to marry Rachel. After being tricked, he agreed to work seven more years for her. The most important goals and desires are worth working and waiting for. Patience is the hardest when we need it the most, but it is the key to achieving our goals.

* * * *

At times we want things out of life, but it takes a long time to get those things. Following God also takes time, but patience is the key. Since coming to God, I've had to learn patience. In the beginning, I wanted fulfillment in my life through God, but it took time, and I had to be patient. Whatever you're looking for out there, be patient, and turn to the Lord to seek that patience. God's timing may not be what you want, but with faith you can get through anything. Don't try to go too fast or you'll miss so much, as I did. I lost years of life because I blamed God for everything, but now my patience has brought me closer to God. Be patient, my brothers and sisters, and watch all the good that God has to offer you.

4/12/20

Jan,

Greetings to you, my brother! Hope this finds you and Karen doing well and God is blessing you with good spirits during all this uproar on COVID-19. Things are a bit strange. They are doing everything they can to keep prisoners from other units seeing each other. What gets me is why go out of your way and waste so much energy keeping prisoners apart. We are not the ones that will spread the virus. We have to worry about a guard bringing it in—not a prisoner. It's all in God's hands so I feel our day to day shouldn't be altered except for certain things like contract workers coming in or any volunteers coming. The rest should run normal. God knows what's up so let Him do what He will and worry about the things you have control of and not what you can't control.

Right now I'm listening to a little country music and relaxing. Still waiting to be approved for medium. They told me I'd be approved on the 3rd. Come to find out—that's not the case. So am waiting for the 17th. It's not that big a deal really 'cause none of the extra privileges we are supposed to have— have come through. So I'll just relax and let God get me where I'm supposed to go when the time is right.

I made a lampshade the other day. I glued the frame of a box together and put pictures on the inside of the open spaces. Now the light shines up into the box and the pictures light up. They are pretty cool. Besides that I've been studying and reading this fantasy story. Also been playing some chess and Scrabble. Helps kill a little time which we have a lot of out of our cells.

I'm really curious to read the final writing of the book. The only concerns I have are putting anything other than what I've put down on the suicides. Nobody needs to know how I've done some of them. So if anything in my letters have anything on that subject we should not put any specifics. I may be retired and on God's path—but it doesn't change the rules of prison life.

Want to thank you and Karen for getting me a new TV. Thank you both for everything you are doing for me. Now we just need our visits. I miss seeing you and kicking it.

That's about all the excitement here. I pray for you, Karen and the family and hope you all are well.

With love and God's blessings,
Jody
Jody Mobley #60021
PO Box 999
Canon City, CO 81215

4/20/2020

Dear Jody,

Hello, my brother! Good chatting with you the other day; I just wish it could be longer. Ironically and sadly, when we were talking Sunday morning, a little after 8 a.m., Ron passed away. He actually passed at eight fifteen, so I'm thinking we might have actually been talking about him when he died. A great Christian and simply a great guy. You would have loved him. So pray for Eunice and his family as they mourn his loss. I know I'm going to miss him. (Ron was an usher at our church who died from COVID-19 and had been very moved by Jody's story at one of my talks to the church men's group.)

That's pretty cool you made a lampshade out of a box. You've got some talents I was never blessed with. As for the book, I'm hammering away, and like I told you, it will be a little slower process, but that's okay; at least I can do it.

I don't know if I've mentioned this guy before, but I have a good friend named Rick Fisher, who I've known for probably fifteen years or so. We met through baseball, and I always liked him but had no idea what his life had been like. In many ways his life paralleled yours, only it was his mom who died early, and his father was very abusive to Rick and his brother. Rick served in Viet Nam, got hooked on drugs, then came home and started using and selling drugs and attempted suicide four times. The last time he drove up to Lookout Mountain with every intention of driving off the edge. He only remembers driving up there, and the next thing he knew, he was in a buddy's front yard begging for help. His buddy took him to his church and introduced him to the pastor there. Rick said for forty-five minutes he cussed and swore at the pastor and God, then fell to his knees and asked the pastor to help him. The pastor told him he couldn't help him but knew who could...God! That was Rick's come-to-Jesus moment, and ever since he's been a very strong Christian. A mutual friend then wrote a book about Rick's life.

They let me write a special chapter at the end of the book called "Extra Innings." Once the book was out, they started looking for someone to make it into a movie, and I did all I could to help Rick out. For almost two years, nothing happened, but Rick has now found a Christian movie production company, and they are in the process of making the book into a movie. He sent me a trailer of the movie, which is not yet completed, and it looks awesome. Rick and I were talking yesterday on the phone about the movie and how it's progressing, and, of course, he knows about you and your story, so I mentioned I'd love to talk to the owner of the movie company when the time's right, and he said he'd hook me up with him. Now, Jody, I have no idea where this could go if it could at all, but as we know, these don't seem to be coincidences, so if this is part of God's plan, it will happen. Again, I have no idea if the guy would even be interested, and obviously we're still a long way from talking about a movie, keeping in mind that it's probably been four to five years since Bill started writing Rick's story. Just food for thought, but maybe it's part of God's plan for your life.

I'm attaching all the questions I created for the kids a couple of years ago. Take a look at them, and if you have ideas, comments, or suggestions about any of them, let me know. I'll check into the GTL family visits and let you know. It would be great to see you, albeit on a small screen and for only ten minutes, but that's better than nothing. Take care, my brother—I'm sure we'll be talking soon.

God bless you, Jody!

Jan

Chapter 42

Genesis 12:10—when famine struck, Abram went to Egypt, where there was food. Why would there be a famine in the land to which God had just called Abram? This was a test of Abram's faith. Abram didn't question God's leading when he faced this difficulty. Many believers find that when they are determined to follow God, they immediately encounter great obstacles. The next time you face such a test, don't try to second-guess what God is doing. Use the intelligence God gave you as Abram did when he temporarily moved to Egypt and wait for new opportunities.

* * * *

During the past few years, my faith has been tested pretty hard. I believe God has put me in a place I didn't particularly like to test my faith. Well, I passed the test, and life isn't as bad as I thought it was going to be in here. I've gotten a job, and I will be moving to a place in the facility called the dorms. It's for people who do good, stay out of trouble, and want to do an easier time. At times I've struggled, while other times have been great. If you ever feel God is testing your faith, ask yourself why. He has a reason, so try not to falter, stay strong, and things can turn out for the better, as they have for me.

5/14/20

Dear Jan and Karen,

Howdy! What have you two young'uns been up to lately? Oh, not much here. Spending time talking to the Lord and waiting to see what's next in life's journey He has me on. He has certainly done wonders for me and I'm excited to see what the future has in store.

265

Well—all this coronavirus stuff has really did a number on how things are in here. The attitudes of people have changed. Some for the better—others not so good. My past is haunting me to no end here. Of course we knew this would happen. Most will never believe the change. However it's not something I let get to me as God will see me through whatever is going to happen.

Now that the weather is getting nicer out we are working outside on my workouts. I've done a lot of what they call circuit training. Been doing that style for over a year now and in that year I've done a lot of the same exercises but not the same routine in over a year. I just make them as I go.

Lately they have been playing DVD movies on TV. Most I've seen—but there have been one or two good ones I haven't. Beats channel checking—which is something that happens most days. I miss my sports.

Other than that things aren't too bad. Even some of the things they stopped serving for meals have changed. We now have been getting big delicious cinnamon rolls and fried eggs. And the Lord surely knows I love both.

Well I sure hope God is looking after you both and the rest of the family—and I sure hope you all are well. Take care and God bless you all.

Love,
Jody

Jody was moved from Freemont Correctional Facility to the Buena Vista Correctional Facility between these two letters. He said they'd called him into the office at FCF and told him they were moving him to BVCF and into medium security, which he wanted so he could have a little more freedom. When he told them he needed to go back to his cell and pack his stuff, they told him it had already been done, then cuffed him and put him on a DOC bus, and drove him to Buena Vista, where he found some of his stuff was missing or had been broken, plus he was still sick from food poisoning while at FCF. He'd served time at BVCF many years before. Having had a rough time there previously, he was nervous about going back; I told him that it might be the same facility, but he was a completely different man now.

5/25/20

Dear Jan and Karen,

May this find you in great love and grace of the Lord! As for me—I feel God is testing my faith. It's been a struggle ever since they moved me. I've been laid up in bed for about four days battling that same stomach ordeal I went through at FCF. There have been a couple of nights where I felt so bad I wanted to just go to heaven where I wouldn't have to deal with this. It was something I ate in the chow hall. The food here is absolutely terrible and makes me sick. To top that off they took some of my property and busted my headphones. But that's not all. I turned in my laundry the night before they moved me. So I am having to pay for a set of greens to replace them and I lost what T-shirts—socks—and underwear I turned in. So I'm not feeling too good at this point. I don't get this move at all. I was doing good and was not getting into any trouble. Why did they move me—even though it's from closed custody to medium? They should've left me there and put me on the medium side there. This is one heck of a test. I pray He shows me the way and we get past this whole ordeal. Sorry things aren't as good as we would like—but I trust God's path for me.

There are some positives. I get to wake up to beautiful mountain scenery and we get to go outside a lot more. The music is good also. Some good things. We can also get jobs for something to do.

How has life been for you and Karen? Hopefully all's well and you're staying safe from COVID-19. Pretty crazy times huh? My prayers are always with you. The Lord sure did bless me by letting us meet. For now I gotta lay down. Take care and God bless!

Love,
Jody
Jody Mobley #60021
PO Box 2017
Buena Vista, CO 81211

5/29/2020

Dear Jody,

I just got your letter from BVCF, and I'm so sorry you're having to deal with illness and the move all at the same time. It seems God's tests never end, and sometimes when we feel we're drawing closer to Him, for some reason we don't understand, we're tested even more. You, my brother, are certainly being tested once again. As I told you on the phone, I'd been reading how patience is such an important quality in our walk with the Lord because it is only through adversity we truly learn patience, and you and I both know we have to have staying power to walk with God. There is no doubt in my mind you can and will get through this, Jody, because you are a new man in Christ, and you have God and the Sumner clan on your side from beginning to end!

Here are some thoughts from David, a true man of God:

David was a man who truly experienced the highs and lows of life. He knew seasons of great busyness, blessing, and victory, and he also knew seasons of despair, grief, and guilt. Yet through it all, David's heart was sustained by a right perspective in the Lord.

David knew how to pause and praise well. Time and time again, David paused to take notice of the Lord's creation, and he praised the mighty work of the Lord's hands. This practice not only reminded David of his humble place within creation but also God's authorship and authority over creation, his life, and his circumstances.

Dear Lord, You are our Lord, sovereign over all. I desire to praise You as creation does. Forgive me for the times I have become nearsighted in my own endeavors, and remind my heart to look upon You first today. In Jesus' name. Amen.

All our love and prayers are with you, Jody—my brother in Christ!

Jan

Chapter 43

Acts 1:12–13—after Jesus ascended into heaven, the disciples immediately returned to Jerusalem and had a prayer meeting. Jesus had said they would be baptized with the Holy Spirit in a few days, so they waited and prayed. When you face a difficult task, an important decision, or a baffling dilemma, don't rush into the work and just hope it happens the way it should. Instead, your first step should be to pray for the Holy Spirit's power and guidance.

* * * *

I could not visit Jody in 2020 due to COVID, and our letter writing diminished to only an occasional letter. Instead, we began talking on the phone once or twice a week, which was far better than letters. By now we talked like great friends, which in fact, we'd become. Although we could only talk for twenty minutes at a time, it was far more personal and informative. We could laugh and kid around, or, depending on the prison situation, he could just vent. We thoroughly enjoyed it and do to this day.

After several months at BVCF, Jody was moved back to the Colorado State Penitentiary and put in medium security. The moving around of prisoners, at times, seems random, but they are at the mercy of the system. His spirits were good, and his faith continued to grow. We were talking around two times a week. I continued to marvel at Jody's upbeat attitude and faith in the Lord while still confined to an eight-by-twelve cell and no foreseeable way out of prison.

In June of 2022, there was a dustup in his pod, and although he wasn't directly involved, he was injured and sent to segregation, along with a large number of prisoners in his pod. I got a call from him while he was in seg, and I could immediately tell something was drastically wrong. He told me what had happened and that he didn't think he could go on. Prison life was just too relentless and hard. Needless to say, I was alarmed because here was a man who'd attempted suicide five times and was telling me he felt hopeless again and saw no point in continuing his life. He was on the edge, and I wasn't sure how to talk him off. I listened and told him I was there for him, and then suddenly, it was as if God had planted an idea in my head. I told him to write a letter to God. Tell Him how mad, depressed, and frustrated he was, and ask Him why these roadblocks kept appearing. He thought for a minute and said, "What a great idea. I'll do it." I told him to write it and put it away for a week or so and then take a look at it again and see what he thought. Then he could keep it, tear it up, or send it to me. A couple of weeks went by, and on one of our calls, I asked him if he had written it, and he said he had and wanted to send it to me. Here is the letter he sent me on July 10th.

My Father,

I'm writing You because I've had a lot on my mind lately. It all revolves around my faith in You, my place on earth, my purpose in this life and why I'm put in bad situations on a continuous basis. To me, there doesn't seem to be any realistic reason, or justification for You to keep testing me, or having me go through all of these negative situations. What point does it serve?

Time and time again I lay out a course to follow, with all these positive goals and plans to work on bettering myself. I try to show You that my faith is real and in good times or bad, I can stay the course and believe things will get better. Yet, every time I get close to fulfilling my goals and getting to a better place in life, a roadblock is placed in my path. We both know You know these things are going to happen, whereas I on the other hand, have no idea these things are coming. However it has gotten to the point that if I'm doing well for a long period of time, I find myself waiting for that roadblock. Knowing that at some point it's coming. Are You trying to prove something to me? If so—what? Are You trying to teach me something? If so—what? What is the purpose of suffering over and over and over again?

I'll be perfectly honest with You, all these ups and downs are really taking a toll on me. I'm tired, worn down and with no end in sight, the hope for a better future is fading. Throw in the mental health problems and things are intensified tenfold. Life just isn't enjoyable anymore. I'm asking for some kind of clarity on things. Anything to let me know this isn't all for nothing. Not to mention I'm tired of being a failure in the eyes of Jan and Karen. I mean it was You that brought us together. You blessed me with a really good friend and brother in Christ. It hurts when you feel you're a burden on those you love and care about. And yes, because of You my Lord, I've come a long way. The love and blessings You've given me has changed my entire life. But with having to navigate through all these obstacles, makes me feel like I still have a long way to go. Would love it if You would bless me with an opportunity to show everybody the real changes You made in my life. My faith, heart, and soul is Yours to mold and guide. You know this. Let me be the person You can be proud of. It's not my faith this is faltering, it's hope. I really need to know there is still hope and meaning to my life, instead of constant suffering, feelings of being a failure and a burden. I pray every day You show me the way. I could go on and on, You know how much I'm hurting right now. So please consider my words and help guide me through all this negativity. Thank You for listening Father. I will continue to pray for Your guidance. I love You unconditionally my Father!

Love, Your son,
Jody

I got Jody's letter about two weeks after he wrote it. As you can see, it's heartfelt, sincere, and desperate. Here's a man who had grown to trust God and had seen the fruits of that trust grow but now was questioning why he kept being beset with what seemed to be never-ending setbacks. To be honest I was at a loss as to what to do or say to him.

Several days after receiving the letter, I was checking on Facebook about a new book I had out, and there was an ad by Trilogy Christian Publishing, which is part of the Trilogy Broadcast Network, stating they were looking for Christian writers. I had written Jody's story three times, finally using his letters as the essence of the book. I sent the introduction to TBN, and within hours they got back to me and stated they wanted to talk about publishing his story. I talked to a gentleman there by the name of Terry Cordingly several days later, and we agreed on going forward with *Prisoner of Faith*. I remember thinking immediately after our conversation, "I wonder how long it will be before Jody calls." It was literally only a few minutes, and he called. As I've mentioned, we can only talk for twenty minutes; I can't call him, and I never know when he's going to call me, so the fact this happened only minutes after my conversation with Terry was…well, you draw your own conclusion.

Needless to say, Jody was speechless and couldn't believe it had actually happened. In our next conversation, he was over the shock of it and was now beyond enthusiastic about what was happening. We now believe God has once again taken us in a direction of His choosing. A few discussions later, Jody told me he felt this was God's answer to his letter. I couldn't agree more!

Epilogue

Psalm 69:13:
"But as for me, my prayer is to You, O Lord, at an acceptable time;
"O God, in the greatness of Your loving kindness,
"Answer me with Your saving truth."

The epilogue of a story is supposed to be the final word or end of the story. That's certainly not the case here. I hope my journey with Jody will continue through eternity, and as Reggie, a dear homeless man I know, loves to say, "God willing," it will.

It says in Romans 11:25–36, "*God works in mysterious ways, His wonders to perform,*" and I can't think of any other way to describe what has transpired since September of 2017 in the lives of two men so completely different in virtually every conceivable way. But given these decidedly different upbringings, God found a way to bring us together to serve Him. A miracle is defined as a phenomenon, wonder, or vision, and I would have to say what Jody and I have gone through is all that and more.

For a kid who was kicked to the curb at age twelve and then spent the next fifty years blaming God for his plight and was just trying to survive day by day, his resurrection from felon to follower of Jesus is nothing short of miraculous, and Jody would be the first to tell you that...now. I have been both a participant and observer on this mission, and to watch a man who was once so full of hopelessness, shame, and anger go through a complete rebirth under the guidance of God has been nothing short of astounding. This has not been a one-way street with God changing just Jody. I, too, have gone through a rebirth of my own. As God changed Jody's heart and soul, so He did with mine as well. If someone had told me several years ago

273

that I would grow closer to the Lord by way of a prisoner and home-less people, I'm not sure I would have believed them, but here we are, and once again I learned never to underestimate God and our Lord and Savior, Jesus Christ! As the Bible implicitly states, and Jody loves to say, "God is always there waiting; all you have to do is let Him in."

May God bless you!

Jody Mobley and Jan Sumner

Printed in the USA
CPSIA information can be obtained
at www.ICGtesting.com
LVHW041922031023
759781LV00061B/1062